Effective Management for Engineers and Scientists

Effective Management for Engineers and Scientists

Leon A. Wortman, D.B.A.

A RONALD PRESS PUBLICATION

JOHN WILEY & SONS, New York • Chichester • Brisbane • Toronto

Library of Congress Cataloging in Publication Data:

Wortman, Leon A
    Effective management for engineers and scientists.

    "A Ronald Press publication."
    Includes index.
    1. Engineering—Management. 2. Psychology, Indus-
trial. I. Title.

TA190.W58   658'.001'9   80–19665
ISBN 0–471–05523–9

Printed in the United States of America

10 9 8 7 6 5 4 3 2 1

To Dorothy, Alan and Chris

Preface

Not everybody wants to be a *manager*. But practically everyone wants to understand what a manager is and does. Is the manager merely a person who has been elevated to an exalted position in his company, division, department, section, or group? Is he in this "exalted position" because of *what* he knows, or because of *who* he knows? Does he have to marry the boss's daughter, or be related directly through blood or marriage to become a manager?

The answer to the last question is really very simple: being part of the boss's family doesn't hurt one bit if all you care about is being called "manager." But whether you became a manager because of *whom* you know or through coincidences of birth and luck, it is *what* you know that will determine whether you are effective as a manager. By effective, I mean *able to achieve desired results.*

The *effective manager* is one who is able to achieve positive, productive results through the fulfillment of his role as the supervisor or leader of people who are responsible for performing technical work. The trick—but it isn't really a "trick"—in performing as an effective manager is in practicing the "arts" of interpersonal communication and of understanding the interlocking needs of the subordinates who are necessarily responding to demands coming at them from multiple directions. These demands include the needs of the group to which the subordinates belong within the organizational hierarchy, the demands or needs of their peers, their supervisors, the leaders and managers throughout the hierarchy, and the company taken as an entity with an image and a series of plans and objectives the subordinates must support.

An "art" is a skill acquired through experience, study, and observation. "Communication" is any process by which information is exchanged between individuals and groups. However, communication is much more than people talking to one another. It is people *working together* toward the attainment of common objectives. It means commitments to the plans, to the group, and to the company and its goals.

The work of the *effective manager of engineers and scientists* is not easy. It cannot be done in a casual or intuitive manner. The "arts" of management must be highly developed and the skills must be prudently practiced. At no time in this book do I ever indicate that a manager's work is easy. Being an effective manager just isn't easy. It is much easier to *become* a manager than it is to *remain* a manager. Some of you reading this book may already be managers. Others may one day become managers. Not everyone will be an *effective manager*.

The manager is *accountable* for people who are *responsible* for technical work. The manager is a person who must skillfully balance his concern for his people with his concern for the task. He must learn to be effective in the development of morale and attitudes that motivate his people to achieve. In this area he has a strong concern for his people. The hard data that define the series of actions for which his people are responsible also define the task for which he has concern.

Being an effective manager of engineers and scientists, I repeat, is not easy and is never simple. It is not my intention in writing this book to make the job of the manager *easy*. I don't think any book can do this. This book is intended to help the new and the veteran manager become more effective managers. I think a book can do that.

Throughout the book I have tried to be consistent in my use of the male pronouns: he, him, his. However, this is done solely as a matter of convenience and to eliminate the awkwardness of having to use expressions like "he/she," "him/her," and "his/hers." I do hope you will not think that my use of the male pronouns to the exclusion of the female or dual pronouns is sexism or discrimination on my part. As have so many other authors, I am sure, I have unsuccessfully struggled with this modern language problem. Effectiveness as a manager, of course, has nothing whatsoever to do with gender.

LEON A. WORTMAN

Palo Alto, California
August 1980

Acknowledgment

I am grateful to many of my co-workers, who contributed in important ways to the knowledge, expertise, and insights that have enhanced my career and enabled me to write this book. Several of the managers to whom I reported directly had particularly positive influences on my development. They have earned and deserve special mention.

Harry Daniels, my first engineering manager, taught me the value of honesty in dealing with subordinates. Paul W. Fuelling, chief engineer of radio station WHN and WHNF in New York, taught me the importance of flexibility in style. William A. MacDonough, retired president of the Kudner Agency, ranks as one of the most effective managers I have known. Indeed, he is my role model for the *effective manager*.

Leonard J. Smith, executive director of Training Services, Inc., Rutherford, New Jersey, encouraged me to combine my academic education and "hands on" experiences in management and organization development into a series of "Effective Management" seminar/workshops. He has taught me a great deal more about two-way communications techniques than he may realize.

Michael J. Hamilton, my editor, earns special acknowledgment for the encouragement and enthusiasm he shared with me in putting my concepts and practices into book form.

L.A.W.

Contents

Introduction

Many organizations use a rather simplistic definition of the word "manager." It is not unusual to read in a policy manual or a collection of rules referred to as S.O.P. (Stand Operations and Procedures) that a "manager is an individual with at least two other individuals reporting directly to him." Not much more is offered beyond the description of the channels of communication that must be observed and the documents that must be completed in order to (a) make a proposal, (b) obtain an authorization, or (c) put some other documents into the storage files.

Not much more is given in the way of guidance on how to be a manager, what is expected of him, or how his effectiveness will be evaluated. A "manager" is simply that, a *manager*. I recall quite clearly the time I tried to find out more about the significance of the title "manager."

My boss, a top executive in a Fortune-500 company, called me into his office and with a beneficient smile told me he was promoting me to department-level manager. Until then, as an employee with that company, not a single person had been reporting to me. My position had been purely *staff* to a staff executive, senior level. Suddenly I was designated a "manager" and would have more than 100 people reporting to me through a hierarchal structure of professional staff, group, and section leaders. I asked what seemed to be an important question: "What's a 'manager'?" I really was quite serious. My employer seemed to be equally serious when he said, "You'll learn!"

Now, many years later in my career development, my heart and thoughts go out to those poor souls who were accountable to me. The only guidance I had been given was "You'll learn!" I did learn, by trial and error. My errors were trials to my subordinates! If only we could redo history. If only we were born smart. But we cannot. And we are not.

For the most part, we are products of our childhood environments. We learn by imitation, sometimes unwittingly imitating those things we despise and people we disavow. This imitative learning is carried into adulthood—chronological "adulthood"—and forms our behavioral patterns and, when we become *managers*, it distinguishes our *management styles*. Without instruction or guidance from a respected and omniscient teacher, we tend to replicate the imprint of those styles that made their deep impressions on us during our formative years, the impressionable stages of growth.

Perhaps the strongest imprint is made by our relationships with our parents, many of whom seem to have an unfortunate inability to cope with their own children and, as though attempting to survive a traumatic experience, take a position of total authority over their offspring. The parent is expected by the social community (and spurred by his own ego needs) to "cope" effectively. The style or technique for coping—probably handed down from grandparent to parent—is quite simple: "I am your father (or mother) and you will do as I say!" The message is clear: "I may not be right all the time, but I am your parent all the time! Honor me. Do as I say—or else!"

There are no quantifiable standards for performance as a parent, no specific measure that determines the effectiveness or success of parenthood. If there were published standards, who would implement them? There are books and seminars on "how to be a parent." Many contain theories and suggestions for practice. But there is no way to impose, insist that the books be read or the seminars be attended by any parent, or that the concepts that are offered be practiced. The parent is the ultimate authority figure who shapes the patterns of growth in the child that emerge later as dominant life styles. The parent may appoint surrogates, such as schoolteachers who spend at least as much time with the child as the parent does each day. Thus, the child grows up surrounded by authority figures. And when the child exits the family and enters society as an *adult*, thinking he is at last free and on his own, he is often traumatized by the discovery that in place of his *parent* who used to tell him what to do all day he now has a *boss* who tells him.

If we view the parent as a *manager*, we view an organizational unit, the family. From whom have the parents learned to be "managers"? Of course, from their own parents who learned from theirs, and from theirs, and so on. The pattern tends to repeat itself over and over again through each generation of the organization. One day a member of the family unit becomes a *manager* of an external unit, a unit whose productivity will be measured quantitatively in very specific and explicit terms.

This *manager* must now interact with a new series of human organisms, each an individual in his own right. The new manager takes control and applies his authority. He mandates. Issues orders. Commands, with a pointing finger, that his subordinates shall "perform." He demands obeisance; "respect my rank, if not me!" Without conscious thought, he behaves as though the members of his work unit, group, section, department, division, or company are his own "children." He is usually totally unaware that, in effect, he is treating his subordinates in a parent-child relationship, "coping" as did his parents in an effort to satisfy his own needs. Without awareness, he is imitating his parents and their surrogates, using authority born of rank as opposed to authority that is born of knowledge, skill, and expertness.

We have depicted the *manager* as a dominant, unreasonable, demanding person, wielding huge power, yielding to no one other than his own supervisor (his "parent"?). The manager is not always in this mode. However, although many preach democracy, given an opportunity they practice dictatorship. But the objective for the manager is to be *effective*—to achieve desired, positive results that are beneficial to all people and entities involved with the company or organization to which they belong or with which they identify.

The *effective manager of engineers and scientists* has an especially difficult set of challenges. He is coping, generally, with people who are skilled in their professions, knowledgeable, creative, ingenious, independent, and who are always asking questions that cannot be ignored, evaded, or avoided by the manager. Each individual in the technical work unit has a unique set of needs that must not be ignored. The manager, in order to be *effective*, must know how to deal with the intense dynamics of interpersonal and intergroup relationships. An inability to achieve the desired results will certainly be noted by his subordinates, peers, and superiors as *managerial* failure. He will be considered *ineffective*. His career or his job may be in jeopardy. The effective manager of engineers and scientists makes judicious use of the human and physical resources that have been placed under his control in order to accomplish the objectives of the work group as a part of the whole organization.

In order to lead and control the engineering and scientific activity effectively, the manager must identify, evaluate, and accommodate five distinct sets of needs and interactions—his own plus those of his superiors, subordinates, peers, and the separate groups or units of activity within the total organization. The manager must be effective in these relationships, which are diagrammed as the *Wheel of Interaction.*

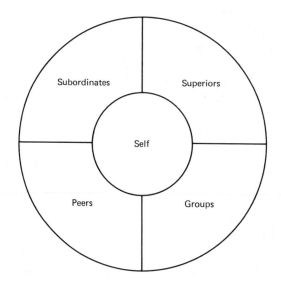

Within each quadrant of the outer circle that surrounds the inner circle, "Self," are the specific needs and characteristics of others with whom the manager ("Self") must interact. Without successful interactions, the manager, the "Self," cannot perform, cannot gain the level of productivity for which he is accountable.

It is not enough to become totally familiar with "Self" and "Subordinates." It is vital to be able to accurately identify, define, and accommodate the needs and characteristics of the "Superiors" (the *managers* of "Self"), the "Peers" or colleagues, and those of the "Groups" or work units. Only then is the manager, "Self," able to begin to satisfy that which ties together individual engineers or scientists, project work units, and activities that represent the needs of the organization as a holistic society. This "society" of human and physical resources contains the objectives and goals toward which all efforts are in reality dedicated, and toward which attainment all contributions of the manager will be noted, measured, and sometimes appropriately rewarded.

A move upward in the organization, from member of the professional staff to the managerial level, demands modifications in appearance and behavior, use of new language, new modes of self-presentation, and adjustments in perspectives. Although such elements may appear to be superficial, they are, nonetheless, influencers and imprinters of the ability to recognize that roles have a new significance when the word "manager" is prefixed or suffixed to the job title. If the manager is to succeed, he must recognize the new focus, adjust to, accept, and learn everything conceivable about the new environments and the expectations of all those with whom he must interface. He must learn to deal effectively with conflict and to nurture the communications processes.

In many interactions there are winners and losers. Everybody admires a winner. Although we may feel great empathy for the under-dog-loser, nobody wants to be a loser. The *effective manager* uses techniques that result in *no-lose* interactions.

Every manager is constantly confronted with potential and actual conflicts. Ideas, concepts, innovations and people—especially those who are creative—are often in conflict, in the sense of disagreeing with one another's beliefs. The *effective manager* manages conflict. Conflict does not manage the *manager*. He has learned the theory and knows how to practice the *no-lose* principles. Those who have not learned to manage conflict constructively may have learned how to suppress or evade conflict. Supression or evasion—as opposed to managing—may extend the tenure of the manager. The prognosis, however, is for eventual failure as an *effective manager*.

The suppression technique will probably remove from the scene— voluntarily or involuntarily—those engineers and scientists who have innovative ideas, unusual concepts, and approaches to technical work that tend to generate conflict. These people often do not conform to the group's perception of itself, or to a strong-willed individual's or manager's directions. It is not often recognized that people who cause conflict may be the truly creative members of the staff. And the manager who does not encourage creativity, ingenuity, and innovation for fear of the potential for conflict may, in the long run, destroy the group for which he is accountable. Although it is certainly not his intent to do so, this manager may find himself surrounded with subordinate engineering and scientific personnel who may be, at best, mediocre in aspiration and performance levels. Free from conflict—but where have the good people gone?

Inadvertently, communications may be discouraged by the *ineffective* manager. In so many ways, it is possible to destroy the openness of communications, to make it a one-way process instead of the desired and essential two-way superior-to-subordinate/subordinate-to-superior flow. Once the two-way channel has been interrupted, and it is a fragile "channel," special skills and time-consuming efforts are required to reconnect it.

It is the intent of this book to fully detail the theories, the means, and techniques by which an incumbent *manager* of an engineering and scientific professional staff can improve his effectiveness. The new or future manager may learn how to avoid the "error" inherent in a trial-and-error approach, get off to the right start, minimize the time and energies expended in patching things together and, because he is *effective*, thoroughly enjoy and find great satisfaction in the manager's role.

This book will develop the *Wheel of Interaction* as an important basis for defining the interpersonal relationships that surround the manager of the professional staff so that he may be enabled to continue on his way to growth and opportunity by demonstrating his unique skills in the optimum utilization of human resources. This book will discuss and describe the optional management styles available to the manager and how and when to apply them to the job. The styles recognize that people are the vital elements in meeting technical work objectives.

Practice is based on theory. This is known as fact to the communities of engineers and scientists. Before one can become a productive professional, one must have a firm foundation in theory. The *effective manager* must have a firm foundation in the theories of human behavior and needs. The view is not from that of the clinical psychologist but is from that of the pragmatist, the working *manager* who, in dealing with his people, must comprehend the inferences that have been drawn from observed behavior and from the experiments with the laws and theories that have evolved and that have found general acceptance. Thus, without pretending that in order to be effective the manager must acquire credentials as a psychologist, we will understand the practical significance and applicability of the most commonly accepted theories of the behavioral scientists. Most important, the *manager* will become involved with how to put these theories to use in communication, conflict prevention and resolution, motivation and productivity, in interpersonal, intergroup, and intragroup relationships.

The reader will learn how to identify his own management styles and those of his peers and superiors. The reader will learn how to modify, where necessary, his own styles, making them flexible and appropriate to each new situation. In this process, the reader will acquire a new understanding and working knowledge of the dynamics of the group, the formation and development and growth of the technical work groups for which the *manager* is accountable.

Case histories and examples of problem situations and people who test the skills of the manager will be presented along with discussions of the alternative courses of actions available to the manager, the probable results of each of the alternatives, and the implementation of those actions that offer the greatest promise for successful resolution.

This is a workbook, a how-to discourse with a specific thrust toward the special requirements of the *manager of engineers and scientists*. This book provides a learning opportunity for the future, brand-new, or veteran *manager* in how to be *effective*, how to achieve desired and desirable results.

Too often, a member of the work unit is victimized or even abused by the ineffective, power-based manager. Another, more fortunate member may have been nourished and inspired, motivated by a manager who uses the positive strategies that are described in this book. At one time or another, any of us may have been an abused victim, may have been the "power boss," or one of the better kind of managers. Abused or abuser, democrat or dictator, we all have much to learn.

1

What makes them tick?

You know you are a *manager*. How do you know it? Your supervisor told you that the word "manager" was to be part of your title. And the personnel file supports it. Further, you are invited to meetings that others in your department do not attend and other "managers"—now they are your "peers"—talk directly to you with a degree of respect they do not show to the people who report to you. Yes, all the *physical* evidence exists that you are a *manager*, accountable for the work performed by others who are your *subordinates*.

In the absence of hard data, we will make the assumption that the managerial title and position are well deserved. We will make another assumption, very important, that no one in the company has given you any instruction in just what a "manager" is, what is expected of a "manager," or how to be a "manager." Simply, you were told, "You are now a manager. Go out and manage!"

A *reductio ad adsurdum*? Not really. It happens!

It is possible that you were named as a replacement for a manager who was promoted, moved up, down, or out and, therefore, a job description of some sort does exist. The first thought you might have: "I certainly (don't want to) (or do want to) follow in that guy's footsteps." But then, you are an individual, not a carbon copy of your predecessor. You have your own assets, liabilities, behavioral patterns, personality, technical skills; you are no doubt the product of a substantially different heredity, environment, and set of experiences. Certainly, therefore, you bring your own style to the management of the tasks and the people who, according to the memorandum that has been circulated, report directly to you.

There is another possibility, one of many actually. The organization is undergoing change, the result of growth or a need for organizational redevelopment. And, in the shakeout, you were named to manage a new activity, department, or project, one that never existed before in its format, with people who, for the most part, never worked together previously as members of the same group. Possibly, a job description hasn't yet been written for the manager's position. If it ever is, it will probably be done after the "job" has been started. The document formalizing the position will be written by personnel to satisfy the demands of the bureaucracy and the S.O.P. manual that, like a bible at a religious university, is installed in every bookcase and, sometimes, is actually read and referenced.

Physical and human resources

Recognize, imprint it indelibly into the conscious forefront of your mind, that you are accountable for only one thing—tasks. You are required to get things done, to meet objectives: specific, quantifiable goals, spelled out elaborately in units of money, time, specifications, and facilities. You are provided with *physical resources* intended purely to provide you with some of the means to attain the *quantified* objectives.

As a *manager*, you have another resource assigned to you—*people*. They are always quantified as units: head count, if you will. But, this particular resource, the *human resource*, is much more complex than any *physical resource* that has been made available to you.

Consciously or otherwise, when two people meet for the first time they "size up" one another. They instantaneously and, they hope, unobviously take physical, quantified measurements. "He's about so tall, so fat, has a mustache, beard, twelve (or whatever) people report to him and he reports to 'Jones.' " Within the time frame of high-speed data-absorption capabilities of the mind, the data is collected and stored for retrieval and processing at a future time. The quantified data is entered into the human system's memory bank dedicated to *hard data, facts*.

The soft data bank

Then another process begins for the two people, the acquisition of qualitative information, impressions of one another. "He's a threatening person. Better watch out for this guy, he's too sharp, probably wants my job." Or, "Nice person, friendly, knowledgeable, experienced, knows what it's all about. He can help me be effective in my job." This information cannot be quantified. Good or bad, you get only one chance to make a first impression on each other, and this soft data is entered into the human memory bank dedicated to *impressions, pro and con.* From that point on, each encounter activates the human management information system (HMIS) instantaneously recalling bits from the two memory banks: *data* and *impressions*. Our responses take the form of a) recognition (hard data) and b) reaction (soft data). By his hard data, we recognize the form factors identified as "Smith." Our response to Smith is governed by the soft data.

The two memory banks can be re-entered at any time. If Smith removes his mustache, the quantified-data bank erases the original entry and accepts a new information bit. Obviously this is so, because if the data could not be altered after its original entry, any change in Smith's physical data, a new suit, a haircut, or growth of a beard, would make him unrecognizable. Smith would not "compute." So, we are continuously updating the "hard data bank."

Interactions

What about the "impressions bank"? That's part of another complex system. The *impressions bank* is much more difficult to re-enter than is the *data bank*. Once a bit of information is entered into this memory bank of impressions, it is extremely difficult to erase it, edit it or make a new entry. The information contained in this part of the human system is that which tends to control reactions and interactions with people, with those who report to us, those to whom we report, and with our peers . . . those not required to report to us, nor we to them, according to the organization chart. But it is important to know that somewhere there is an organization chart that also displays the interrelationships among peers. The *Wheel of Interaction* summarizes the intent of the organization chart, the intent to organize all resources, physical and human, in such a way that the objectives of the organizational entity are attained or surpassed.

Management is all about the Wheel of Interaction, the successful planning, organizing, directing, and controlling of resources toward the objectives of the entity. We will assume that the objectives have been clearly defined, quantified, and that they have been recognized and accepted by you, the manager of resources. Your effectiveness, perhaps your future, certainly your personal satisfaction and need fulfillment, are directly related to and measured by how well you manage the resources.

People orientation

We will make a further assumption: your technical skills are well developed. You are efficient, effective, and totally competent in the management of physical resources. Your engineering skills, your knowledge of physical techniques and processes have been proven to be among those at the top among professionals. Your credentials are beyond challenge—as far as physical resources are concerned. But you recognize that people, a subject not covered in any one of your engineering classes (and that one semester in "human relations" now seems to have been inadequate) are the most complex resource assigned to your set of accountabilities. As individuals they are extremely complicated, sometimes unpredictable, always changeable, evasive or direct, unidentifiable, argumentative, resistive or compliant, cooperative or competitive, puzzling, and at times downright perplexing. And you are expected to manage them as individuals and as part of a group of task-doers. It can be a frightening and overhwelming experience.

More than one manager has failed, not for the lack of people or time or money with which to start the assault on the tasks, but for having run out of time and money as a direct result of the ineffectiveness of "people." It is a fact, too, that some managers have trouble recruiting people, either from inside or outside the company. *Nobody wants to work for them!* People problems are among the most common causes of management and project failures. Why? Because tasks are accomplished through people.

The manager who does not understand his people, who has little comprehension of the fact that his people are individuals with private needs that inexorably seek satisfaction, who fails to recognize that people are intensely complex, who does not add people orientation to his task-oriented management style, is in serious danger of creating an environment for failure instead of for success, of frustrating his own needs as well as those of his group members. It is predictable that such a manager may never get the desired results despite long hours of dedication, trail, and tribulation.

First the theory

A manager doesn't have to be a psychologist or a behavioral scientist in order to be an effective manager of engineers and scientists. However, in order to become a knowledgeable and practicable engineer or scientist, one must first become well acquainted with theories and laws. Likewise, in order to become an effective manager of human resources, one must first become familiar with some of the theories that attempt to define and interpret human behavior and personalities, formation of habit patterns, needs, and motivational drives, and direction (or redirection) of human energies in positive and productive directions.

The fact that one carries the title "manager" does not automatically convert him into an exemplary human being. Alongside those of his subordinates and peers, are his own hangups, behavioral patterns, needs, and motivators. If he can learn to understand his own actions and reactions at the interpersonal level, most certainly he will gain constructive, valuable, and effective pragmatism, be able to strike that desirable balance between principles and practice that tends to meet the quantified objectives of the work group and the organization, enrich the lives of those individual engineers and scientists for whom he is accountable and, importantly, enhance his personal growth as a human being and advance his career in management, his company, profession, and industry.

A single person may have so many variables operating on his behavior that we may never be able to recognize, much less control, them in order to predict his actions. Certainly within the business environment, the demands that compress all time frames make the thought of becoming engaged in a psychoanalytical process with the individual, superior, subordinate, or peer totally unreal. One might suppose that the reaction variables would increase in some direct relationship with the size of the group.

Predicting group behavior

One might draw the pessimistic conclusion that, if each of us is so individualistically complicated, it becomes virtually impractical for the manager of a group to "manage" the group. Take heart, however, in the belief of psychoanalysts that while it is almost impossible to predict, accurately and precisely, the behavior of a single individual, it comes closer to possibility to predict the behavior of a group of individuals who perform within the same environment at the same time. The phenomenon is that the individuals contained in a group will tend, as the size of the group increases, to have more and more of the same variables operating. The prediction of group behavior, of special interest and value to the manager of the group, becomes somewhat simpler because the variables become more apparent and therefore more identifiable.

Some individual members of the group will always be at opposite poles, if behavior can be identified as being polarized, but most will cluster at the middle as the size of the group is extended; responses, in the behavioral context, will be similar and predictable. Behaviorists contend that, the bigger the group, the more successful the manager can be in his predictions. Perhaps here we have a partial explanation of the success some managers exhibit as they move upward in the accountability for work groups, seeming to become more competent as the head count of their sections, departments, or divisions is increased. In order to *manage* people successfully, one must *comprehend* people. From a study of the behavior of the individual we may develop a knowledge, limited perhaps but useful knowledge, of the behavior of the group. True *authority* and *power*, for the effective manager, are gained through *knowledge*. It is appropriate, therefore, to explore several of the more widely accepted theories of personality of the individual.

Theory as a basis for action

The scientists and the engineers of Hollywood, television, and the comic books are generally portrayed as and considered to be a species apart from so-called typical people. They are concerned exclusively with superscientific development, nuclear energy, mind-control machines, space travel, and other means for advancing their own special interests, which, strangely enough, are usually dedicated to or causative of fantastic levels of destruction. Perhaps the only realistic element in these portrayals is that these fictional scientists and engineers are forever proving that theories can be converted to hardware and machines uniquely capable of meeting clearly defined, even though diabolical, objectives.

There is little doubt that the enormous amount of special training required for competence in today's disciplines has tended to make the construction of theories seem to be an esoteric puzzle. It is possible that some of the work of the theorist has been alienated from the day-to-day activities of people who must perform activities with measurable productivity or output levels. Often, it is difficult to determine whether a theory is developed as a rationalization of an activity or as a basis for the prediction of probabilities that an event will occur or, once having occurred, will reoccur in a way that has been predefined.

The most general requirement for the language of theory is that it be understandable by other people. It would be too much to hope that the theorist's formulations be understood by everyone, or at least by those who have earned advanced degrees through college and university education. It is valuable in any examination of theories to accept these fundamental notions about all theories: through a set of definitions or rules for interpretation, they have empirical references; they provide complex anticipation systems that permit predictions; they must be stated in ways that are communicable. Restated, *theories are sets of statements, understandable to others, which make predictions about empirical events.*

With these simplistic comments as the basis for accepting the limitations and delimitations of theories about the incredibly unsimple functionings of the human organism, we begin our discussion of some of the leading theories of personality, what personality is, how it is formed, grows, and influences the behavior of the individual and, in turn, the effectiveness of the work group.

Personality theory

Freud.   In any discussion of personality theory, one must begin or end with the work of Sigmund Freud, often referred to as the father of psychoanalysis. But we are not really interested in becoming psychoanalysts, so we pass by this fact and recognize that he is also called the father of *personality theory*. It is sometimes claimed that a majority of well-known theorists use the basic premises of Freud as the foundations on which they build their own theories; often they are explained by the manner in which they depart from Freud. Freud invented many words, developed a language in order to communicate his theories, many of which were originally misunderstood and vilified, especially those concerned with the sexuality of the human organism. As managers of scientists and engineers we have little practical interest in delving into sex drives and how they may motivate the individual. But we do find valuable interest in several of Freud's concepts that have been redescribed by others as *principles*.

Pleasure principle. Freud contends that man is a pleasure-seeking animal, that every act is motivated by the desire for pleasure and to some degree by the avoidance of pain. Freud was a highly moral individual who used the word "pleasure" not in the hedonistic sense but in the sense of living in a pleasant state of being, striving to avoid pain if at all possible, or, failing this, to reduce it. The search for pleasure is instinctive to animals.

Reality principle. Man not only seeks *pleasure* but is bound by limits of reality that tell him on occasion that he must postpone an immediate pleasure in favor of a future, more important pleasure. Freud believes man is aware that life is bounded by rules that, if followed, will create other pleasures for him. The principle of reality is considered to be learned, and is neither inborn nor instinctual.

Tension reduction principle. Any object in physics that is pulled in two opposing directions becomes taut, tense. The Freudian principle subsumes that man will become tightened or tense when he too is being pulled in two diametrically opposed directions. When such opposing forces are being felt, man attempts as best he can to reduce them, or to become so strong that the pressures become relatively weak and tolerable. To succumb to the pressures invites self-destruction, and instinct does not allow this. However, because man cannot ignore either the *pleasure principle* or the *reality principle*, tension becomes part of his day-to-day existence. How he copes becomes manifest in his interpersonal relationships, how he relates to his superiors, subordinates, peers and the group within his work environment.

Repetition compulsion principle. Man is a habit-following animal, inclined to repeat that which is successful. The longer he does this the more fixed the habit becomes as a part of his daily conduct. In fact, the habit can become so fixed that he may compulsively and repeatedly follow it as a method of coping with each new problem, whether or not the habit leads to success.

Id, ego, and superego.   Three terms, coined by Freud, that are especially popular among people applying his principles.

The *id*, part of the human mind, governs the part of personality that attempts to satisfy one's impulses immediately—demanding, selfish, inconsiderate. It is the total personality at birth, animal-like, uncivilized, uncultured, primitive.

The *ego* attempts to satisfy the demands of the *id*, mediating continuously between the demands of the *id* and the realities of the outside world. When the environment threatens a person's psychological security and thereby causes tension, the *ego* attempts to remove the tension. The *ego*, related to the *reality principle*, may use realistic techniques for successfully solving problems, or it may distort the realities of the situation in order to defend the sense of security. These "distortions" are known as *ego defense mechanisms.*

The *superego*, functioning as the conscience and the personality's reminder of the moral principles of society, tells the person what is and what is not acceptable behavior. According to Freud, the *superego* is formed in childhood as the result, generally, of observations of the behavior of parents or guardians, absorbed and accepted as the individual's own principles of conduct and morality.

We readily recognize in others the personality traits that have been described as *ego defense mechanisms* by Freud and others. Sometimes we recognize them as our own. These are responsible for many of the actions with which the manager has to deal on a day-to-day basis. These are distinctive manifestations of behavioral patterns that tend to cause us to apply labels to people's personalities, to like or dislike them as individuals and, of special importance to the manager, to produce personality conflicts that are counterproductive to the attainment of the group's objectives.

Defense mechanisms (according to Freud).   *Repression* prevents a prohibited desire, such as murderous anger, from attaining a conscious level of action. The repression of an impulse can produce tension. For example one person in the group, section, or project may become extremely angered by the actions or statements of another, causing an intense desire to fight back verbally or physically; but fear of the consequences causes the emotion to be unconsciously repressed. As a result of *repression*, tension may exist mutually between the two parties, or it may be felt by only one. Certainly, it has a negative effect on the job performance; it is a distraction from the work objective and the manager must recognize and deal with the situation. "Dealing with the situation," from the manager's viewpoint, may mean doing nothing, or simply allowing time to ameliorate the condition; or it may mean physical separation of the parties; or it may mean controlled confrontation as an attempt (which will probably fail) to *manage* the conflict. We describe specific techniques for managing conflict in later chapters of this book.

Regression as an ego defense mechanism, in most of Freud's writings, is concerned with returning to the behavior characteristics of one's childhood. However, it is possible to return, to regress to an earlier form of behavior that is not of childhood but of later maturity. Regression is a manifestation of the *repetition compulsion principle* discussed earlier. An engineer may take a design approach to a project that replicates a similar attempted design, although the previous effort might have ended in failure. The engineer may be emotionally smitten with his concept and, despite the previous experience, will try it again. Reasoning plays no part. The action is compulsive. The engineer then is considered to be stubbornly persistent and, thereby, may present special problems to his manager who must accomplish the task through the engineer.

Projection is a mechanism for protecting one's own *ego* from feelings of guilt by casting one's feelings toward another individual and, totally unwittingly, blaming him for the very faults or characteristics that one has himself. The individual may comment that two other members of the group strongly dislike each other, or that one of the two dislikes him. The fact may be that the individual dislikes, or even hates, one or both of the other two but to admit it to oneself may generate such feelings of guilt and tension that the *tension reduction principle* comes into play and provides the defense for the *ego*.

Reaction formation is a complex mechanism defined by Freud for the defense of the *ego*. It resembles *projection* to the extent that the individual in whom this defense mechanism is operative does not express his feelings accurately. The behavior may be considered extreme. For example, one person may overdo things by continuously repeating how delighted he is to be working on a particular project or with a specific project leader. The true feelings that are being protected by the *ego defense mechanism* are that the person actually dislikes, even abhors the project or the leader. To admit it to oneself could produce intense internal pressures, tensions that could seriously interfere with the individual's work performance and, of course, the *pleasure principle*. Shakespeare reveals his awareness of this phenomenon of personality in his frequently quoted line, "The lady doth protest too much, methinks."

Rationalization is another *ego defense mechanism* that prevents disturbing thoughts and actions from reaching the consciousness, replacing them with acceptable substitutes. The manager may encounter this in statements from an engineer or scientist that attempt to explain that the workload and the nature of the task make it impossible for a human to stay on schedule. Recall the phrase, "A poor workman finds fault with his tools." While this may be an accurate description of the situation, it is possible that, in reality, the protester is deliberately causing the work of the group, section, or department to fail. This feeling may have been caused by his conviction that he has been passed over, was neglected, or is unappreciated. The manager must learn to differentiate between an ego defense that may be an unconscious behavior and deliberately destructive activity.

Jung. Carl Jung, a student of Freud, broke with his teacher in 1911. Jung felt that Freud overemphasized the impact of instinct and sexual factors in human motivation. His own theory of personality emphasizes the idea that personality development and structure involve a pattern of opposite traits and tendencies, such as passivity versus aggressiveness and thoughts versus feelings. The popular interpretations of this, the best known part of Jung's theory of personality, is the classification of people as extroverts or introverts. The extrovert is outgoing socially, concerned mostly with the external, objective world. The introvert is more withdrawn socially, concerned with the inner, subjective world. While both of these characteristics are found in each of us, one or the other becomes dominant and forms the extroverted or introverted personality.

Adler. Alfred Adler was a follower of Sigmund Freud. They broke their relationship in a dispute over basics. Adler believed Freud understated the significance of feelings of *inferiority* and *superiority* within the individual. He formulated a theory of personality development in which they receive more attention. Adler noted that real and imagined inferiorities stem primarily from *organ weaknesses* and the specifics of the *family constellation*. An "organ weakness" can be anything from small hands to a heart with leaky valves, any physical characteristics that might restrict the capabilities of an individual in attempting to meet a competitive situation. The "family constellation" generally refers to the person's status with regard to his siblings. Relative inferiorities and superiorities of the children in a family may stimulate a complex network of rivalries that might be expressed in direct intellectual competition or in an avoidance of the intellectual domain in favor of some other areas less dominated by a sibling.

In his theory, Adler argues that a basic human drive is the need for superiority, the full development of one's potential abiltiy. Some people with a specific weakness often develop feelings of inferiority about it and try to compensate for it by developing a superior capability that is not restrained by the weakness. Thus an intensely cerebral engineer or scientist, obviously superior in his field, may have evolved from a family of athletes, a physical capability for which he may have had an organic weakness.

Horney. Karen Horney analyzed the anxiety that a child may develop through an insecure or uncertain relationship with its parents and the ways in which this anxiety may manifest itself in interpersonal relationships. Horney contends that needs for affection, approval, power, admiration, prestige, independence or personal achievement can be excessively strong in an adult who as a child was dominated, did not receive appropriate attention, respect, warmth, and admiration, or who was overprotected or discriminated against.

Sullivan. Harry Stack Sullivan studied the interpersonal processes that shape personality. He believes that the individual's personality is never separate from all other human personalities. All that the individual's personality has been, is, and will be is the product of the interpersonal contacts he makes through life. To Sullivan the world is an anxious place. Fundamentally, the world of anxiety creates tension. Out of the anxiety grows much of the basic fabric of a person's personality. Sullivan observes that at no time in his life is man free from the pressures of tension for any appreciable length of time. Tension is considered by Sullivan to be an interior system that holds man together to face the struggles of life. To the engineering manager this emphasizes a necessity to recognize that human tensions are conditions of living and, because of their underlying anxieties, the manager must be aware that peaceful coexistence within his group may not have permanence. In fact, it can be forecasted with a high level of confidence that conflicts will arise. How the manager responds to these interpersonal orientations will have a quantifiable effect on the task.

Fromm. Erich Fromm studied the relationships between the psychological processes and the social systems and social conditions under which man lives. This is referred to as *humanistic psychology*. Fromm concluded that some people or societies may becomes members of a cause, perhaps a cult, turning to a leader who promises to satisfy their social needs. Such people join and follow with extreme degrees of devotion. Fromm used humanistic psychology as an interpretation of the rise of Hitler and Nazism in Germany.

In part, Fromm's theory may explain the intense dedication to the company one witnesses from time to time on the part of people working in relatively low-level positions. Although their physical rewards may be small, they find fulfillment of social needs through their identification with the company or the department or the manager. To the manager, such devotion can be a very mixed blessing. If the devotion is to the company or the department, the manager may find himself excluded from the loyalty he seeks from the employee. He is subordinate in the mind of the devoted one. On the other hand, if he becomes the personification of the object of devotion, he may find himself faced with a personal responsibility that consumes time and energy.

In an example, one the author witnessed, the employee was a secretary overwhelmingly devoted to serving her supervisor, a division manager in a high-technology company. She became so protective of his office as to effectively build an isolation wall between her supervisor, the manager, and his people. How did the supervisor cope with the situation? A set of rules of conduct were agreed upon and written down for both the secretary and her supervisor to observe. It covered such mundane things as the techniques for handling telephone calls, requests for appointments, and the freedom of access by subordinates to the supervisor's office for communication. At least once a week, time was taken for an exchange of ideas between the secretary and her supervisor in which she was given full recognition for quality of work performed and an opportunity to contribute to the improvement of the supervisor's productivity, and for the supervisor to contribute to her continued need fulfillment.

Learning theory

Pavlov.   The experiments of the Russian scientist Ivan Petrovich Pavlov are often referred to, sometimes with cynicism bordering on sarcasm, by those who are responsible for teaching others to perform routine tasks. For example, in the series of experiments that is probably well known worldwide, he made discoveries concerned with conditioned canine behavior. While studying the digestive process in dogs, he noted that one dog would begin to salivate before food was actually put in its mouth. Eventually, he showed food to the dog before each feeding, and it became clear that the dog would begin to salivate at the sight of food. But if the food was shown and then withheld repeatedly, the dog would eventually stop salivating when shown the food. Pavlov went on to experiment with associations and stimuli such as a bell and a light. He demonstrated that under rigid laboratory controls a dog could be trained to salivate, twitch its hind leg, or perform other reactions to the sound of a bell, the sight of a light, or other properly conditioned stimuli. Pavlovian conditioning started a school within psychology known as *classical conditioning*. It found followers all over the world. Others, of course, continued this class of experiments and gained fame for their developments of theories that tended to describe the means by which humans acquired behavior or learned to perform tasks.

Watson.   Scientist John B. Watson contends that all human behavior can be analyzed in terms of stimulus and response, in that a stimulus is any change in the environment and a response is the behavioral reaction to the stimulus. He believes that there are certain inherited, innate, or inborn connections between particular stimuli and responses. An example is Pavlov's dog salivating when meat was presented. Watson also holds that the act of salivating at the sound of a bell or the turning on of a light is a learned response. His faith in his concept of conditioning was so great that he is reported to have said, "Give me a dozen healthy infants, well-formed, and my own specified world to bring them up in, and I'll guarantee to take any one at random and train him to become any type of specialist I might select—a doctor, lawyer, artist, merchant-chief and yes, even into a beggarman and thief, regardless of his talents, penchants, tendencies, abilities, vocations and race of his ancestors." Needless to say, the real world, as we know it, does not make such an experiment feasible.

Skinner.   B. F. Skinner is probably one of the best known of behavioral scientists. To the scientists involved with behavioral theories, Skinner has been a pioneer in the interpretation of the phenomena of *operant conditioning*, a learning process through which behavior is acquired, maintained, or eliminated by the consequences of that behavior. To the layman, Skinner is the scientist who taught pigeons to do such amusing things as play Ping-Pong and bowl. In his book *Beyond Freedom and Dignity* (1971), Skinner discusses behavior modification through the use of reinforcers. He argues that, instead of describing an individual's psychological state in terms of "crises," "alienation," or "low ego strength," we should focus on the behavior that characterizes such states. Once the behavior has been identified, it becomes possible to manipulate the contingencies that maintain it.

The contributions of many of the psychologists responsible for the development of acquisition or learning theories are actually in the explanations of the conditions that affect the formations and retentions of the associations between stimuli and responses. These explanations are considerably more significant than the discovery of such phenomena as salivating in response to the tinkle of a bell or the flash of a light. As a practical procedure, these methods may have been known to animal trainers long before Pavlov noted them. It is reported that gypsies trained bears to dance to music by a conditioning procedure. The bear would be chained to a surface under which a fire was built to heat a stone on which the bear stood. The gypsies would play music while the bear moved about to relieve the pain in its feet. The music became associated with feet pains. Music was the condition stimulus. Thus the sound of the music caused the bear to make foot movements that resembled dancing, the conditioned response. Of course the bear was in reality doing that which it had learned as an activity that would relieve pain when music/heat was heard/felt. Do you suppose the bear really enjoyed "dancing"?

It is possible for man, as well as the lower orders of animals, to acquire a habit, a reaction, either in an effort to avoid discomfort (anxiety) or to gain a reward (pleasure) for work performed.

The engineering manager, through the stimuli of his power to reward and his power to punish (or nonreward), may elicit the response of positive or negative behavior on the part of an individual or of the engineering group as a whole. When the response is positive, one often refers to those who react as being "motivated." When it is negative, one says they are "demotivated."

Tabular description: Personality and learning theories

Theory/Principle	Author	Definition
Pleasure principle	Sigmund Freud	The search for pleasure and the avoidance of pain are instinctive and highly motivational
Reality principle	Sigmund Freud	In the search for "pleasure" and the avoidance of "pain," man learns that reality may delay fulfillment
Tension reduction principle	Sigmund Freud	Tensions are generated by the opposing forces of the "pleasure" and "reality" principles; tensions are reflected in the interpersonal relationships of the individual
Repetition compulsion principle	Sigmund Freud	The tendency to repeat an initially successful experience may readily become a "habit," causing the individual to repeat the experience whether or not it is successful each new time it is attempted
Id	Sigmund Freud	The primitive personality with which we are born; causing us to be demanding, selfish, and inconsiderate
Ego	Sigmund Freud	The "intermediator" between id and reality whose prime function appears to be to reduce tensions
Superego	Sigmund Freud	Formed in the childhood years, the superego keeps us aware of

Theory/Principle	Author	Definition
		the demands of societal behavior; self-protectively, the superego may cause the ego defense mechanisms to take control
Repression*	Sigmund Freud	Restraining one's self, holding back a desire to take an action, or controlling an impulsive desire to do something that is prohibited by society
Regression*	Sigmund Freud	Returning to the behavior of one's childhood or of an earlier experience; related to repetition compulsion
Projection*	Sigmund Freud	Protecting one's own ego, particularly against feelings of guilt; often by refusing to admit one's own deficiencies to one's self and often manifested by a tendency to pass the blame to others
Reaction formation*	Sigmund Freud	An overstatement of projection, manifested by a tendency to disguise negative feelings by being quite vocal in positive proclamations
Rationalization*	Sigmund Freud	Protecting the ego by finding substitutes for feelings that may be personally disturbing; such as blaming tools or the environment for an unsuccessful effort
Extrovert/Introvert	Carl Jung	Each of us has the characteristics of the introvert and the extrovert; however, one of the two will become more dominant at times
Inferiority/Superiority complexes	Alfred Adler	A basic human drive is the need for superiority; some people with specific weaknesses or inferior capabilities in one area may compensate by becoming superior in another

*Ego Defense mechanism.

Theory/Principle	Author	Definition
Anxiety neuroses	Karen Horney	Anxiety may develop through an insecure or uncertain childhood relationship with parents; exhibited in adult life as a powerful search for affection, approval, power, admiration, prestige, independence or for personal achievement
Anxiety/Tension	Harry Sullivan	Anxiety creates tension; we are never free from either and therefore conflict is inevitable
Humanistic psychology	Erich Fromm	People and societies become members of cults or join causes whose leaders appear to promise to satisfy perceived needs. A subordinate may become intensely loyal to a supervisor because of a personal need that may be fulfilled through this relationship
Classical conditioning	Ivan Pavlov	Associations of stimuli and responses that tend to describe the acquisition or development of behavior or learning how to perform specific tasks
Continuation of conditioning	John Watson	All human behavior can be analyzed in terms of stimulus and may be conditioned deliberately to respond in a desired (if not desirable) way to a programmed stimulus
Operant conditioning	B. F. Skinner	Behavior modification can be achieved through a learning process; an individual's behavior can be modified or maintained through the development of a system of rewards and punishments for responses to stimuli that reinforce the recognition of the consequences of specific behaviors.

Note the considerable similarity among the theories and principles of behavioral scientists such as Pavlov, Watson, and Skinner; however, their experiments and conclusions independently performed tend to verify one another and extend the depth of understanding of human behavior, how it may be developed, learned, modified, or maintained through appropriate stimuli. The effective manager of engineers and scientists recognizes the part he must play in the process of "conditioning" in order to satisfy the needs of all elements of the Wheel of Interaction.

2
The search for satisfaction

We now move beyond the aspects of personality formation, habits, and instincts into the realm of adult behavior—adult from the chronological standpoint. *Growth theory* emphasizes the human need to advance as an individual, to move in the direction of realizing one's maximum potential. In this stage, man is concerned with personal needs, achievement, self-fulfillment, and need satisfaction.

The manager who is accountable for the work performed by others has several choices as *the manager*. He can "pull rank," commanding his subordinates to perform. He can ignore the individual as a complexity of needs, anxieties, and conflicts and insist on the rule of "eight hours' pay for eight hours' work"—you owe your soul to the company store. This power is born out of a company document. On the other hand, he can develop a knowledge of the intricate human organism and use that knowledge in an endeavor to satisfy the separate and combined needs of the individual, the group, the company entity. This power is born out of knowledge. There is no hard and fast rule that any one of the alternatives is correct. In fact, they are all correct. But at times one may be more "correct," more *effective*, than any of the others.

The manager, a human organism with his own sets of needs and intricacies, cannot be expected to play "God," and he would be operating on very soft ground if he were to attempt to be a psychiatrist or a psychotherapist. What is expected of him is a great abundance of flexibility of managerial style. Tough or democratic, when necessary.

People have needs

What about the *needs?* Does man work solely for pay? Does he live for bread alone? How does one explain the phenomenon of the engineer or scientist who, having been made two job offers, each with the same pay and equivalent fringe benefits and geographic locations, is able to make a choice of one over the other? What factors influenced the decision? There are, of course, theories that attempt to explain the elements that do come into play. These are the theories of leading behavioral scientists Frederick Herzberg, Abraham Maslow, Douglas McGregor, David McClelland, and others. We will discuss those that have found the greatest support in the psychiatric and managerial communities.

Behavioral sciences

Herzberg. Frederick Herzberg was concerned primarily with motivation when he conducted a study that has become both well-known and controversial. He used the critical incident method of obtaining data for analysis from among approximately 200 accountants and engineers employed by eleven firms in the general area of Pittsburgh, Pennsylvania. The professional subjects in the study were given these directions:

> Think of a time when you felt exceptionally good or exceptionally bad about your job, either your present job or any other job you have had. This can be either the "long-range" or the "short-range" kind of situation, as I have just described it. Tell me what happened.

Responses were fairly consistent and have been widely published, quoted, accepted, and challenged. Do recognize the important fact that the statement was put to professionals, not to hourly production-line people performing routine tasks, but to people who, in their daily work, are expected to exercise judgment and initiative, possibly some creativity. *Good* feelings that were reported were associated with job experiences and job content. *Bad* feelings were generally associated with the physical environment, lack of opportunity for advancement, and other peripheral aspects of the job. An example of the *good* feelings was reported by an accountant who had been given the responsibility for planning and supervising the installation of computer equipment. He took pride in the knowledge that the new system would have an important effect on the overall functioning of his department and that he had been selected for the assignment. An engineer gave an example of *bad* feelings. His first assignment had been to keep tabulation sheets and manage the office when his supervisor, the engineering manager, was away. It seems that the manager was always too busy to provide what the engineer believed was adequate training. Further, the manager would become annoyed and impatient when the engineer tried to ask questions in an attempt to learn. Within this context, the engineer reported he felt frustrated by the job, unrecognized and in a dead-end situation.

Herzberg developed a theory, on the basis of this study, that is known as *Herzberg's Two-Factor Theory*. He defined the two factors as *satisfiers* and *dissatisfiers*. The satisfiers were labeled *motivators* and the dissatisfiers were called *hygiene factors*. It is important to understand the concept and remove any ambiguities that might be created through the semantics. First, let's tabulate Herzberg's Two-Factor Theory.

Hygiene Factors (Dissatisfiers)	Motivators (Satisfiers)
Policies and administration	Achievement
Supervision	Recognition for accomplishments
Working conditions	Challenging work
Money, status, security	Responsibility
	Growth and development opportunity

A "dissatisfier" is a factor that, if inadequate in quality or quantity, can lead to unhappiness, tension, conflict, and frustration in the employee. Converting a *dissatisfier* to a *satisfier*—for example, increasing an employee's salary in reaction to a complaint, or moving his desk closer to a window where the light is better—may alleviate the causes of dissatisfaction, improve the *hygiene factors*, but they do not necessarily *motivate* the individual to better performance levels. While there may be a short upward spurt in interest, it is not likely to be sustainable in the form of increases in output or productivity.

The respondents to the study keyed *good feelings* to the specific tasks being performed, the job itself. When they had *bad feelings*, they were usually attributed to a sense of being treated less than fairly, the administration of policy, and the environment in which the job was performed.

While *motivators* have a positive uplifting influence on morale and attitudes that are demonstrated through increased output, the *hygiene factors* produce no such direct improvement. It is probable that *motivators* cannot operate effectively or at maximum potential when dissatisfiers are prevalent. The *hygiene factors* are imperatives for positive morale and attitudes, critical elements of a base upon which the *motivators* may be constructed.

The manager of engineering and scientific personnel has learned from experience that the greatest attractions he can offer to desirable candidates are the qualities listed as *motivators*. And he has learned from experience that in order to retain these valuable staff members, there must be a continuum of *motivators*. The engineer and scientist must know that when the current project is completed, there will be another stimulating project onto which his talents, knowledge, and skills can be transferred, continuing to offer challenge, growth, development, recognition—the act of being transferred to a new assignment in itself can represent recognition—and opportunities for achievement and increased responsibility.

One of the conclusions that may be drawn from the Herzberg study is that in the basics of the need for specific *motivators*, engineers and perhaps other professionals do have much in common. It is vital that the manager recognize this and know how to respond. A typical response from many of the personnel managers of small and big companies is: "There is a wide diversity of needs among all workers and most employees don't know what they want."

Such thinking condemns one to take the "easy" way out. Deal with dissatisfiers! Do so by telling the employees what it is they really want. This is demonstrated in the popular "employee communications programs" one sees in the form of bulletins attached to boards in each department and work area. The bulletins, in order to constitute a program, take the form of a periodical publication. They usually describe the fringe benefits, management's leadership skills, and the wondrous merits of working for the company. Note the photographs of employees posing with their supervisors receiving plaques and cash awards for ideas contributed that saved money; the bowling team; the softball team; "good old Joe" at his retirement luncheon; the new building or employees' lunchroom. These, in effect, may be attempts to create satisfaction or to eliminate dissatisfiers by showing the employees how well the company is meeting their needs.

According to Herzberg's theory, if the intent is to motivate, the point will surely be lost. But communications programs are not all negative or wasted effort. The engineering manager can use such programs, such bulletins to give *recognition* for accomplishment within the company. He can ask or persuade the communications manager to do a profile on a member of his professional staff, reporting on special accomplishments such as the award of a patent, the presentation of a technical paper, the successful completion of a project or task with information on the special noteworthiness of the occasion, a promotion within the department, or the arrival of a new staff member. Such communications are concerned with the job itself and the significance of the individual or of the professional group in relation to the content of the work—what the staff will do for the company, as well as the converse.

Maslow. Abraham Maslow suggests a classification of *needs* and the relationships among them. He believes that man naturally tries to satisfy his unmet needs and that therefore unsatisfied needs are *motivators*. The simplistic conclusion one might draw from this statement is that if management can identify the operant needs and create an environment in which the employee sees the possibility for satisfying these needs, performance and productivity should improve. This is "simplistic" only because of the impracticability of rapidly identifying each individual's needs as they come to the fore, or those of a group as its needs become evident, and the severe difficulty in rapidly developing actions that will simultaneously satisfy the needs (even if they have been accurately identified) of individual, group, manager, subordinate, superior, and the company.

Nonetheless, Maslow arranges needs in a progression, a *hierarchy of needs* that ranges from those that are *primary*, or unlearned, those with which all animal life is born; to those that are *secondary*, or acquired from the environment.

Examples of *primary needs*, all natural, include hunger—the need to consume food; thirst—the need to drink fluids; sleep—the irresistible need to lie down, close one's eyes and enter a comatose state. Other biological functions are natural, and do not have to be learned.

Examples of secondary needs include status—the need to impress one's neighbors or friends, possibly by owning a large and impressive home, fancy clothes, a new automobile, and country-club membership; power—the ability to influence others, become a leader instead of a follower; acquisition of material goods and wealth—more than is necessary to satisfy the basic, primary needs. These are not instinctive or innate; they are learned through the environment in which the person is reared and to whose influences he is exposed.

One can readily describe the motivational effect of a primary need such as hunger or thirst. Who hasn't been so hungry or thirsty that he would have given almost anything for a cracker or a mouthful of water? How many times have manager's meetings had to be interrupted for a break for lunch, coffee, or what have you? At the moment of intense hunger or thirst, that primary need is dominant and becomes the critical driving force. One can hardly wait for the food to arrive, not because of the need to return to the meeting room but because of the physiological drive to eat and drink. Then, having had one's fill, having satisfied the need, other needs come to the fore and demand satisfaction. In fact, if one has oversatisfied the need for food by overeating, there is virtually no inducement or incentive that can be found that would make one eat another morsel. The need, once adequately satisfied, ceases to be a motivator or driving influence.

Maslow's hierarchy of needs can be diagrammed.

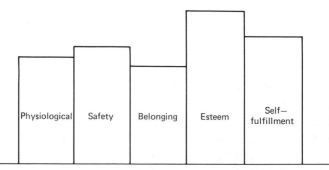

Figure 1 Hierarchy of needs, according to Maslow. The five basic needs are diagrammed in sequence from left to right. However, the heights of the needs vary to indicate that they are not always equal in demanding satisfaction. At any given moment, the dominant need would be depicted as having the greatest height and would be the motivating force, influencing individual and group behavior.

1 *Physiological.* The unlearned primary needs.

2 *Safety.* Emotional, as well as physical shelter and security. Imagine the cave man or the warrior in the field searching for a place to rest and sleep where he will be safe from peril. Having found the safety, having satisfied this need, his search stops and another need becomes manifest.

3 *Belonging.* The need to be loved, feel needed and wanted, to identify with a group—societal, social, or business—is the third level in this hierarchy. The need for "love" is not intended here in the context of sex, which is actually a physiological need.

4 *Esteem.* At this level in the hierarchy, reference is usually made to the "higher order" of needs. The first three needs are, thus, the "lower order." This is the arena of the *ego*, where self-esteem and gaining respect, admiration, and recognition from others become important motivators. The needs for power, achievement, and status (real or symbolic) are part of this level.

5 *Self-fulfillment.* Often called "self-actualization," this need may be aroused as a motivator within a person who has satisfied all other needs or who, through frustration at not being able to satisfy some of the other needs, must attempt to make a reality of the perception he has of himself.

More than one need may be operating at the same time.

Needs do not necessarily occur in this sequence. A person lost in the wilderness, caught in a snowstorm, may successfully overcome the physiological need for sleep, which, if responded to under the circumstances, could result in death. The need to find shelter would become the motivating need instead.

Assume that a staff engineer or scientist is being adequately paid for work performed. He is able to satisfy his physiological needs, including those of his family. Assume, also, that the economy is such that the engineer or scientist can readily find employment in his field. An attempt to offer him the security of a pension plan while he is, say, in his thirties or forties will be virtually meaningless, and thereby fail as a motivator. When the engineer's or scientist's physiological and safety needs have been taken care of, he may seek *belonging*—identification with a company known for its technological superiority, for its engineering orientation. In our society's continuing growth as a *technological* society, many companies recognize this need on the part of the professional and actively publicize and advertise the company's accomplishments. In addition to influencing the financial community of investors and advisors, the objective is quite often to retain those outstanding professionals already on the staff and to attract others who are motivated to satisfy the need for participation in the superior professional society the company represents.

The engineer-manager can aid in *esteem-need* satisfaction by encouraging the professionals to actively participate in the relevant professional societies and associations, to deliver technical papers at society meetings, to hold office, to attend conferences (with the financial support of the company), and by providing various forms of recognition and opportunities for advancement.

The satisfying of the *self-fulfillment needs* is a matter of individual drive and/or frustration and a simple formula for managing a person with this dominant need cannot be stated. It will certainly provide a test of the manager's skills in comprehension and the invention of responses. Effective means for satisfying the needs of those who actively seek self-actualization, whether because they have already satisfied all other needs (unlikely) or because they have been frustrated in attempts to satisfy other needs (more likely) and must attempt to realize their own perceptions of themselves, include encouragement to take advanced studies and pursue advanced degrees at colleges and universities (with the financial support of the company), job enrichment as opposed to job enlargement in the form of challenging work tasks for which they may be uniquely equipped.

As we progress more deeply into the how-to of management we will explore specific manifestations and appropriate managerial responses. It is important to note that the satisfaction of any need is transitory. Satisfaction of any one of the needs is indeed rarely permanent. It is interesting to note that high productivity and low turnover are often found where professionals have low security, but where good opportunities for self-fulfillment are continuously present.

McGregor.   Douglas McGregor observes that the professional person, the engineer as he designs equipment, draws upon the knowledge of science and of his colleagues, and upon knowledge gained through personal experience. The degree to which he relies upon the first two rather than the third is one of the ways in which the professional may be distinguished from the layman. McGregor observes that the typical manager has been slow to utilize social science knowledge, feeling that his own personal experience with people has been so rich that he has little need to turn elsewhere for knowledge of human behavior. He often feels that the social scientist's knowledge is theoretical while his (the manager's) experience is quite related to reality. This is a dichotomous viewpoint wherein, despite the fact that he is a professional engineer or scientist, the manager favors the validity of personal observation and challenges the body of scientific knowledge, even though it may be theoretical. Without conscious awareness, the majority of industrial managers tend to divide their beliefs about human behavior into two theories, labeled by McGregor as "X" and "Y."

Theory X reflects a belief that management must counteract the human tendency to avoid work—that man has an inherent dislike of work. McGregor comments that a good deal of lip service is given to the ideal of the worth of the average human being, but that a great many managers privately support the assumption that the average person prefers to be directed, wishes to avoid responsibility, has very little ambition, wants security above all. Those who follow the assumptions of Theory X believe that because of this characteristic dislike of work, most people must be coerced, controlled, directed, threatened with punishment to get them to put forth adequate effort toward the achievement of organizational objectives. The dislike of work is so strong that even the promise of rewards is not generally enough to overcome it; only the threat of punishment will do the trick. The manager who buys the assumptions about human nature as described in Theory X generally adopts a management style that is sometimes described as the "carrot-and-the-stick," a style that has also been colorfully described as "pat them on the head while kicking them in the rear!"

Theory Y, on the other hand, assumes that the average individual has great potential for growth, that the limits on the integration of workers' needs with those of the organization are not limits of human nature but of management's ingenuity in discovering how to realize the potential of its human resources. The assumptions that McGregor refers to as Theory Y are completely counter to those of Theory X. Theory Y assumes that the expenditure of physical and mental effort in work is as natural as play or rest; that work may be, depending on controllable conditions, a source of satisfaction or a source of punishment.

Further, according to Theory Y, man will exercise self-direction and self-control in the service of objectives to which he is committed; external control and the threat of punishment are not the only means for bringing about effort toward organizational objectives. Commitment to objectives is a function of the rewards associated with their achievement—the satisfaction of ego and self-actualization needs, for example. And the average human being learns, under proper conditions, not only to accept but to seek responsibility; avoidance is generally one of the *consequences of experience*, not an inherent human characteristic. The capacity to exercise a relatively high degree of imagination, ingenuity, and creativity in the solution of organizational problems is widely, not narrowly, distributed in the population. And, finally, under the conditions of modern industrial life, the intellectual potentialities of the average human being are only partially utilized.

Theory Y, if one sincerely accepts its assumptions about human nature, places causes for laziness, indifference, avoidance of responsibility, intransigence, lack of creativity and an uncooperative attitude squarely in the lap of management and its methods of organization and control.

McGregor's theories about human nature may not be difficult to accept, but they do challenge a number of managerial habits of thought and action. The manager may proclaim he personally believes in the assumptions of one theory over the other, but practicing those styles of management that are implied by either theory can be exceptionally difficult. The manager's belief in the "goodness" of man (Theory Y) and the practice of this belief is the same as the belief in the physical phenomenon of creating a perfect vacuum; it has not yet been achieved in general practice. Integration of individual and organizational objectives demands more skill of the manager than does an autocratic approach to the individual. It is the manager, more than the subordinate, who must accept responsibility and self-control if he would implement his faith in Theory Y.

McClelland.   David C. McClelland is one of the leading investigators of motivation. His studies have been conducted on a worldwide basis, with diverse societies, cultures, and ethnic groups. McClelland was strongly influenced by the findings of earlier investigators of the 1930s. He began his investigations in the 1950s and out of these came his theory that each of us possesses three needs—*power, affiliation,* and *achievement.* McClelland believes that people differ essentially in the degree to which these needs or motives dominate their behavior at any given moment.

1 Need for power. The word "power" is used in the sense of one's ability to influence the thoughts and actions of another. The actual achievement of a desired goal is secondary in its importance to the individual whose *need for power* is dominant. What does matter is the exercise of *power* itself.

This is demonstrated in meetings and conversations that may originally have been intended for the purpose of creative thought, problem-solving, defining a course of action or scientific investigation, or for the development of consensus. In such a situation, the person with a dominant need for power will attempt to influence, persuade, or control the thought processes of other professionals in the group. It is not the rightness of his technical approach as an engineer that matters to the power-need person, it is the satisfaction he derives from having successfully persuaded the other professionals in the group to his way.

The phenomenon of the expression of the *power* need will often emerge in a brainstorming session, disobeying the brainstorming rule that forbids on-the-spot critiquing of another's idea. The individual who seeks satisfaction of his need for *power* has great difficulty in participating in such a democratic process. He is compulsive about putting his own ideas and concepts before the group or the individual and pressing for acceptance, while simultaneously "putting down" those presented by others.

The engineering manager who finds himself confronted by a member of his professional staff at the moment when the member's *power* need is dominant faces a great potential for conflict and frustration. By recognizing the situation, being consciously aware of the psychological forces that are in play, the probability is great that a course of effective managerial action will be found that will satisfy, at least in part, the needs of the individual, the group, the company, and the manager himself who, one must not forget, has his own set of needs that seek satisfaction. If the manager and his subordinate are simultaneously trying to satisfy the same need, and if the concepts or approaches to the work problem are severely divergent, there is potential for conflict between them. There are several approaches, as there usually are, to the successful handling of the situation. One may be to "pull rank" and order the subordinate to follow his "leader." Another is to give in to the subordinate, allow for complete satisfaction of his needs and accept one's own frustration as part of the price of being a manager. Yet another is to attempt a compromise between the manager's and his subordinate's positions, which may frustrate the objectives of the individuals, the group, or the company. We will explore other routes that offer maximum probability for success when we deal with the specifics of *conflict resolution.*

2 Need for affiliation. Those whose needs are dominated by affiliation, who derive satisfaction primarily from social and interpersonal activities, are motivated principally by a sense of belonging to or identification with a group, a company. If given the choice of working with people who are technically competent or those who are their friends, they will choose their friends. They are, at times, recognized as compulsive talkers who are invariably part of a group, even a clique. They are active in the department's or the company's bowling league, softball team, and other social activities that enable them to gain satisfaction of the *need for affiliation.*

The engineering manager who does not recognize the existence of the *affiliation* need is the one who is totally surprised at the strongly negative reactions of some of his people when, in a desire to provide what he considers to be a degree of privacy, he has partitions installed between work stations and desks. The person who has a strong need for *affiliation* views the partitions as threatening, as counter to his motivation, his need for societal participation; the partitions will most certainly generate grumbling, can even cause a fall-off in his productive output. On the other hand, others may welcome the relative isolation and the improved degree of privacy as an aid to meeting their different needs.

3 Need for achievement. Reaching their goals, the attainment of specific objectives, are the motivational influences of individuals high in the *need for achievement.* High achievers are not necessarily motivated by money per se; however, they use money and the acquisition of material goods as visible, physical measurements of levels of *achievement.*

High achievers require immediate feedback, statements of their progress against goals. They will avoid tasks and projects that are at the extremes of "easy" and "difficult." They prefer assignments that are of moderate difficulty, with at least a 50-50 probability for success (or failure). Also, they tend to be loners, preferring to work independently so that performance against objectives can be related quite specifically to their own efforts rather than to someone else's. High achievers avoid gambling situations wherein they do not have control over the outcome. They are the traditional "penny-ante" players if "caught" in a poker game.

It could represent a significant misunderstanding of the individual's motives to believe that his hesitation to accept an assignment, or the flat rejection of it, is caused by lack of self-confidence or of specific skills. Similarly, but conversely, the "young tiger's" eagerness to accept an enormous challenge may be caused by (a) inexperience or (b) the absence of a fundamental *need for achievement*; he has not weighed the risks and opportunities inherent in the challenge as carefully as would an individual in whom the need was dominant. On the other hand, the "tiger" may accept the assignment (not as a challenge) because it satisfies or appears to offer satisfaction of other needs (*affiliation* or *power*).

It is important for the manager to recognize those needs that are dominant in the individual and to make a determination as to whether or not the person fits the job description, the project or task, the group, and the company. To accept enthusiasm as the sole basis for making an assignment is to create a "sink or swim" risk situation for all persons involved, including the manager.

The climate within an organization is both a product and a determining factor of motivation. Climate can be defined as a feedback loop, regenerative or negative, that may satisfy or inhibit the inherent characteristics of the individual. Power-oriented organizations, such as the military, will tend to attract and provide support for those who have a *need for power*. Organizations with reputations for people orientation will attract and give support to those who would satisfy the *need for affiliation*. Supported by McClelland's theory, a manager who believes that the organization is best served by high achievers and wants to attract and keep those who have a *need for achievement* will design a climate directed toward that objective. Such a climate might very well contain the following incentives:

1 A reward system, possibly money, certainly recognition, related to attainment of specific objectives.
2 Emphasis given to the individual's performance rather than to that of the group.

3 A goal-setting procedure that enables each individual to participate in the setting of his own quantified goals in accordance with those of the organization.

4 Rapid feedback on performance and immediate rewards for successful task fulfillment.

5 Relative independence for the individual from other segments of the organization.

Recognize, if you will, that the above incentives are those that are often used by sales-oriented organizations or aggressive and successful sales managers. Perhaps this explains the behavioral rationale and needs of the successful sales engineer. He has a numerical quota, a standard by which his performance will be measured. It is a standard established with his strong participation and acceptance. He receives sales reports with high frequency, usually weekly, as rapid feedback on performance. Commissions, bonuses, or incentive payments are received as quickly as possible after the close of the related time period of the quota. And the sales engineer prefers to be away from the home office, working independently in the field. He "affiliates" with his customers as the means for satisfying the societal need.

Now that a better understanding of what makes the sales engineer "run" has been outlined, it is entirely conceivable that a climate can be created and a series of systems can be generated that recognize the needs of the professional staff, that offer opportunities for motivational development, and that satisfy the complexities of the individual (self), associates (peers), the organization (group), and the subordinates and superiors with whom each must interact.

How do the theories correlate?

It is interesting to note the ways in which the theories of the four most-often quoted behavioral scientists relate to each other.

Maslow is credited with the development of the theory that man's needs can be described in an ascending order, a *hierarchy of needs*. The *lower order of needs* has, for each person, limited value as work motivators. The lower order consists of *physiological* and *security* needs that man has learned to satisfy, either through direct efforts as in pioneer days of self-provisioning or through indirect efforts such as working just enough to earn the wherewithal that might be exchanged for those things that satisfy these needs. The *higher order of needs, affiliation, ego* and *self-esteem*, and *self-actualization*, have relatively infinite value. Some people will cease their efforts when their perceptions of *physiological* and *security* needs have been satisfied. Others will continue to pursue satisfaction of *ego* and *self-actualization* needs to a degree that, at times, may appear to be insatiable. It is these "pursuits" that often become the constructive drives, the manager's motivators. These same drives, when compulsively obeyed, can make executives at high levels of management risk home, marriage, and familial relationships as they attempt to climb (sometimes claw) their way to the top of the organization's ladder.

The *hierarchy of needs*, as defined by *Maslow*, has served as the foundation for theories of growth and adult behavior, the focal point upon which many other scientists have based their studies. *Herzberg* divides his theory into two basic levels, *motivators* and *hygiene factors*. The latter are essentials for positive attitudes and good morale. Herzberg points out that the presence of a *hygiene factor* is a *satisfier* and its absence is a *dissatisfier*. Yet, altering a *dissatisfier* so that it becomes a *satisfier* does not necessarily result in *motivation*. For example, an engineer who feels he is not being paid adequately is *dissatisfied* because of the absence of this *hygiene factor*. However, giving a salary increase, even if it meets the specific "demand" of the engineer, does not necessarily result in improvements in productivity. It may, for a while at least, reduce the dissatisfaction, reduce the "noise level" of griping. Herzberg's *hygiene factors* equate with the *lower order of needs* in Maslow's hierarchy with a discernible overlap into the mid-level, *affiliation* needs. Herzberg's *motivators* may include a degree of need for *affiliation*; most certainly are responses to the *higher order of needs* in Maslow's hierarchy.

McClelland deals entirely with *motivation*, pays little attention to such aspects as *hygiene factors*. His theory of *power, achievement*, and *affiliation* as the prime motivators is easily identified with Maslow's *higher order of needs* in the hierarchy.

McGregor's *Theory X* and *Theory Y* contend that a manager's style reflects his assumption of the nature of people. Those who assume that *Theory X* accurately describes the nature of man assume that man does not have the capacity, certainly is not willing to rise above the *lower order of needs*; material values are virtually all man is concerned with. The manager who makes these assumptions is generally quite *autocratic* in his relationship with his people. His orientation is entirely toward attainment and completion of the tasks for which he is accountable, and which (he probably would say "unfortunately") must be delegated as the responsibility of people who are his assigned resource. On the other hand, the manager whose assumptions are identified with *Theory Y* believes that "man does not live by bread alone, but by faith, by admiration, by sympathy" (Ralph Waldo Emerson). This aligns with the *higher order of needs*. The style of such a manager seeks a balance between people orientation and task fulfillment and is often described as "participative."

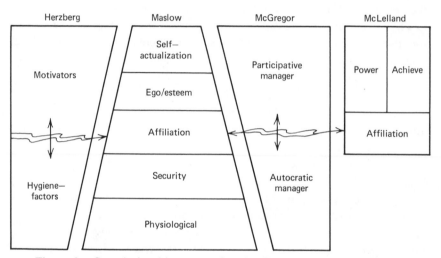

Figure 2   Correlationship among four leading behavioral scientists.

Figure 2 diagrams the correlations, as we have described them, among the theories of behavior within the work environment developed by Maslow, Herzberg, McGregor and McClelland.

In later chapters we will discuss the application of motivation theories and become involved with specific situational analyses and recommendations for courses of managerial action that offer the maximum probability for achieving a desired result.

3
Who am I?

The ability to be objective about oneself is a rare one. It is almost impossible to see ourselves as others do. Our ego defense mechanisms spare us the pain and discomfort of seeing most of our own faults, many of which we can do nothing about.

Yet each of us does have a certain perception of self, a view of his own personality, and a tendency to attempt to predict his own responses to specific stimuli. We are the products of our heredity, environment, and experiences. The complexity of the human mind and the virtually unmeasurable number of variables and interactions that impact on the early formation of our personalities and behavioral systems result in what becomes identified as, for better or worse, our *individuality*.

Few of us react identically to a given set of circumstances that comprise a situation, an interrelationship, an interaction. To add further complexity, most of us do not react consistently to the same set of conditions. For example, the timid, meek, or unassertive person who is a Caspar Milquetoast at work might very well be tyrannical and aggressive in a social or family environment. The converse can also be true. The very same exposures may cause exhilaration, interest, and attraction in some, while causing enervation, ennui, and avoidance reactions in others.

Do we have the courage to ask others what kind of manager they believe us to be? Not likely, for fear that what we might hear could cause anxiety and tension. Man does not like anxiety and tension and will go out of his way to avoid the intense discomfort they are capable of generating. When someone volunteers a description of us as a manager, how do we respond? We like to think "We can take it!" But parenthetically (since we can usually "take it" only when the description flatters and praises), the pleasure-seeking principle and the need for high self-esteem might very well make the volunteered information (and the volunteer) appear to be unfriendly. And because of the possibility that we may harbor self-doubts, a description of us as a highly desirable manager (with suitable amplifying adjectives) can arouse suspicion, thoughts that the volunteer is playing politics, "brown-nosing," "buttering up the boss," and other phrases that pooh-pooh overtly generous comments. We search for covert motives.

How, then, do we gain an honest, overt, unselfish appraisal of ourselves as human beings and as managers? Of course, we can visit a "shrink," a psychologist who specializes in industrial environments. We can satisfy ourselves with observations about our advancements within the company, in responsibilities assigned, in titles given, in salary increases and bonuses awarded. Aren't these evidence of performance as the right kind of manager? They might be, and then again they might not. Our performance might be correct under one form of organizational leadership—hard-nosed chief executive officers may seek out hard-nosed managers. Change the leader and, if the predecessor's style was different (isn't it usually?), is ours appropriate? If not appropriate, can we modify our own behavior without diminishing our effectiveness as a manager of engineers and scientists? Can we do it within a suitable time frame? What is our philosophy of management and people? What are our own needs?

Here are two self-evaluation vehicles. They are free of human foible or politics, incapable of liking or disliking you for any reason. One is based on the theories and assumptions of Douglas McGregor, Theory X and Theory Y, which we discussed in the previous chapter. The other is based on Abraham Maslow's hierarchy of needs and Frederick Herzberg's hygiene-factor and motivator concepts, also discussed in the previous chapter. They present statements and situations to which you are to give your off-the-top-of-the-head response. At the end of each self-evaluation vehicle is the method of scoring yourself and an explanation of the scores through which you develop a picture of yourself as a manager of others, the professionals on your staff. We begin with McGregor as the base.

You and McGregor

Douglas McGregor does not advocate a style of management. He does contend that the assumptions a manager holds about people form the philosophy that leads to a manager's style, his responses to superiors and associates and, especially, to his subordinates. Here we present a series of statements based on McGregor's concepts. Some are controversial and even in disagreement with each other. You may have varying degrees of reaction to some of the statements. This is perfectly natural; many other managers, no doubt, share your agreements and disagreements with what follows. As an engineer or scientist, you will recognize that there are no right or wrong answers, that there are only personal points of view. You will, therefore, be expressing your very own opinion. In responding, it is important that you be as honest and as direct as you can possibly be. Any efforts to depict yourself as you think you should be (or as you think others would like you to be) can introduce a distortion that would render the results meaningless, certainly not applicable to yourself. Check the space associated with each statement that indicates the degree of acceptance or rejection you hold for it.

Statement or Belief	Accept		Reject	
	Much	Little	Little	Much
1 Man has goals that are naturally opposed to those of the organization.				
2 The average human being will avoid work if he can.				
3 Most people work only because they have to.				
4 The average human being prefers to be directed.				
5 Generally, one can trust the subordinates who report to him.				
6 Minimum effort, maximum reward—that's what most people want.				
7 The use of authority is the best way for a manager to get things done.				

Statement or Belief	Accept		Reject	
	Much	Little	Little	Much
8 People, regardless of skills or level in the organization, search for values and accomplishments on the job.				
9 Security is the most important thing to the average human being.				
10 Increased offerings of money are usually not enough of an incentive to overcome people's inherent dislike of work.				
11 The average person in an organization, under proper conditions, will accept and seek responsibility.				
12 The average person has potentials that are considerably greater than those generally recognized in today's organizations.				
13 A cold and objective concern should always be demonstrated toward problems that arise in the organization.				
14 Subordinates must be controlled and directed by their managers if one wants them to work toward the goals of the organization.				
15 Good managers should seek rationality and the elimination of emotional factors in the work environment.				
16 Human beings are primarily self-motivated and exercise self-controls.				
17 It is wise not to be too trusting of others in an organization.				
18 Generally, you can trust your superiors.				
19 The employee who wants security is the type that is most often encountered.				
20 Most employees can handle a cer-				

Statement or Belief	Accept		Reject	
	Much	Little	Little	Much
tain amount of autonomy and independence on the job.				
21 People will try to get away with as much as they can.				
22 People naturally look for their most rewarding experiences away from the job.				
23 On the job, most people are not self-starters.				
24 Managers can depend on the individual to exercise self-control in the performance of many of the organization's tasks.				
25 The average human being avoids responsibility.				
26 The average human being is able to find work a source of satisfaction and fulfillment.				
27 The way they usually are, people have to be coerced, controlled, directed, or threatened with punishment to get them to exert adequate effort toward the achievement of the organization's objectives.				
28 Generally, you can trust your peers and colleagues.				
29 Unfortunately, the average human being doesn't have very much ambition.				
30 Also, he has an inherent dislike for work.				
31 The majority of employees have the capacity to exercise a high degree of creativity, imagination, and ingenuity in solving the organization's problems.				
32 Intuitively, most people are indifferent, or even antagonistic toward the company's objectives.				
33 It is unhealthy, from the organization's viewpoint, to give greater				

Statement or Belief	Accept		Reject	
	Much	Little	Little	Much
independence to most of the employees.				
34 The manager, in order to reduce the potential for conflict, should restrict interaction between subordinates and encourage interaction with him.				
35 Money, fringe benefits, and other such tangible incentives are essential to the motivation of the employee in order to assure productivity.				
36 If the employee has personally committed himself to organizational objectives, he does not need external controls or threats of punishment, but will exercise self-control and self-direction.				

The following numbers identify the statements above that are clearly aligned with *Theory X*:

1	2	3	4	6	7	9	10	13	14	15	17
19	21	22	23	25	27	29	30	32	33	34	35

The following numbers identify the statements that are clearly aligned with *Theory Y*:

5   8   11   12   16   18   20   24   26   28   31   36

Each check mark under the "Accept Much" Column carries a value of 4 points and each check mark under the "Accept Little" column carries a value of 3 points. Each check mark under the "Reject Little" column carries a value of 2 points and each check mark under the "Reject Much" column carries a value of 1 point.

Make separate totals for the statements aligned with Theory X and Theory Y, applying the appropriate values for the "much" and "little" check marks. Now, multiply the total arrived at for Theory Y by a factor of 2.

Theory X totals = _____

Theory Y totals × 2 = _____

Compare the two totals. The larger of these two numbers reflects your philosophical assumptions of the nature of man, favoring one of the two theories. The maximum score you can receive for either theory with *much acceptance* is 96 points. It is not likely that one would be, if one has been completely honest in responding to the statements, so entirely believing in either theory as to attain so large a number. Neither theory is right or wrong; neither is better than the other. However, your philosophy or assumptions will affect your managerial style.

Theory Y consistency. Managerial behavior that typifies those who believe in the assumptions of Theory Y may be described and observed by their subordinates, peers, and superiors as being approachable, open-minded. Also, such managers are generally capable of maintaining attitudes of high expectations among their subordinates. They encourage initiative and risk-taking (being risk-takers themselves, as far as people are concerned). When a subordinate makes a mistake, the manager helps him learn the lesson contained within the mistake. The manager whose assumptions are consistent with Theory Y is willing to share and enjoys giving credit to his subordinates for superior performance.

Theory X consistency. The manager who makes Theory X assumptions about the nature of people is typically dependent upon the base of authority inherent in his rank within the organization. He is not receptive to ideas from subordinates if they conflict with his own. The tendency of this manager is to tightly control, oversupervise, be intolerant of mistakes. He readily casts blame, unwittingly discourages risk-taking as represented by initiative, stresses failure-criticism and overlooks successes. He is uncomfortable when he gives praise to a subordinate.

What are your needs?

Needs are motivators. Your subordinates have them. So do your peers and your superiors. It is the basic *need*, the quest for *satisfaction* of that need, that *motivates* individuals, groups, and organizations (collections of groups) toward productivity. Frederick Herzberg's concept of *hygiene factors* and the ways in which these differ from *motivators* is, in reality, closely allied with Abraham Maslow's *hierarchy of needs*. Both scientists were searching for definitions of the human characteristics that cause people to behave the way they do. A possible result of understanding these human characteristics can be a distinct improvement in the manager's ability to predict behavior, the responses to stimuli, whether generated externally or internally with respect to the human organism.

At the risk of belaboring the point, it is important to recognize that the act of becoming a manager of other people at work does not eliminate the fact that the manager has his own set of needs. Rather, on becoming a manager, it is even more imperative for the manager to develop an in-depth comprehension of his own set of responses to stimuli.

The following is a self-evaluation vehicle. It can identify needs that are dominant, probably operating at this moment. The needs can identify your personal practices relevant to employee motivation toward attainment of the goals of the organization. As you develop an understanding of the probable effects of your managerial practices on your engineering and scientist professionals, you can speculate quite pragmatically about the consequential impact you are having on the group's work objectives.

Evaluate yourself, then evaluate others.   Correlating Herzberg and Maslow, we interpret the lower order of needs within the *hierarchy of needs* as *maintenance* or *hygiene factors* (satisfiers and dissatisfiers, essential to morale and attitudes but not, of themselves, work motivators). The engineer's or scientist's drive for performance and productivity is usually located in the higher order of the *hierarchy of needs* (ego, esteem, and self-actualization). It is the higher order of needs that relates directly with Herzberg's concept of *motivators*.

The following are statements whose responses reflect your needs as revealed by your decisions under conditions that are typical of the dynamics of management and motivation. For each statement two possible responses are offered. As in the previous self-evaluation, the choice is not "right" or "wrong." There are no "right" or "wrong" responses, only perceptions of how you would react or the actions you would take relative to specific conditions. Again, it is of the utmost importance that you be completely honest with yourself. Forget your "skills" at taking "tests." Don't play "games." Make your selections of the alternative responses rapidly, without attempting to second-guess the possible impact on your final score.

Alongside each statement are two circles. Each circle contains a letter-symbol that matches one of the two possible responses. You have a total of three points to distribute between each pair of responses. If you feel that one of the responses entirely characterizes the way you would handle the specific circumstance, put a "3" in the appropriate circle and a "0" in the other. You may use a value on the scale of "3" to "0" for any of the responses, with "3" representing a response that is maximal and "0" minimal or not a likely characteristic of your practice as a manager. The quantities you give to each pair must total "3." You may, for example, assign a quantity of "2" to one response and, therefore, "1" to the other. At the end of the process, you will read instructions on how to interpret the data.

1   The most valuable employee:
    B—does a job exactly as specified, neatly and in   Ⓑ Ⓓ
    an orderly way. D—is ambitious and takes pride
    in his work.

2   When a professional joins my staff, as part of his
    orientation, I:
    B—emphasize the company's fringe benefits, sta-   Ⓑ Ⓔ
    bility, and how easy the job is. E—make sure he
    is aware of the opportunities for growth, freedom,
    and stimulating work.

3   If I become aware one of my people is performing
    below standard, I reemphasize for him:
    D—ways in which he can take pride in what he is   Ⓓ Ⓔ
    doing. E—the significance of the task and how it
    can become more meaningful to him.

4   My approach to morale problems is to provide:
    D—a system of awards for public recognition
    and appreciation. A—improved working condi-   Ⓓ Ⓐ
    tions, possibly wage increases, and a lessening of
    physical strain.

5   When a professional joins my staff, as part of his
    orientation, I:
    C—emphasize the fine sociability of the mem-
    bers of the group, and the opportunity of working   Ⓒ Ⓓ
    with nice, friendly people. D—give considerable
    emphasis to the recognition and the personal
    growth opportunities offered by the content of
    the tasks.

6   Most people evaluate their jobs according to
    whether or not:
    C—the job environment offers friendly condi-

tions for making good social contacts. D—the job
enables rapid advancement on the basis of individual achievements.   Ⓒ   Ⓓ

7   I observe that my professionals become more
dedicated and accomplish more when:
E—the effects of their work provide personal
growth. D—the effects of their work provide tan-
gible rewards.   Ⓔ   Ⓓ

8   My approach to morale problems is to provide:
B—a more orderly, predictable environment and
assurance that seniority rights are observed. C—
improvements in interpersonal relationships that
are more rewarding to each person.   Ⓑ   Ⓒ

9   The most valuable employee:
B—works neatly and in an orderly manner, follows the job specifications closely. A—appreciates good working conditions and a salary that
is fair for the work.   Ⓑ   Ⓐ

10   If I become aware that one of my people is performing below standard, I reemphasize for him:
A—the working conditions and the pay are well
suited to the job description. B—that we may
have to cut back on staff head count if our productivity has a negative effect on profits.   Ⓐ   Ⓑ

11   I observe that my professionals become more
dedicated and accomplish more when:
A—the lab is well equipped and all the physical
needs are well met by the company. C—everybody is enjoying, sharing free time together, and
there are no conflicts.   Ⓐ   Ⓒ

12   My approach to morale problems is to provide:
A—improved working conditions, possibly wage
increases, and a lessening of physical strain. B—a
more orderly, predictable environment and assurance that seniority rights are observed.   Ⓐ   Ⓑ

13   If I become aware one of my people is performing
below standard, I reemphasize for him:
A—working conditions, money, and how we can
make them okay for him. D—the intrinsic value   Ⓐ   Ⓓ

of the work, its importance, and how proud he should feel about it.

14 When a professional joins my staff, as part of his orientation, I:

E—make sure he recognizes the opportunities offered for freedom and growth and the stimulation offered by the specific tasks. A—emphasize how pleasant the work conditions are and how our pay and fringe benefits are better than those of the competitors.

(E) (A)

15 I observe that my professionals become more dedicated and accomplish more when:

E—the effects of their work provide personal growth. A—the lab is well equipped and physical comforts are high.

(E) (A)

16 The most valuable employee:

A—appreciates good working conditions and a salary that is fair for the work. C—has a strong desire to be a part of the group and get along with others.

(A) (C)

17 My approach to a morale problem is to provide:

E—work that stimulates and challenges the mind. A—improved working conditions, possibly wage increases, and a lessening of physical strain.

(E) (A)

18 If I become aware one of my people is performing below standard, I reemphasize for him:

B—that we may have to cut back on staff head count if our productivity has a negative effect on profits. E—the nature and value of the work he is performing and how to make it more meaningful for him.

(B) (E)

19 When a professional joins my staff, as part of his orientation, I:

B—emphasize the company's fringe benefits, stability, and how easy the job is. C—point out how friendly his associates are, how compatible and interesting.

(B) (C)

20 The most valuable employee:

E—is innovative, creative, and work is personally rewarding to him. C—is concerned about the rest of the group, wants to be part of and get along well with it.   Ⓔ Ⓒ

21 My approach to a morale problem is to provide: B—a more orderly, predictable environment and assurance that seniority rights are observed. D— a system of awards for public recognition and appreciation.   Ⓑ Ⓓ

22 The most valuable employee:
   D—is ambitious and takes pride in his work. A—appreciates good working conditions.   Ⓓ Ⓐ

23 I observe that my professionals become more dedicated and accomplish more when:
   C—they enjoy, share good times, and get along well together. B—standards are made clear, stability dominates, and there is little danger of losing one's job.   Ⓒ Ⓑ

24 I observe that my professionals become more dedicated and accomplish more when:
   A—the lab is well equipped and physical facilities are in good order. D—rewards are given in the form of public recognition and appreciation for good work performance.   Ⓐ Ⓓ

25 If I become aware one of my people is performing below standard, I reemphasize for him:
   D—the significance of the work he is doing and the pride he should take in it. C—the fine atmosphere, friendly associates, and the need to do his fair share.   Ⓓ Ⓒ

26 My approach to a morale problem is to provide: A—lessening of physical strain, improvements in working conditions and, if possible, more money. C—improvements in interpersonal relationships that are more rewarding to each person.   Ⓐ Ⓒ

27 My approach to a morale problem is to provide: B—clarification of standards, an orderly and predictable environment, and protection of seniority rights. E—more stimulating and challenging work.   Ⓑ Ⓔ

28 If I become aware one of my people is performing below standard, I reemphasize for him:
D—the significance of the work he is doing and the pride he should take in it. B—that we may have to cut back on staff head count if our productivity has a negative effect on profits.

29 If I become aware one of my people is performing below standard, I reemphasize for him:
A—working conditions and how we are trying to make them satisfactory for him. C—the fine atmosphere, friendly associates, and the need to do his fair share.

30 The most valuable employee:
E—is innovative, creative, and finds his work rewarding. B—does his job neatly, in an orderly fashion, and according to specifications.

31 The most valuable employee:
C—is concerned about his associates and wants to be recognized as part of the group and to get along with the others. B—does his job neatly, in an orderly fashion, and according to specifications.

32 Most people evaluate their jobs according to whether or not:
E—it offers freedom and opportunity for maximum growth. A—it pays well enough.

33 Most people evaluate their jobs according to whether or not:
E—it offers freedom and opportunity for maximum growth. C—it offers a friendly environment and good relationships.

34 Most people evaluate their jobs according to whether or not:
A—it pays well enough. B—it offers job security and employee benefits.

35 When a professional joins my staff, as part of his orientation, I:
E—make sure he recognizes the opportunities offered for freedom and growth and the stimulation offered by the specific tasks. C—point out

how friendly his associates are, how compatible and interesting.

36 When a professional joins my staff, as part of his orientation, I:

D—give considerable emphasis to the recognition and personal growth opportunities offered by the content of the tasks. A—make sure he is aware of the pleasant environment and how well he is being paid.   Ⓓ Ⓐ

37 If I become aware one of my people is performing below standard, I reemphasize for him:

E—the significance and high value of the work, and how we can make it more meaningful to him. A—the nice environment we provide, and how well he is being paid.   Ⓔ Ⓐ

38 Most people evaluate their jobs according to whether or not:

D—it offers recognition and rapid advancement based on his accomplishments. B—it offers job security and employee benefits.   Ⓓ Ⓑ

39 I observe that my professionals become more dedicated and accomplish more when:

E—rewards in the form of personal growth are visible. B—standards are made clear, stability dominates, and there is little danger of losing one's job.   Ⓔ Ⓑ

40 I observe that my professionals become more dedicated and accomplish more when:

E—rewards in the form of personal growth are visible. C—the environment is friendly, good times are being shared, and everyone is enjoying.   Ⓔ Ⓒ

41 The most valuable employee:

D—is ambitious and takes pride in his work. E—is innovative, creative, and finds his work rewarding.   Ⓓ Ⓔ

42 I observe that my professionals become more dedicated and accomplish more when:

B—standards are made clear, stability dominates, and there is little danger of losing one's job. A—the lab is well equipped and physical necessities are well taken care of.

Ⓑ Ⓐ

43 The most valuable employee is:
D—ambitious and takes pride in his work. C— concerned about others and wants to get along with and be part of the group.

Ⓓ Ⓒ

44 My approach to a morale problem is to provide: C—improvements in interpersonal reationships that are more rewarding to each person. D—a system of rewards for public recognition and appreciation.

Ⓒ Ⓓ

45 My approach to a morale problem is to provide: C—improvements in interpersonal relationships that are more rewarding to each person. E—more stimulating and challenging work.

Ⓒ Ⓔ

46 My approach to a morale problem is to provide: E—more stimulating and challenging work. D— a system of rewards for public recognition and appreciation.

Ⓔ Ⓓ

47 Most people evaluate their jobs according to whether or not:
E—it offers freedom and opportunity for maximum growth. D—the job enables rapid advancement on the basis of individual achievements.

Ⓔ Ⓓ

48 I observe that my professionals become more dedicated and accomplish more when:
B—standards are made clear, stability dominates, and there is little danger of losing one's job. D—rewards are given in the form of public recognition and appreciation for good work performance.

Ⓑ Ⓓ

49 When a professional joins my staff, as part of his orientation, I:
C—point out how friendly his associates are, how compatible and interesting. A—emphasize how pleasant the work conditions are and how our pay and fringe benefits are better than those of our competitors.

Ⓒ Ⓐ

50 If I become aware that one of my people is performing below standard, I reemphasize for him:
C—the fine atmosphere, friendly associates, and
the need to do his fair share. B—that we may
have to cut back on staff head count if our productivity has a negative effect on profits.

ⒸⒷ

Determining the nature of your needs.   The statements you have just
completed reflect your own set of needs. They do, to some degree,
reflect your assessment of the needs of people who report to you. In
completing the fifty statements, you awarded point values to the relative
strengths of pairs of alternatives. The "strengths" you attributed to
each of them help determine your needs as you perceive them.

Total the points you have awarded to each circled letter, adding
together those points for letter A and, as a separate group, those for B,
for C, and so on. Enter the points on the chart below. As a double-check
on the accuracy of the completion of the statements and the summation
of all points awarded, the grand total for all five letters should be
exactly 150.

$$E = \underline{\hspace{1cm}}$$
$$D = \underline{\hspace{1cm}}$$
$$C = \underline{\hspace{1cm}}$$
$$B = \underline{\hspace{1cm}}$$
$$A = \underline{\hspace{1cm}}$$

Total   =   150

The letters correspond to Maslow's *hierarchy of needs.* Letters A and
B represent *physiological* and *security* needs. C represents the mid-
level, *affiliation.* D and E are the *higher order of needs: ego and esteem,*
and *self-actualization.*

It is extremely unlikely that anyone would score all points within one
letter-need system. Quite likely, there is a distribution throughout all
the letters. However, one letter will probably have been awarded more
points than another. The relative values applied to each letter indicate
the relative strengths of the needs of your subordinates—as you perceive
them.

In the work environment of engineers and scientists, motivation is
most likely to be effective when satisfying the *higher order of needs* is
emphasized by the manager. Serious disruption of effectiveness of the
work group, possibly high turnover as well, is most likely to occur if the

manager of the professional group places exaggerated emphasis on satisfying the *lower order of needs* when the *higher order of needs* is seeking satisfaction. If such is the case, need-frustration will most certainly occur and become evident in various and individual behavioral patterns, often without obvious consistency from one individual to another. In some, tensions will build and become manifest in resentment, rebellion, and personality conflicts. Others will become apathetic, as though they had "given up" and are just letting things go any way the natural course of events would take them. Some may become total conformists, appearing to have no opinion of their own, following the manager's specifications quite implicitly without exercising ingenuity or creativity.

Yet it is entirely possible that the manager finds himself accountable for individuals and a work group that is operating primarily in search of satisfaction of the *lower order of needs*, letters A and B, and letter C to some extent. If the individuals and, therefore, the group are to become most productive in the completion of the tasks and the work objectives of the organization, the manager must determine the discrepancies between his own point of view and the actual needs. If it is determined that the *lower order of needs* is operating in fact, the manager should develop remedial actions to provide appropriate *hygiene factors*, and then give serious consideration to methods for raising the aspiration levels of the members of the group, possibly through a system of rewards and job enrichment, placing emphasis on the *motivators* defined by Herzberg and Maslow.

Rate your supervisor, your peers, and your subordinates. Every manager belongs to at least two organizational groups. In one he is the superior. In the other, the one to which he is accountable, he is the subordinate and a peer.

As a separate and interesting exercise, do the above series of fifty statements, substituting the third-person approach for the first person; "he" and "his" in place of "I" and "my."

Are the needs of your manager, your superior in the organization chart, consistent with your own?

As another significant exercise, be presumptuous enough to respond to the statements as you honestly believe your subordinates might.

Are your needs consistent with those of your subordinates?

4

Managing the creative mind

Dictionary definitions of the word "creative" are very unsatisfying. Generally, they attribute *creative ability* to Godlike functions such as creating the earth; creativity is *creating*. However, when one works with or encounters a *creative person*, one does not have thoughts or reactions that identify that person as a "god." Is *creativity* a process of the mind, a predictable organization of stimulus-response actions, or is it an unpredictable occurrence, a phenomenon of the human organism that cannot be satisfactorily explained to men of science?

In the worlds of technological development, engineers and scientists who have gained the label "creative" are highly sought after. Yet, how does the manager know the person is *creative*? By what process of evaluation do we contend that "A" is a creative person while "B" is not? The manager cannot afford to overly theorize about and contemplate the question. He must, when faced with a technical problem that demands solution, develop a set of criteria by which he may make a determination with respect to this undefined (or difficult-to-define) characteristic of thought or behavior (whatever one chooses to call it). This "determination," a personal definition, enables pragmatism such as selecting an individual from among the professional staff to whom an assignment will be given that appears to demand creativity.

As a leader of engineers and scientists, the manager has been trained to quantify, to attach measured data to the accomplishments of people. Therefore he develops a set of quantities, criteria, in the process of selecting the person who appears to be best qualified to generate a solution to the technical problem. These are among the specific accomplishments by which a "creative" person is most likely to be identified:

1 Patented inventions.
2 Patents applied for.
3 Publications and oral presentations.
4 Unpublished research reports.
5 Unprinted oral presentations.
6 Improved processes.
7 New instruments.
8 New analytical methods.
9 New ideas.
10 New products.

This is the "tally" method for calibrating the *creativity* of the individual. Yet we lack a clear-cut definition of the process itself, *creativity*. We do make assumptions and there are schools of thought. One school of thought assumes that the creative mechanism is basically the same as for learning and therefore represents a particular aspect of the learning function. Another school of thought assumes that creativity is a higher mental process than learning and so becomes a gift, one that some have and others lack.

Whether gift or learned quality, creativity is often difficult to detect or to predict. The manager who attempts to recruit an engineer who must have "creative" abilities may resort to past accomplishments, quantified by the tally methd previously listed. But at early points in the individual's career path such detailed accomplishments will not yet have become adequately manifest to enable one to confidently apply the label to a candidate.

Would you have offered Einstein a job? The typical job application, resume, or interview hardly qualifies, separates, or identifies the person with creative potential. This inadequacy is revealed in the portions of job application forms that ask for a listing of (a) patents held; (b) professional society memberships; (c) grade of membership; (d) offices held; (e) honors awarded; (f) publications; and, of course, (g) educational record, degrees earned, names of institutions awarding the degrees, and percentile ranking in the class. Professional personnel managers, people who specialize full time in recruitment, enjoy and feel some embarrassed amusement playing a game that might be called: *Would you hire this person on the strength of his job application information?* The majority of leading recruiters would probably reject Albert Einstein's application on the basis of poor education. The players in this game might fail to recommend interviews for such people as Thomas Jefferson, former Harvard president James B. Conant, and physicist Michael Faraday.

Creativity? Ingenuity? Productivity?

Many studies and programs have been planned and implemented in the past, and will most certainly be programmed for the future, in which scientific approaches are taken toward the identification of the ingenious, creative, and productive professional. One of the elements that has come from these efforts is the structuring of three separate categories of definition:

Creativity is demonstrated by bringing something entirely *new* into being. This emphasizes the newness, the lack of previous existence of the idea, concept, process, or product. It may not have an immediate application.

Ingenuity is shown by inventing or discovering a solution to a specific problem. The emphasis in this case is on the accepted existence of a defined problem and the demonstration of a quality of uniqueness in solving it in an unusually clever, precise, or surprising way, adapting existing processes or designs to the situation at hand.

Productivity occurs when many creative and ingenious ideas and solutions are brought forth. It emphasizes both quantity and quality of contribution; it is sometimes called "output."

It appears that the major differentiation among the three terms is one of degree. The *creative* person generates novelty. The *ingenious* person applies experience, adapting, modifying, revising previously acquired knowledge to the solution of a present problem. The two words are often used interchangeably, but this is not accurate. People who exhibit one or both characteristics are highly prized, eagerly sought as members of the professional staff.

The objective is productivity. In order to be meaningful and truly valuable to the manager's accountability for task completion, both *creativity* and *ingenuity* must result in *productivity.* Art for art's sake, invention purely for the purpose of inventing, devising and revising entirely as a demonstration of cleverness—in reality an attempt to satisfy the need for self-esteem—may contribute to the psychological well-being and level of morale of the individual, but may not provide measurable attainment toward the quantified work objective by which the capabilities of the individual, the group, and the manager will be appraised.

Characteristics of creative people. Let's continue with our attempt to identify the *creative* engineer or scientist. Biographies of such people offer two characteristics that are always present: (a) the courage to be different and (b) a dedication to long hours and hard work. While it is true that not all who have dared to be "different" in the history of scientific development have been ostracized, either literally or figuratively stoned or pilloried, literature is filled with the physical and emotional penalties that have been visited upon many who have dared to deviate from the conventional explanations. The biographies of the great do not always support the general contention that hard work and long hours are correlated with scientific creativity. Available data does not clearly describe the work habits of famous researchers. However, a pattern or repetition does appear in reference to the creative scientist's persistence, tendency to ignore or pay scant attention to the everyday demands of society, and, often enough to be noticed, a rigid regularity in the allocation of time for work, and an approach to work that can never be described as casual.

Creativity generally takes three forms: (a) *chance*—the creative act that happens by pure chance can rarely be duplicated and the product of the chance act may not be pragmatic or usable despite its novelty; (b) *planned creativity*—the product of this deliberate act may not meet an immediate physical need, serve no known useful purpose at the moment of its creation (painting, writing, sculpture, and other works of art are examples); and (c) *spontaneity*—the moment of creation of newness through a spontaneous or unplanned response to an identified need or a statement of an immediate problem known to be in need of solution.

Psychologists are in general agreement that the creative person is characterized as self-stimulating, independent, sensitive, goal oriented, and capable of giving direction to his own efforts. Managers who have had the experience of working with or of being accountable for the activities of creative engineers or scientists (as we have defined "creative") will recognize the accuracy and applicability of these delineated characteritics. Depending on the manager's abilities to comprehend, tolerate, go along with, appreciate, stimulate, appraise, and value the contributions of the creative members of his professional staff, the total experience can be gainful, physically and emotionally rewarding—or can bring about sighs of intense relief when the association is ended. The most common mistake made by the manager of the creative individual is that he tries to *manage* the individual according to the same standards he applies to the more conventional members of the group.

There is little doubt that the creative engineer or scientist is a relatively rare person, a scarce commodity in the arena of available human resources. It is pragmatic to combine the definitions of *creativity* and *ingenuity*—the dividing lines are often difficult to discern—and, without coining a new word that might prove to be neither creative nor ingenious, treat both as one. We prefer to apply the word *creative* to the combination of traits. Therefore, when we say "creative" we also mean "ingenious."

Managing the creative engineer and scientist

It appears that the creative engineer or scientist conforms to the assumptions that MacGregor labels *Theory Y*. It would also seem that such people's motivations are operant at the high-level in Maslow's *hierarchy of needs*: self-esteem and self-actualization. Herzberg would certainly agree that both the creative engineer and scientist gain their *good* feelings exclusively from the *motivators*, certainly not from the *hygiene factors*.

It is especially interesting to note that the creative engineer or scientist, in his career and growth aspirations, may have little interest in becoming a manager, in assuming the cloak of accountability for the performance of others. As has been stated previously, he wants to be evaluated strictly on the basis of his own performance as an individual. This is not in the least a reflection on ambition, technical capability, or on value to the organization.

Another aspect of managing creativity is worth discussing here. Should the manager of creative engineers and scientists be an engineer or scientist himself? Should he be a humanist, skilled in interpersonal relationships, communications and needs-satisfaction? The answer to both questions is "Certainly, yes!" However, the emphasis on the latter answer should be greater than on the former. The function of the engineering manager, director of R & D, vice president for engineering—or whatever the manager's title might be—is not to show the creative engineer how to perform his function. It is primarily to create the ambience and the relationship that motivates, stimulates the creative process of the individual who is responsible for the work task.

The creative engineer will not have been employed merely because the manager doesn't have enough hours in the day and has to augment the available number of man-hours by adding to the professional staff. No, the creative person has been brought into the group or department because of his potential for contributions that are unique. It is the role of the manager to provide the stimuli that produce the desired responses in the form of extraordinary productivity, possibly a kind of productivity of which the manager might not be capable, even if the day were to be made long enough. The scientist remains first a scientist, second, as a

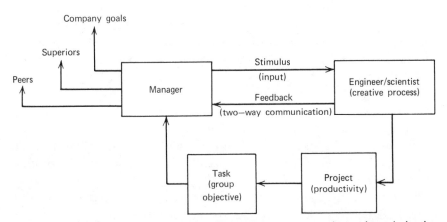

Figure 3 A stimulus flows as an input from the manager to the engineer/scientist who, motivated by two-way communications, provides continuous feedback to the manager. The creative process results in fulfillment of the task that is the group's objective. This performance is coordinated with peers, superiors, and the company's master objectives.

remote possibility, a supervisor. The former acts as the receiver of stimuli, the latter as the transmitter.

It goes almost without saying that engineers and scientists, especially those who are identified as *creative*, must have positive regard for the professional skills and knowledge of their managers in reference (not deference) to the technological areas in which they operate. The creative person often needs someone with whom he can "think out loud," "bounce ideas off of," and in his own way generate a regenerative loop of transmission and reception of thoughts that are germinating. In order to participate as a valid "transmitter" of stimuli, it is requisite for the manager to have developed a meaningful set of credentials that bear witness to his personal capabilities, knowledge, and reputation in the field of scientific endeavor with which the task and the creative engineer or scientist are operant. The ideal combination of creative scientist combined in the mind and frame of an effective manager is indeed the rarest of resources. We deal therefore with the person who has elected to become the manager—or fortune has designated him a titled "manager"—of creative people.

Managerial qualifications.   In supervising the creative person, motivation and stimulation will vary from person to person, more so than with those who are performing routine, albeit productive tasks. Each individual's motivation, if the manager has more than one "creative" staff member in his group, requires separate identification. If this "identification" is accurate, it will rarely change the characteristics of the person's needs for stimuli; they will remain fairly constant.

Integrity.   At times interchangeable with "courage" and "guts," the use of the word integrity implies the moral strength to make unpopular decisions on findings, progress reports, and forecasts of success as modified by probabilities of successful achievement of the specific objective. How hard, how sorely one is tested when, at monthly report time, the manager must write "no progress." An even greater test of moral fiber occurs when the manager must report failure, in the form of a recommendation that a project be abandoned, even though the reason is not related to competence of the professional staff but is a prudent judgment concerned with budget and priorities. Such a level of integrity is vital to the intelligent control of the project, the organization, and to the personal respect of the creative people who, being achievement oriented, will be frustrated by a task with a low probability for successful completion.

There are a number of other qualifications or traits that must characterize the manager of creative professionals. These include a talent for imbuing in others his own enthusiasm and interest in the work that is being performed, a *leadership* quality that is essential to the successful performance of all managers, no doubt. The manager must be *supportive* of the efforts of the individual, as well as of the group; however, the manager must have a *single-mindedness* concerning the project or task, be able to resist the temptations of pursuing a tangential effort that offers great interest as a scientific endeavor but whose pursuit would significantly distract time and energies from the primary objective. This is the basis of the cliché that has become popular among R & D people: when one is surrounded by alligators, it is difficult to remember that the original assignment was to drain the swamp! The effective manager must not forget, must keep his people on the track through the persuasive powers of his personal charisma, warmth, friendliness, and agreeable manner. The use of authority on the basis of rank in such situations is generally significantly counterproductive.

Creativity and logic.   Have you ever asked the creative engineer or scientist how he thought of or came up with the "idea, concept, or solution" to the problem on which he was working? Usually, the response will take one of two forms, both quite sincerely and honestly believed: (a) "I don't really know; it just came to me suddenly;" (b) "Well, I tried approaches *a, b,* and *c* and then I thought . . . and that led me to the answer."

Creative process is elusive.   What *creativity* is and why some people are more creative than others are questions that behavioral scientists have been trying to answer for years and years. Attempts have been made to correlate *creativity* and levels of intelligence such as are measured by *IQ tests.* However, it seems that all tests of intelligence levels are challengeable and do not find universal acceptance among psychologists. Thus, because assumptions do not find acceptance, the studies and their conclusions are rejected. Whether in the arts or in the sciences, creative productivity seems to be recognized *after the fact* and its occurrence is virtually impossible to predict, either in quality or timing.

The creative person usually cannot describe how the creative event occurred or what process was employed as a stimulus. Certainly, if asked for a deadline for delivery or a commitment as to exactly when he will be able to provide a solution to the problem or task at hand, he is placed in an anxiety-producing position. He is unable to provide a reliable answer and, because of his native integrity, he is reluctant to become specific with respect to the exact moment of productivity. Yet it is recognized by many behavioral scientists that tension of the internal type, self-stress, may be one of the fundamental requisites for creative production. Therefore it behooves the manager to develop a mutual agreement, even if informally expressed, on the time and nature of the sought-after solution. In a nonthreatening manner, the manager must insist on quantified targets by which he and the creative person will measure performance. Both persons will profit from such an agreement on objectives. This refers back to the earlier statements concerning integrity, moral strength and fiber that enables the manager to report "progress" or "no progress."

When the creative process is completed and the solution is admired and prepared for implementation, the creative person may, in response to the question, "How'd you do it?," develop a narrative of *logic* that attempts to explain the process he followed in arriving at the successful stage. Often, this is rationalization. This form of rationalization may be an *ego defense mechanism*—because the person *is* a scientist and scientists possess knowledge—or it may be the romantic development of a path of logic that attempts to explain the facts, after the fact.

The nonconformist.   One often hears of such people, employees who refuse to conform to the behavioral patterns described by the organization. Some managers, peers, and even superiors resent the nonconformist whether or not his credentials and his performance record indicate he is a valuable member of the work group. Some of this resentment may be based on the manager's own fears of inadequacy. The nonconformist threatens the manager's ability to manage. The situation becomes especially demanding of the manager's abilities to cope, stimulate, motivate, discipline, and communicate. How nice it would be if all people were alike. How much nicer, if all people responded positively and equally productively to the personal style of the manager. How simple the task, how light the manager's burden. Fortunately, or unfortunately, depending on one's viewing position, it is never this way, never at all so nice, simple, or light.

Group pressures. A group will often exert pressures on its members to conform to the consensus of what constitutes the norms of the group. These *norms* may consist of working in such a way that the individual does not appear predominant, neither superior nor inferior, in relation to others within the group. This characterizes an aspect of the philosophy, culture, and behavioral pattern of the Japanese work group. Attempts on the part of an individual member of the group to perform tasks that make use of his superior talents may be perceived to imply that others in the group are inferior. In many Japanese work groups, an individual who ignores the group consensus may be ostracized by his peers, and be on the outside, unable to find affiliation, operating as an unwelcome soloist.

Group pressures can serve to help the group (a) maintain itself as a group, fulfilling the need for affiliation; (b) accomplish the goals of the group with respect to the defined tasks and objectives that have been accepted; and (c) provide itself with a forum for expression, definition, and validation of opinions and points of view related to the work project and of the role of the group within the overall organization. The attractiveness of the group to the individual is directly related to the individual's needs, the strength and nature of these needs, and how the individual perceives the group's ability to satisfy these highly personal needs.

Qualify the nonconformist. The nonconformist is not a rare person. Almost every manager of engineers and scientists has had experience with individualists, persons who resist the attractions of the group. Such an individual may have, at one time, been totally accepted as a member of the group, but then, for no apparent reason, appeared to deviate from the group's standards or society. This can be the result of a feeling of comfort and self-assurance on the part of the individual, in that he has earned the respect of the group's members, which, at least temporarily, may not demand this individual's participation and, without ill feeling, will not be distressed by the separation. Within the individual who has separated himself from the group's normal affiliation, there may be the responses that we call "creative beginnings" and, regardless of the stimulus or source of initiative, the individual finds he must move at a pace that diverges significantly from that of the group as a body. Superficially, or to the naive observer, there is a cessation of communication between the individual and the rest of the group. The astute manager recognizes the variant possibilities that are causing the behavior and responds accordingly, accepting that the separation may have an indefinite duration, measured in days, weeks, or months. It is not predictable. But it is manageable to the extent that the needs of the individual, the manager (self), the peers, superiors, and the organization are satisfied.

Recognize individual personality.   No one is continuously creative. The cartoonist's favorite method of depicting the creative moment is to draw a light bulb glowing above the head of the individual, together with a look of something akin to surprise on his face. Creativity is very unpredictable. In timing it must be given breathing room. In practice this often means "Leave him alone, he'll come home." The manager must discipline his patience during the "waiting" periods.

Give him time to be alone.   While the creative person does not necessarily want to be isolate, he does want to have periods, which he can choose, in which he may find mental seclusion, separation from real-world pressures. The manager may have to accept an oral report, rather than the routine, normally mandatory weekly written report. As a professional, the creative engineer or scientist will probably keep his lab notebook up to date; however, if he misses a day or two, don't nag! In all likelihood, the manager will become more frustrated than will the individual. The nagging will most likely be tuned out, totally unheard. Certainly, not a motivator. Doomed to failure.

But don't let go.   This may sound contradictory, following the previous paragraph. However, the creative person doesn't want to be ignored. In no way is he seeking total independence of the kind that says, "Buddy, you're on your own!" The noncreative person, although a conformist to the norms of the group, may be a rebel against authority, might welcome being left completely alone. In fact, he doesn't really want feedback on his performance; it represents a potential threat to his security to have appraisals. Yet the truly creative individual welcomes frequent contact and communication with his superior. He finds comfort and reassurance in knowing that he has open access to an "ear" that is both sympathetic and knowledgeable, an "ear" to which he may give voice concerning his critical paths of exploration, his puzzles and momentary frustration, a sounding board that provides ventilation of thoughts and additional stimuli. The manager must keep contact, with discretion.

Allow latitude, but apply pressure.   Again, we seem to have an anomaly of ideas. The creative person seems to want to work at his own pace and in his own good time; however, he usually needs the kind of reassurance that comes from careful applications of pressures and reminders. He doesn't want continuous pressure because his work pace is intermittent—go, stop, go, stop. The manager of the creative person makes his presence felt, but without the slightest trace of oppressiveness.

Tell him how you feel.   The creative person has an ego need, just as all people do. His need is not for idle flattery, for he will immediately recognize an artificial compliment or a social ritual. If his progress appears to be slow—and you will know it because he will tell you so with a sense of frustration—give encouragement that offsets the letdown feelings. Redefine the objectives with him to make certain the original goals are still being pursued and that energies are not being diverted onto a scientifically fascinating route, but one that is apart from the real purpose of the effort. Tell him how others feel about his work, especially the thoughts of those for whom there is mutual respect. Even though he doesn't complain, be alert to signs of depression or resentment; these might reveal some of his innermost feelings, those that are being protected by *ego defense mechanisms*. And, of course, attend to the *hygiene factors*, the environment, the physical facilities and other systems that affect morale and attitude. He may be a brilliant, ingenious, creative person. At the same time, he is very human.

Defer to his source of stimulation.   It may be a manifestation of the manager's own insecurity when he is overly concerned with what others might think if they were to come into his department and see one of his people doing isometric exercises, one sitting with his feet on the desk appearing to be asleep, one standing on his head or sitting on his desk in the Lotus position of the yogi, or another jogging in the parking lot. If one were to have a department with nothing but classic geniuses, virtually any behavior is possible. It would take quite a lengthy book on management practices to attempt to provide guidance to the person fortunate enough to be surrounded by and accountable for such stimulating, but totally unpredictable, people. The fact is that the nonconformity of the creative engineer or scientist may very well extend to his physical behavior while he is engaged in thought processes.

The most common conduct is generally found in a divergence from the usual business hours. He is rarely an 8-to-5 person. He may show up at any time before noon; although he usually does develop a habitual "reporting" time it may be hours later than anyone else's. On the other hand, he seems to lose track of time, either skipping lunch altogether or erratically bringing a "brown bag" or suddenly racing out for a quick sandwich. For him, the work day ends at any hour, usually long after it has ended for others. This may be distracting to other staff members. But the manager should be aware that all efforts to make him conform to an 8-to-5 day—"It's for your own good"—will most likely fail. Support it. Don't fight it. If he is into yoga, meditation, or jogging, don't try to force your own philosophies or beliefs on him. In all likelihood, while doing "his thing" he is stimulating his thinking machine. Measure his productivity, not his idiosyncrasies.

Be patient with his failures.   The creative engineer or scientist is a willing explorer of the unknown and unproven. Learn to control your own fears of failure. Be secure in the knowledge that your creative person is resourceful and refuses to quit just because the path he was pursuing, and which you defined in your monthly report, came to a dead end. If we could know which of our ideas were good without putting them to the test there would really be no such thing as "bad" ideas. Support it. Don't fight it. If he is into yoga, meditation, or jogging, tience. Let him know he has your support. If you don't, his innate fears may dominate his conduct and his initiative, stifling his inventiveness. Tell him how you honestly feel. If you can no longer support him, whether because of budget or your own insecurities, discuss it with him and explore alternative courses of action.

Provide public recognition for achievements.   That's where he is "at." The creative engineer or scientist has a high energy level that is directed toward satisfying the self-esteem needs. The satisfaction comes, in reality, from the esteem in which others hold him. All accomplishments, small and large, should be given full recognition, brought to the attention of the group, his peers, superiors, and the organization. Do let him know that you have spread the good word about his latest "discovery." This will keep the energy level high and stimulate further creativity. Recognition is a vital food for the soul of the creative person. Without it, his response system may wither, lose its freshness, force, and vitality.

Provide instant feedback.   McClelland's studies of known high achievers indicated that such people require rapid and frequent feedback on performance. This is not demanded in the sense of "ego food." It is in the sense of confirmation that the performance is good, bad, or indifferent. When the creative person provides you with a report of progress, a request for assistance, or any other communication, it is essential that the response be given as soon as possible. Of course, take the time necessary, but no more than that, to evaluate the information and develop a suitable response. The absence of reaction will be seen as a sort of reply in the form of a negative recognition, a most demoralizing, if not degrading, action (or inaction). The manager must respond speedily and intelligently.

Innocent foibles have a place. So what if he is always making tea and never drinking it? If he never lights the pipe that's constantly in his mouth? Or drinks soda pop continuously? Can't work without two short, sharp pencils on his desk, but he always uses a pen. A terrible housekeeper? Remember, he is invariably a *nonconformist.* Not deliberately. He can't explain it any more than you can understand it. Such foibles are innocent, hurting no one, but serving some indefinable purpose. He's entitled to have them as part of his private individuality. The manager must recognize that they will prevail over all efforts to eliminate them. If you feel you must rationalize them, the problem is yours, not his. He will inexorably march to his own drumbeat. And the professional, competent manager of the creative engineer and scientist monitors the "beat," but does not try to change it.

No, don't "baby" him. The foregoing guidelines may read as though the manager of creative professionals is a baby-sitter, a mollycoddler, supposed to indulge all the whims of his best people. This is far from the need. The manager must be empathetic, comprehending, adult in his dealings. The manager is not expected to perform as a nurturing parent, nor is he to play the enthusiastic child. The manager never departs from being the adult member of the team, never departs from reason and logic. He sets goals, high goals, and he keeps the efforts moving in the direcion of attainment of these high reaches. When necessary, he is able to be tough, the stern adult who resorts to paths of logic, breaking through emotional barriers without becoming emotional. Without the use of pom-pom girls or cheerleaders, the manager of the creative person maintains enthusiasm for the problem that requires solution, regardless of how elusive the solution might be. By dint of his unusual understanding of personality, learning and growth patterns, and his ability to apply the lessons derived from the behavioral sciences, he continuously transmits stimuli that generate the appropriate responses.

How creative are you?

Engineers and scientists, by virtue of training, experience, and inclination, make every effort to quantify theories and concepts. Data, if it can be developed, becomes a universal language through which all engineers and scientists can communicate. Thus, the question "How creative are you?" is a valid attempt to quantify, attach specific values, or defined levels to the intellectual behavior associated with those people who, because of observed processes and productivity, we tend to label "creative" or "ingenious."

Test yourself. A consulting/research organization specializing in creative problem-solving, decision-making, and organizational improvement has developed methods and systems for maximizing the generation and use of new creative concepts and ideas. As an integral part of its methodology, the firm, Princeton Creative Research, Inc., has developed screening instruments for the recruitment and selection of creative managerial and technical talent. With the express permission of the firm's psychologist and president, Eugene Raudsepp, we have adapted the unique test-instrument, "How Creative Are You?", so as to enable you to determine whether or not you have the personality traits, attitudes, values, motivations, and interests that creative individuals generally have. The original test-instrument consists of over 310 items that indicate your position on the creativity-originality-imagination continuum.

The instrument is easily self-administered and self-scored. It can also be used to identify and, to some degree, predict creative behavior and the potential for creative productivity in others.

How to take the test. Fifty statements are given here. They are not complex, nor are they intended to be "tricky." Therefore do not try to second-guess how a creative person might respond to each statement. Answer as accurately and frankly as you possibly can. After each statement indicate with a letter the degree or extent to which you *agree* or *disagree* with it. For example: A = strongly agree; B = agree; C = in-between, have no opinion, or don't know; D = disagree; E = strongly disagree. The scoring instructions are given at the end of the series of statements. Do not look ahead to the scoring instructions.

1   I always work with a great deal of certainty that I am following the correct procedure for solving a particular problem.   _____

2   It would be a waste of time for me to ask questions if I had no hope of obtaining answers.   _____

3   I feel that a logical step-by-step method is best for solving problems.   _____

4   I occasionally voice opinions in groups that seem to turn people off.   _____

5   I spend a great deal of time thinking about what others think of me.   _____

6   I feel that I may have a special contribution to give to the world.   _____

7   It is more important for me to do what I believe to be right than to try to win the approval of others.   _____

8   People who seem unsure and uncertain about things lose my respect.   _____

9   I am able to stick with difficult problems over extended periods of time.   _____

10   On occasion I get overly enthusiastic about things.   _____

11   I often get my best ideas when doing nothing in particular.   _____

12   I rely on intuitive hunches and the feeling of "rightness" or "wrongness" when moving toward the solution of a problem.   _____

13   When problem-solving, I work faster when analyzing the problem, and slower when synthesizing information I've gathered.   _____

14   I like hobbies that involve collecting things.   _____

15   Daydreaming has provided the impetus for many of my more important projects.   _____

16   If I had to choose from two occupations other than the one I now have, I would rather be a physician than an explorer.   _____

17 I can get along more easily with people if they belong to about the same social and business class as I do. _____

18 I have a high degree of aesthetic sensitivity. _____

19 Intuitive hunches are unreliable guides in problem-solving. _____

20 I am much more interested in coming up with new ideas than I am in trying to sell them to others. _____

21 I tend to avoid situations in which I might feel inferior. _____

22 In evaluating information, the source of it is more important to me than the content. _____

23 I like people who follow the rule "business before pleasure." _____

24 One's own self-respect is much more important than the respect of others. _____

25 I feel that people who strive for perfection are unwise. _____

26 I like work in which I must influence others. _____

27 It is important for me to have a place for everything and everything in its place. _____

28 People who are willing to entertain "crackpot" ideas are impractical. _____

29 I rather enjoy fooling around with new ideas, even if there is no practical payoff. _____

30 When a certain approach to a problem doesn't work, I can quickly reorient my thinking. _____

31 I don't like to ask questions that show ignorance. _____

32 I am able to more easily change my interests to pursue a job or career than I can change a job to pursue my interests. _____

33 Inability to solve a problem is frequently due to asking the wrong questions. _____

34 I can frequently anticipate the solution to my problems. _____

35 It is a waste of time to analyze one's failures. _____

36 Only fuzzy thinkers resort to metaphors and analogies. _____

37 At times I have so enjoyed the ingenuity of a crook that I hoped he would go scot-free. _____

38 I frequently begin work on a problem that I can only dimly sense and not yet express. ——

39 I frequently tend to forget things such as names of people, streets, highways, and small towns. ——

40 I feel that hard work is the basic factor in success. ——

41 To be regarded as a good team member is important to me. ——

42 I know how to keep my inner impulses in check. ——

43 I am a thoroughly dependable and responsible person. ——

44 I resent things being uncertain and unpredictable. ——

45 I prefer to work with others in a team effort rather than solo. ——

46 The trouble with many people is that they take things too seriously. ——

47 I am frequently haunted by my problems and cannot let go of them. ——

48 I can easily give up immediate gain or comfort to reach the goals I have set. ——

49 If I were a college professor, I would rather teach fact courses than those involving theory. ——

50 I'm attracted to the mystery of life. ——

Scoring instructions. Make certain you have responded to each statement. Using the following table, circle the numerical value given to each response, according to the respective number of the statement and the letter-grade you have assigned to it. Compute your score by adding the numerical values in each letter-column. At the bottom of the table is the interpretation of the score in terms of degree of creativity.

	A	B	C	D	E		A	B	C	D	E
1	−2	−1	0	+1	+2	26	−2	−1	0	+1	+2
2	−2	−1	0	+1	+2	27	−2	−1	0	+1	+2
3	−2	−1	0	+1	+2	28	−2	−1	0	+1	+2
4	+2	+1	0	−1	−2	29	+2	+1	0	−1	−2
5	−2	−1	0	+1	+2	30	+2	+1	0	−1	−2
6	+2	+1	0	−1	−2	31	−2	−1	0	+1	+2
7	+2	+1	0	−1	−2	32	−2	−1	0	+1	+2
8	−2	−1	0	+1	+2	33	+2	+1	0	−1	−2
9	+2	+1	0	−1	−2	34	+2	+1	0	−1	−2
10	+2	+1	0	−1	−2	35	−2	−1	0	+1	+2
11	+2	+1	0	−1	−2	36	−2	−1	0	+1	+2
12	+2	+1	0	−1	−2	37	+2	+1	0	−1	−2
13	−2	−1	0	+1	+2	38	+2	+1	0	−1	−2
14	−2	−1	0	+1	+2	39	+2	+1	0	−1	−2
15	+2	+1	0	−1	−2	40	+2	+1	0	−1	−2
16	−2	−1	0	+1	+2	41	−2	−1	0	+1	+2
17	−2	−1	0	+1	+2	42	−2	−1	0	+1	+2
18	+2	+1	0	−1	−2	43	−2	−1	0	+1	+2
19	−2	−1	0	+1	+2	44	−2	−1	0	+1	+2
20	+2	+1	0	−1	−2	45	−2	−1	0	+1	+2
21	−2	−1	0	+1	+2	46	+2	+1	0	−1	−2
22	−2	−1	0	+1	+2	47	+2	+1	0	−1	−2
23	−2	−1	0	+1	+2	48	+2	+1	0	−1	−2
24	+2	+1	0	−1	−2	49	−2	−1	0	+1	+2
25	−2	−1	0	+1	+2	50	+2	+1	0	−1	−2

Score	Interpretation
80 to 100	Very creative
60 to 79	Above average
40 to 59	Average
20 to 39	Below average
−100 to 19	Noncreative

5
Building positive
interpersonal relationships

COMMUNICATE! It is not feasible to estimate the number of times managers have used this word as though it were an "Open sesame!," an order to a subordinate, a section leader, project manager, or other key members of his group. How many times has it failed to produce the desired result? How many times has the speaking (or shouting) of this simple word done little more than add frustration for the manager and his people?

Why? There must be, and there often are, very important but not necessarily obvious, reasons "why."

A misused word. One of the most important reasons is found in the fact that *communicate* is an overused, frequently abused, and misused term. The dictionary defines it in a literal sense: *to transmit or convey something intangible, as information or feelings, so that it is satisfactorily received or understood.*

In this sense, communication is a technology, a process by which there is an exchange of information through a common system of symbols and signs. A language.

When a manager in a work environment says, "We've got to improve communications around here!" his message is no doubt clearly understood—*semantically.* As evidence of this, he is overwhelmed by the day-books or letter-books of his people, each of which displays numerous examples of communications—memoranda, notes, and other correspondence. The literal response, therefore, would be to increase the volume of information exchange, expand the stack of paper work, with no visible increase in productivity. Also, there could very well be an enhancement of the frustration, tension, and anxiety levels as a direct result of a highly inaccurate exchange of information.

Say what you really mean.   Of course, written exchanges of communications are necessary to assure that information has been accurately transmitted, received, and understood. When you say *COMMUNI-CATE!*, you really mean, "I perceive a need to improve the ways in which we work together." You aren't actually interested in the details of how the activity or project work is carried out.

As a manager of engineers and scientists you are most interested in productivity, output—the fruit of units of input. That's one of the ways in which you too are being measured. Isn't it?

The group communicates.   A group is a number of individuals assembled together for reasons of unifying relationship. That relationship is not to exchange signs and symbols. It is to become, as a result of the unifying relationship, capable of adding to the effectiveness of each individual so that the objectives or tasks are accomplished. The members, the individuals, are additives—one plus one plus one . . . equals *n*. They are not multipliers. One times one, times one, times one . . . times one, is still *one*. When the individuals are activated in the former mode, they are a *group*. In the latter mode, they are merely a collection of individuals, probably noncontrollable, operating at random. No further comment is necessary.

Desirable leadership characteristics

Think back to the days when you were at the very bottom of the professional ladder, a subordinate, probably with no one reporting to you. All of your communications were upward. Those directed toward you always came from a higher level in the organization, moving downward. Recall the supervisor whom you believed to be most effective, the one you enjoyed working for better than for other leaders. In all probability he practiced, whether by intuition or intent, these behavioral traits:

- Open and honest communications. Told you what he honestly thought.
- You trusted the things he said; respected his opinions and comments.
- Authority was delegated, indicating a trust in you and in the group. He relied on the judgment of his people. Demonstrated faith in the creativity of others.
- Exercised the appropriate amount of authority based on his rank, but did not oversupervise. Rarely, if ever, did he become dictatorial.
- The team approach was predominant. Showed decision-making methods to the group that improved your decisions. Encouraged friendly competition and made cooperation easy.
- Backed up his decisions and those of his people.
- Knew how to listen. Made your comments seem important. He took time to work out problems, on an individual as well as on a group basis.
- Always willing to discuss problems and usually showed you how to solve them by yourself.

Weren't the effects very positive? He probably brought out the best in you and in others. Helped you develop. Shared growth opportunities with you. Productivity, esteem, recognition, and job satisfaction were probably high for you and your colleagues.

You may not be able to precisely emulate this leader whom you recall so gratefully. You could be still better than he was. Your own personality, heritage, and environmental experiences have made you an individual with your own very special traits and characteristics. You most certainly have "something on the ball" or you wouldn't be where you are today. The continuing questions include, "How do I become a more effective leader, remain a leader, and continue my own development and growth in the organizational hierarchy?"

You are surrounded by challenges. Each of the people reporting to you represents a challenge. "A challenge," some say, "is an opportunity in a heavy disguise." That's all well and good for the observer. But for the person who is being "challenged," it can mean "stormy times" as well as occasions to demonstrate one's leadership qualities. Just as you are an individual, so are each of your subordinates. The immediate task is to provide a positive influence on the behavior of your people.

You have two levels of authority.   Merely by definition, you, as the manager, outrank your people. Inherent in this is *authority* based on *power*, A_p. You may issue commands. They may, or they may not, be obeyed. The military hierarchy is based on power-authority. The subordinate to the military officer has no option but to obey. His training has taught him obeisance to the commands, the orders of his superiors. He has no choice but to subordinate his individuality. In the military, the individual is suppressed as such until he conforms to the group behavior. This is not necessarily wrong, except outside the military.

There is another type of authority, that which is based on *knowledge*, A_k. It is true that when the leader speaks his people must listen. Because he has inherent *power-authority*. However, when, in addition, he has *authority* based on *knowledge*, his people will *respond* with positive actions. This is true, I daresay, in both the military and in commercial/industrial/technological communities. A_p, then, assures that the subordinates will *hear* the leader's communications. They may even take some sort of action. A_k assures positive *action*.

The myth of management.   Somewhat facetiously, although I believe there is an underlying seriousness, engineers and scientists have been heard to comment that "The first myth of management is that it exists!" The existence of management is made apparent by the *authority* it uses to achieve its objectives: *power-* or *knowledge-based*, A_p or A_k.

Power-based authority depends on the manager's ability to infuse fear, and to exercise coercion. A manager who depends on the power of his rank uses his A_p to deprive or punish his subordinates as the primary means for achieving his personal and professional goals. He perceives his subordinates as being dependent upon him for punishment and reward. His attitude is plainly: if you will do something good for me I might/will do something for you in return, such as give you something you need (as the manager perceives the need). The power-authority manager is entirely task oriented, has little concept of people orientation. His subordinates may comply. If they do comply it is usually out of fear of being deprived of the rewards, which deprivation is a form of punishment. An environment of fear derived from a power-authority manager may operate with a quantifiable degree of success among hourly nonexempt production laborers. They will not like the environment but, possibly because they have low aspirations or low self-esteem, they will tolerate it. On the other hand, in prosperous times it doesn't take much to make these people quit and move to another place that appears to offer a nicer, more comfortable environment.

In times of severe recession or industry layoffs, even the professional engineer or scientist will appear to tolerate the power-based environment, resigning his emotions to a bitter, hopefully temporary fate. If need-frustration occurs, the ego defense mechanisms will become operative. Productivity will probably be poor.

Older employees with dependence upon the forthcoming retirement plan also may put up with the A_p figure rather than sacrifice the pension benefits. Productivity will certainly diminish and the manager will complain that older people just can't "put out!" What would Herzberg say to this?

On the other hand, knowledge-based authority, in order to be effective, depends on the manager's ability to appropriately blend task orientation with a sensitivity to the fact that tasks are performed and objectives attained through people. He has knowledge of the needs of his people and, in order to assure positive motivation, attempts to operate with a tendency to fulfill these needs. And generally he has technological knowledge, an expertise, a set of credentials as a professional that enhances his acceptance within the community of professionals who are his subordinates, colleagues, and superiors. His authority, then, is A_k, based on knowledge of people and of tasks.

Coping with a negative personality

As a manager of a dynamic situation, you don't have time to perform the functions of a minister, priest, rabbi, social worker, or psychotherapist. Quite likely, you don't even have the inclination or desire. Tasks have to be done—through your people, like it or not. The "negative personality" is a nonconformist who challenges your authority, regardless of its base, power or knowledge. He is aggressive, rebellious, and at times openly hostile. Yet he has demonstrated that he is extremely intelligent, pushes himself to furious levels of concentrated activity and productivity, and his solutions to problems are often ingenious or creative. You don't want to lose him, not only because of his unique capabilities but because, if he leaves, your competitor might grab him.

To carry the problem further, he not only challenges you directly, he has conflicts with others in the group on whom he refuses to lean and of whom he is highly and outspokenly critical.

Such a person usually has little confidence in others. It is not that he feels superior to others; in fact, his attitude could be concealing a low self-esteem. He has set extraordinarily high standards for performance, for time usage, and for the method of operation. Unrealistic, perhaps. But if these standards could be met, the quality and level of output of the group would certainly exceed the manager's highest aspirations. Unfortunately, they usually cannot be met.

To further amplify his uniquely positive qualities that increase the desirability of keeping him within the department, this "negative personality" is keenly analytical. He cuts rapidly through the superficial aspects of a problem, right to the heart of the matter. But on the other hand, he is impatient with people who cannot follow his line of thinking or who cannot express themselves as openly as he does. Obviously, he is not a leader. But he thinks he is qualified to be one of the best of leaders purely on the basis of his technological skills. He has little understanding, at this time in his development, of the complex role the leader of other people must play.

This same person, the negative one, is intensely competitive, sometimes causing him to expose his rival in an unintentionally unkind way. Others feel inadequate when assigned to work with him. They express this as resentment. In group meetings he attempts to dominate the train of thought and conversation. It is interesting to note that his superior, you, his manager, may not even be aware of the extent of the resentment because he is often highly political, almost fawning to you, to those who are your peers, or even to your superior in the organization. He has an extraordinary need for acceptance, applause, attention, and affection.

His behavior contradicts his need fulfillment and drives him further away from gaining satisfaction. If this person does not learn to cope with his problem, to modify his behavior, to alter his apparent mind-set, it may one day be too late. He will move from job to job, because few managers will be able to "handle" him and the conflicts he creates and, rather than continuing the struggle, they will "wish" him onto their competitors. And when retirement eventually comes, he will be incapable of adapting to the serendipitous environment. He will probably become a self-righteous "grouch."

Solving the problem. If the problems introduced by Mr. Negative Personality above can be solved, everybody can become a winner; the "negative" becomes a positive. The effects of the abrasions are removed from the peers. Each learns from the other about patience and technology, and the manager remains in control of the essential blend of people and task orientation. Here are several actions that you should pursue if you are the manager accountable for this person:

- Assume that this person is doing the best he knows.
- Recognize the needs that the individual is trying, although unsuccessfully, to fulfill.
- By all means, avoid expressing the anger you may feel under these trying circumstances. You are, after all, going to exercise authority based primarily on knowledge, not on power.
- Initiate frequent nonthreatening discussions with the individual. Allow him to speak his mind, to make his critical comments, but within the privacy of your office. Do not argue. Do not allow your human feelings of wanting to spring to the defense of others to take over.
- Without being hostile or critical, state the way you perceive his behavior. Without wearing an intense, disapproving frown, describe an incident in which he was involved or had created. Ask him how he thinks others feel about it. Does he want them to feel the way they do? Are the reactions those he really wants? If not, what action does he think would be most likely to achieve these reactions, the ones he really wants? How would he react if another member of the group were to say or do the things he did under the circumstances?
- In a sincere and friendly manner, make him aware of how highly you value his participation, how much you want to help. However, make him aware that in order to gain all the rewards of his efforts, he must take others into account. His progress within the company is related to this fact, as it is for all future managers. Perhaps by example, tell him that each of us experiences disappointments and defeats. But add that we do learn from each effort.
- Let him know how frequently his behavior has been negative, that you are concerned that he may be developing a behavioral

pattern and a mind-set that can operate against him as well as against the group.

- He may challenge or try to debate your perceptions. He may even accuse you of open hostility toward him. Don't let his outspoken comments "hook" you. Don't fight back. Express your observations at the very moment that he is being negative. Talk in terms of his own goals. Reemphasize that you want to help him attain them. Doesn't he want to? The decision is his alone. You want to provide the opportunities and guidance.

- Emphasize your belief that all encounters do not have to result in winners and losers. It is possible to have situations in which there are no losers. (More on this later.)

- Don't expect to accomplish behavior modification in one session with him. Expect to have to repeat the process over and over again. However, in each session, do articulate your notice of improvements he has made since your last discussion. These are positive reinforcements. Give examples so that he will know you are sincere and will begin to have models to emulate.

- Teach him to be patient with himself. This instruction may surprise him, but he will soon become aware of the fact that he is compulsively demanding of himself and, therefore, impatient with the imperfections that others might exhibit. Explain that objectives are attained in a step-function process rather than in a single all-out high-pressure push.

We recognize the stubbornness that seems to possess some people. Despite all the good attempts to modify the behavior of the "negative personality," nothing seems to change. This is usually not a failure on the part of the manager. Sometimes people with uncontrolled drives have enormous difficulties accepting what others perceive to be reality. The ego defense mechanism just won't allow the personality to accept the critique, however gently and pragmatically it has been set forth.

If there is little or no response.   It may be necessary to go beyond the gentle counseling described above. It may be necessary to have a confrontation. Now, by "confrontation" we do not mean a shouting contest, recriminations, accusations, and counterattacks. We do mean getting Mr. Negative to admit that a problem exists that is causing harm. He must be made aware, way up at the front of his consciousness, that he is his own worst enemy, undermining his own progress. This takes considerable self-control on the part of the manager. He must maintain a composure that continues to be nonthreatening, constructive, all the while appearing to verbally discipline the subordinate. This will probably generate some anxieties in the subordinate's temperament at the moment. Many managers will withdraw at this moment, fearing a scene. The "scene" rarely comes. What does usually happen is Mr. Negative, feeling a loss of esteem in the eyes of the manager, his supervisor, will suddenly change his manners during the conversation in an attempt to recapture the esteem he fears he has lost. This is the moment the manager can use to everyone's advantage. The need for acceptance and affection, the fear of rejection, are high just then. Mr. Negative, although he may be playing it political, is in a listening mode. Now the manager can renew his attempts to induce behavior modification. He does this by repeating the process described above under *Solving the Problem*. However, now he works from a position of greater strength, a combination of A_k and A_p.

Sometimes we admit defeat. You have given Mr. Negative all the time and counsel you can, more than you can afford to in view of the many pressures under which you must operate . . . and he isn't the only one in the department with difficulties. So despite all original and all renewed best efforts to help him modify his behavior, the subordinate persists in behaving as a "negative personality," an abrasive to his peers and to you. It is time to take formal action, to assure the support of the personnel department in the event of a drastic action (involuntary termination).

Two things will probably occur. One, the abrasive person will feel he has not been treated fairly, his skills and competence unrecognized. Second, you will feel angry and at your wit's end with respect to this situation. All that time and energy for naught.

It is possible Mr. Negative will complain to the personnel manager about his "unfair treatment." Possibly, also, he will try to go over your head to your superior in the organization chart, the person to whom you report.

Fortunately, you have kept a logbook, a record of the dates and times of the discussions, together with some notes on the nature of the discussions and the reactions exhibited. Now you will begin to hold formal short-interval performance appraisals with copies of the written review being sent to personnel for insertion in the employee's file. The first appraisal will call for a second review and appraisal within a short period, perhaps two weeks to thirty days. You will have discussed the matter with personnel and your supervisor, gaining their support and recognition of the fact that you have made every conceivable effort to guide and improve the employee's opportunities. Personnel will review policy with respect to the appropriate appraisal periods before which termination, if absolutely necessary, should be implemented.

Thus, you will be adjudged by your subordinates, peers, supervisor, and, it sometimes happens, a labor court, as having been proper, fair, equitable, having exercised good judgment. Too, your conscience, your superego, and your ego will not keep you awake at night coping with guilt and unanswered questions.

Do you have an abrasive personality?   You may not be immune from an unconscious tendency to irritate your subordinates, your peers, and your supervisor. Here are ten questions you may ask yourself. They are not to be scored. They are merely to be considered seriously, introspectively. Conclusions are apparent.

1. Are you quick-on-the-trigger or short-on-the-fuse in discussions with others?

2. Do you feel an irrepressible urge to debate many of the statements others make? Do many of your discussions become arguments, and you wonder why?

3. When you talk about your activities, do you constantly use the word "I"?

4. Do you use such expressions as "whip them into shape" and "straighten them out" in conversations that are critical of others?

5. Do you consider yourself to be more competent than your colleagues and your boss? Do you let them know you feel this way, by word or deed?

6. You want to be liked, but do you wonder why you don't seem to be accepted by the others? Do all your efforts at friendship lead nowhere?

7. Do you manage to avoid responsibilities?

8. Are you giving a lot of emphasis to acquiring status and power symbols?

9. Are you reluctant to share or to allow others to have the same perquisites as you?

10. In meetings with your colleagues, do your comments take a lot of time? Do you try to stand out in meetings as being especially clever and perceptive?

Conflict management—an opportunity to excel

Problems offer hidden opportunities to the manager. The effective manager views a problem as an opportunity to prove his skills. The unskilled manager, the ineffective manager views a problem only in the light of potential for failure. Conflict among individuals within a section, department, division or company—or among sections, departments or divisions will surely test the manager's knowledge, temperament and capability. It is probable that the inability to properly resolve conflict is one of the most frequent causes of managerial failure or breakdown.

What is "conflict"?

We do not use "conflict" in the sense of armed or physical battle. Conflict is the frustration of the needs of an individual or group by the attempts of another individual or group to satisfy its own needs. Conflict is a mental struggle that results from an incompatibility of ideas, needs, desires, wishes, interests or demands.

Conflict, as we use it and as virtually all managers meet it, is mental, not physical. It is incompatibility at the intellectual level. The existence of a conflict may become quite apparent when it reaches the "shouting" stages, as it sometimes does. However, the prudent manager notes the potential or reality of conflict long before tempers are lost and—very important—long before it has a negative effect on productivity or hinders the attainment of objectives or fulfillment of the tasks.

People who are experiencing conflict may break rules in attempts to satisfy their own needs. The effective manager recognizes his role in conflict management and resolution. He helps his people identify their needs. He does not stand by, hoping it will all "work itself out." (Suppose it doesn't "work itself out"?) The effective manager recognizes and accepts the critical importance of his role in resolving conflict.

He neither ignores the situation nor loses his "cool" when he recognizes conflict.

Win-Lose? Lose-Lose? No-Lose?

The manager may very well be involved in a conflict "of his own." Managers of professional staffs of engineers and scientists may have disagreements (or conflicts) with their peers and with managers of other departments, with marketing, with manufacturing, with finance, with superiors, with subordinates, and so on. No one, at any level of the organization, is immune from the potential of a destructive conflict. The individual who is superior in rank has authority (based on power-of-rank) on his side. But superiority in this sense is only a relative term. One is not automatically endowed with superior knowledge because one has been promoted within the hierarchy. "Pulling rank," ordering those who are in conflict to "cease and desist" may terminate the conflict. Or so it might appear. The command "cut it out, you guys!" carries a message that says "you both lose!" Because the conflict has not been resolved—possibly merely driven underground—everybody, including the person holding superior rank, loses.

The manager may, after making himself familiar with all "sides of the issue," decide in favor of one side of the conflict over the other. This seems like the easiest, most natural thing to do. Perhaps it is both easy and natural. But, unfortunately, this response creates a *winner* and a *loser*. And the *effective* manager may very well become the "loser" himself when the person, section, department or division that "lost the decision" loses its motivation, sense of commitment and fair play, or leaves the company. Certainly, the "winner" may feel triumphant and trumpet the success story. "See—I knew all along I was right!" The probability is that the manager who resolved the conflict by creating a *winner* and a *loser* will become a loser himself.

No-Lose is Win-Win

The effective manager chooses the best option of all, the one that ends with *no losers*. This is equivalent to everybody *winning*.

Achieving this state—No-Lose—is not easy for most managers. But, for the effective manager, it is the only one that is acceptable. It requires special care and programing and the long-term payoff can be quite significant for all who are involved. The *No-Lose* method accurately implies: "*everybody wins!*" The No-Lose method accurately depicts the manager as a person who is restrained, intelligent, understanding, compassionate, and very effective.

The method can be reduced, on paper and in practice, to a 7-step procedure; a formula for effective management . . . a formula from which one must never stray in the management of conflict. We will list and discuss the *Seven Steps To No-Lose Conflict Resolution.*

1. Acknowledgement and Acceptance. The persons involved in the conflict must be guided to the point where they will admit to themselves, to their manager, and to their adversaries that a conflict does exist. This admission is usually a difficult one for people to make. It is essential those who are in conflict acknowledge the disagreement.

Having made this admission, they must be further guided to the point where they will accept the need to bring the conflict to a conclusion; the situation is not beneficial to anyone and must be resolved. We are not looking for an amicable solution. We are not concerned with a buddy-buddy resolution. We are concerned only with a conclusion from which all parties will benefit. No winners. No losers.

This first step may take time to accomplish. But, there is no shortcut-option. Take the time. Move to the second step only after there is a solid belief that all parties have acknowledged the existence of a conflict, and are willing to work toward and do accept the importance of achieving a No-Lose resolution.

2. Description. Now that all participants have acknowledged the conflict and have expressed an acceptance of the need to resolve it, move to this step wherein the nature, the detail of the disagreement is elaborately described. The manager is especially careful not to give the slightest indication of prejudice in favor of or against one or the other of the viewpoints that are in conflict.

There is great value, at this point in the process, of using a chalkboard or a large easel-mounted pad and marker pen to list the viewpoints and the "pro" and "con" arguments for each. It is quite probable that none of the people who is in conflict has taken time to display his views. Even if they have been put into memorandum form for internal distribution, it is unlikely they have had the opportunity to examine the written arguments.

Again, the manager is careful not to give any indication that he favors one position over the other. In a No-Lose process, it is the adversaries in the conflict who will arrive at the resolution. The role of the manager is exclusively that of a catalyst—the agent for positive change.

When each of the adversaries agrees that his (an adversary may be an individual or a group) views have been accurately defined, the manager moves the discussion to step 3.

3. Pathing. For any of the arguments there always are several alternative paths to solution. They may all be right, so to speak. But, generally, one is better than all the others. And it is the "better" or "best" path that must be identified and pursued. Again, the manager does not choose the path. He guides, suggests and proposes alternatives. The persons or groups who are in conflict with one another will decide the optimal path.

The manager, on the basis of his greater experience in conflict resolution, points out the dangers, the pitfalls, the hazards and obstructions that may be met along each path. The manager does this in a way that avoids the appearance of rejection or acceptance of any one of the alternatives that are proposed. The group continues to use the chalkboard or pad to display the key points. This reduces opportunities for misunderstanding or misinterpretation of the spoken words. Evaluation of the alternatives, the discussion of the merits and demerits of each path is the next step.

4. Assessment. As we noted, only one of the paths or alternative routes to a No-Lose resolution is best. Despite the apparent appeal that several of the paths developed in Step 3 may offer, time must be dedicated to a thorough evaluation of each of the paths that has been displayed on the board. The discussion continues until consensus is reached among the people who represent the conflicting views. This will demand time and effort "up front." But, the long-term results justify the means.

5. Selection. Consensus leads to the selection of the path the participants will pursue. Because there is consensus, there is commitment. There is, also, recognition and realization that it is possible to resolve a disagreement, a conflict, in a way that can result in No-Lose, Win-Win. Now that we have consensus and commitment to a specific path, we move to Step 6.

6. Action. The time has come for implementation, for moving forward along the selected path. How we shall proceed is the theme of this step. At this point in the discussion, the manager takes a stronger position than he has in steps 1 through 5.

The persons who are in conflict are responsible for resolving the conflict—while performing their work-tasks. The manager is accountable for the actions and the productivity of the individuals and the group. However, in this step, the manager makes certain that company policies and standard operating procedures are observed so that, in resolving one conflict, another new conflict is not created. If company policy or S.O.P. stands in the way of a No-Lose resolution, the manager may consider and, if necessary, take action to temporarily modify the policy or procedure. Needless to say (but I say it), the manager avoids taking the initiative of modification without obtaining support and guidance from his own superior.

In this Step 6, a timetable, a series of critical events is plotted to serve as benchmarks for the measurement of progress toward the No-Lose resolution. This enables Step 7.

7. Evaluation. The participants meet at intervals specified as "critical events" to evaluate progress against the standards and controls that were defined in Step 6 as part of the "Action" plan. The manager anticipates that there will be perturbations and interruptions in the progress-curve. He is not alarmed by this fact. He prudently makes certain, during the evaluation meetings, that each of the participants evaluates the causes and effects.

Perhaps the standards and controls are not realistic? Should they be revised? Tightened or loosened? Have we lost sight of the original objective? Have we strayed from consensus?

The manager again becomes the catalyst, enabling the participants to come to a renewed position of consensus, commitment and motivation toward successfully resolving the conflict.

Does it always work?

"Work" means result in a No-Lose Win-Win resolution. There can be no guarantees of success. However, the possibility is great, the probability is high that the effort will succeed. The possibility also exists that the nature or the makeup of the groups will change. Some people are quite inflexible, unwilling to examine an opposing viewpoint. Even though they may publicly proclaim their ability to appreciate the positions that others may take in disagreement with theirs, they secretly retain their own views and endeavor to put them into action. What is the manager to do?

Back to square one

If the procedure does not appear to be meeting expectations, the manager and the group must search for the cause. This may require a reexamination of the conflict. It is appropriate to call the participants together for a review of the situation and ask these questions:

- Did we sincerely admit and accept the existence of conflict?
- Did we accurately describe the nature of the conflict?
- Did we develop and adequately examine all the alternative paths of action available to us?
- Did we select the optimal path? Does this path, in the light of current relationships, continue to be "optimal?"
- Did we miss a step in the path?
- Did we establish the appropriate standards and controls?
- Or, is our evaluation of progress in error? Are we expecting too much? Too little?
- Perhaps we should go back to Step 2 to assure ourselves that our assumptions are accurate?

Benefits are derived

The advantages to the individuals, the group, the manager and the company derived from the above approach may be summarized. They produce:

- increased commitment to the resolution.
- high quality action paths.
- warm relationships and temperaments that are contained and restrained.
- high probabilities for success, increased motivation and productivity.
- proof that the manager is effective.

6
Constructing two-way communications

Communications within an organization can go in any direction—upward, downward, and lateral. Managers who communicate *downward* are certainly doing (part of) their jobs, informing, advising, giving guidance to their engineering and scientist professionals. However, if there is no feedback, no *upward* communications from professional staff members to their managers, there is only *one-way* communication. The manager might just as well be talking to himself.

There *must* be an easy way! Well, nobody told you that being a manager was going to be *easy*. Your people depend on information inputs and data feedback. So do you. This is further evidence that there is a mutual dependency between manager and subordinate. So why isn't it easy? Why, when you are eager to get verbal progress reports, are they reluctantly delivered? Or why do you sometimes have to go into the lab and find out yourself? Why isn't the information volunteered? Doesn't the staff realize how important it is to give you feedback? Possibly, they do not.

Are your downward communications correct?

What you say is not always what people understand you to mean. For example, because you are a totally honest person who is achievement oriented, you may say to a project leader, "I am afraid if we don't show more progress, and we're in this together, the project may be canceled."

What your project leader may have heard is, "I may be laid off if we don't do better work." In reality, although this event is always a possibility, you meant to say, "I'd like to learn more about the progress on the project, the barriers, problems, and how we can work together to overcome and solve them and meet our objectives and commitments to the front office. I'd like to discuss the details with you."

You didn't mean to be threatening. But the threat was implied by the words, if not by the inflection. If the subordinate is already feeling frustration, the last thing he wants to hear is a threat about his future with the project. He may not be insecure, basically, but a canceled project may be equivalent to a loss of recognition and a blow to self-esteem.

Weigh, measure your words carefully so that you do not come across as a power-authority (A_p) figure. Many people have a dread fear of authority. Whether or not this fear developed in their childhoods is not important. The fact it exists is important and, although you are not a clinical psychologist, the negative effects of such "fear" must be recognized. Your approach must be nonthreatening. Ivor Catt, in his book *The Catt Concept* (G. P. Putnam, 1971), in which he describes strategies engineers sometimes use to hold their jobs while others are losing theirs, refers to the technique of making sure nobody else in the organization knows as much about the project as you do. In other words, the engineer may deliberately avoid *upward* communications. The boss does not fire him because of the boss' own fear of a resultant loss of ability to communicate upward to *his* supervisor. Certainly not a healthy situation. But if you have had to deal with one like it, you know it did indeed test your skills in communications.

Another potential cause of the absence of upward communication can be found in the fact that high achievers usually are not risk-takers. Upward communication often does involve elements of "risk" for the individual who initiates the communication. The subordinate who presents a concept or a proposal for a project will attempt to evaluate the upside opportunities and the downside risks that may be his lot in the event his presentation is accepted, staffed, and budgeted. The opportunities are present for recognition, in the event of successful attainment of the objectives. The negative risk is the potential loss of esteem that may befall him in the event his concept or idea proves to be wrong or unworkable. To allay such fears of consequences, you must provide sincere and strong assurances of the fact that you recognize that all *opportunities* also involve elements of *risk*. Let him know that in the event of success he will receive full recognition for his contributions and, in the event it doesn't work out (do not refer to "failure"), he will continue to have your strong backing and support.

It is entirely possible that you do not recognize the "opportunities" to be as strong or as great as your subordinate feels they are at this time. Your judgment, based on superior experience (not your own fear of failure) and knowledge of the technology, is that the time or personnel or budget are not currently available, or not available in the appropriate quality or quantity. Perhaps the idea and the project should be reviewed at some later date for possible positive action. It is important that you be completely honest about the situation with respect to the company's current position in the matter. Do praise those elements of the subordinate's presentation that deserve laudatory comments. Recognize that the subordinate did devote time and energies to ways in which to make contributions to the group, department, or the company. Also, do give an honest critique of those elements of the concept or proposal that you feel would benefit from additional investigative thinking. Again, avoid expressing a threatening nonverbal attitude bodily or facially, as well as in your voice. Thus, you will demonstrate that you have *recognized, listened, understood,* and *do invite further communications* with your subordinate. If, on the other hand, the dialogue between you and the subordinate is regarded by him as a "put down," he will be very hesitant to expose himself in the future to a repeat performance. Creativity and ingenuity will be suppressed.

Facts and feelings. Many of our thoughts and actions are a combination of facts as we know them, plus our feelings toward people. A subordinate may feel he is being manipulated by your spoken reaction and a perceived lack of action. For example, out of fear possibly, a subordinate sort of "tosses" an idea to you over a cup of coffee in the employees' lunchroom. He "fears" meeting with you in the more formal environment of your office wherein reside all your *power symbols.* Further, in the environment of the lunchroom he feels more your "equal" and can terminate the discussion at any time he so desires. His control is greater at the moment than it may be at other times or in different places. If you become sensitive to this kind of experience and if you notice it seems to be happening more often than you would like, it may be well worth your while to examine your own downward communications for possible unintended but implied threatening postures.

A subordinate will feel he is being manipulated if there is no action taken on a suggestion he made with the best of intentions. If you respond to a suggestion or to a formal presentation with, "I'll look into it and get back to you," make certain you do follow through on both of those statements. They are perceived as promises. The combination of "facts" as your subordinate knows them and his own "feelings" can be the product of a reputation you may have acquired as a manipulator, a manager who says "I will," *but doesn't.* This product can become *fact* to the subordinate who converts it to a firm belief that there will be action, or inaction, depending on your "reputation."

Be consistent. Even though you may be under tremendous pressure to get to a meeting called by your own supervisor, the manager of managers, avoid giving short shrift to one of your own subordinates who has a desire and a pressing need to express an idea and to get your reactions. Do not rush away from him, shouting back over your shoulder, "Can't talk now! Gotta get to a meeting!" Take a few of your important seconds to let him know how interested you are in hearing what he has to discuss and make a specific appointment for the discussion. Rushing away from him is rejection, a deterrent to future communications. Taking a few moments (seconds are all that are necessary) to make the date is for him a form of recognition and encouragement for continued communications. Your subordinates must be aware that you are always attentive to what they want to say.

Build your credibility. The basis for good communications, in both directions, is a trusting and credible relationship between you and your subordinates. The confidence of his subordinates will not be crushed when the manager has to tell an achievement-oriented engineer or scientist that his favorite project is being terminated because of lack of budget or because of changes in priorities. The subordinate will certainly be disappointed by the news and want the opportunity to assure himself that all efforts have been made to avoid the termination. When he is confident of his manager, he feels free to ventilate his thoughts without animosity, comfortable with the feeling that the facts are accurate, that his manager did everything possible to support the individual member of the group, the group as an entity. Each feels supportive of the other.

Morale and attitudes remain positive in a participatory environment. Without this constructive environment many might engage in self-pity, feel severe personal loss or discrimination, become defeatists, lose motivation. No one can afford such self-punishment. The individual, the group members, all become *victims* where no victimizing was intended.

Be a responsive listener. Talk is cheap. The failure to listen is expensive. In the social environment, the person who talks all the time and rarely listens may soon become an outcast, ostracized by others who feel the need for expression, who want to be heard from. People enjoy the opportunity for giving as well as for taking. "Taking" is listening. "Giving" is responding. The conversation "hog" soon becomes a soloist, loses the audience because he frustrates the needs of others to be "heard from."

The business environment is similar in the "give and take" aspect. The subordinate and the peer need and search for opportunities to speak up and speak out—assuming the manager's style is not suppressive. The willingness on the parts of the subordinate and the peer to speak to the manager must be considered complimentary, beneficial, valuable, and useful to the growth of people and accomplishment of tasks. The manager must be willing to "take," listening closely and accurately to what is being said. He must be capable of understanding what is meant by the speaker's words. This willingness to listen accurately encourages and stimulates two-way communications. The implication is correct that to do the opposite will discourage two-way communications and impair the effectiveness of the manager.

Responsive listening encourages the person who is doing the talking to continue, to become creative as well as communicative. *Passive listening*, attentive but silent and without reaction, is a "turn-off." It is the opposite of *responsive* listening. It silently and eloquently reveals to the talker that you would just as soon not have a discussion, would cut it short, or wish he would go away. Passive listening is totally unrewarding, unsatisfying if not frustrating. If it is not intended to be a rejection of the talker, it comes quite close to this condition.

People in search of solutions to problems often need an opportunity to ventilate their minds, to talk things out. When they are given an opportunity to express their feelings to the manager, they expect and should be given acknowledgment of their expressions. Under such conditions, the manager should engage in eye contact with the talker. Look directly at the person's eyes, certainly not out the window or at the wall. Doodling is a form of body language that says the doodler is not really listening but is trying to create a mental "escape hatch" from the reality of the moment. Almost intuitively, the speaker will recognize that he has not obtained undivided attention and the session will be brief, the need of the speaker will be unfulfilled. This is one way to cut short or to end a conversation with an unwelcome visitor. There are times when such actions, at the risk of being considered rude and impolite, are useful. However, if your intent is to encourage the speaker to give constructive expression to his ideas and feelings, *responsive* listening is the only way to go.

Do not sit in silence, staring into the eyes of the speaker. Encouragement is contained in briefly spoken footnotes to verbal paragraphs. The "footnotes" are such periodic comments as:

> "I understand what you say."
> "Very interesting."
> "Do go on."
> "Is that right!"
> "I hear you talking."
> "Tell me more."

Send "I" signals. Be careful of responses that begin with the word "you." For example, "You don't say!" can be taken to mean, "I don't believe you!" when interjected during a conversation.

Better to say a phrase such as "I hear strong feelings from you." This does not imply agreement or approval or censure. It merely acknowledges that which is actually happening and, because of the judicious use of the pronoun "I," clearly acknowledges the fact that you are listening closely to what is being said to you. "I understand what you are saying," is another "I" message that indicates empathy without commitment. It encourages a continuation of the conversation and keeps it from becoming a monologue.

Express that which you perceive, that which you hear, in terms of "I perceive from what you are saying that . . ." and two-way communications are assured. Remember, the dialogue may be intended only as an information-sharing or gathering event.

Determine whether or not a decision is necessary at the very moment. Better still, continue to be a responsive listener while asking for time to consider all viewpoints with an "I" statement such as, "I have certainly learned a great deal from you and I do appreciate the time you took to bring this matter to my attention. I would like to dig into it more deeply.

I'll get back to you by (specific time) and we can go on from that point."
Responsive listening should be habit forming.

Twelve "do nots" in communication

The most common abuses caused by power-based authority (A_p) will be
recognized in the following twelve cautions, things to avoid in the way
the manager talks to his subordinates.
Do not:

- *prosecute by interrogation.* Avoid questions that take the form
  of implied accusations, that put the subordinate on the defensive. This type of format must not be used: "Did you ask
  anyone before you went ahead?" "Who told you to do that?"
  "Why did you ever do it this way?"

- *pass judgment.* Be careful not to be accusative or judgmental.
  You wouldn't like someone to tell you: "You are way out of
  line!" "Boy, are you ever wrong!" "You acted without thinking!"

- *respond inconsistently.* You may have learned as a parent of
  growing children that consistency in words and actions are
  essential to the development of a child's or young adult's
  construction of self-esteem and the maintenance of two-way
  communications. We never outgrow this need for *consistency.*
  If we did not find it in our childhood, we may continue the
  search for it well into our adulthood. If we do find it, how
  fortunate we are. Having been so fortunate, we search for
  maintenance of this environment and, if we do not succeed, the
  ego defense mechanisms may very well come into play. We
  become inconsistent in our behavior toward others when we
  allow ourselves the unaffordable luxury of self-indulgence in
  moodiness, short temper, and unpredictable relationships.

- *lose your "cool."* If one of your subordinates has made a
  serious error—one that may have caused you personal embarrassment or that endangers the progress of the project—and if
  you feel your temper rising do *not* try to discuss the situation
  with the offender *at this time.* If *he* is upset about the situation,
  do *not* try to discuss the situation *at this time.* Wait! Wait until
  you are both cool, relatively free of emotional pressures. Even if

time is of the essence—*cool it!* One or both of you might say
things that will be regretted, things that might have been better
left unsaid at any time.

- *raise your voice in anger.* Certainly, never use a threatening
  tone to one of your subordinates within the view or hearing of
  his peers, or of yours. He will be humiliated by the experience
  through a sense of loss of esteem in the eyes of his peers. You
  will most certainly suffer the same loss, although it may not be
  expressed, in the eyes of your peers. You are the leader, the
  setter of exemplary behavior and self-control. Wait, and discuss the subject privately. Make certain you do not exhibit the
  kind of inconsistent behavior that characterizes those who have
  short tempers or, in the vernacular, "short fuses." Such people
  are shunned by subordinates and peers because one cannot
  predict the timing and volatility of the "short fuse." Also, such
  people are not regarded highly by their supervisors because the
  results, or lack of results, from inconsistent or unpredictable
  behavior soon become apparent.

- *threaten.* Ominous expressions of warning should never be a
  deliberate or an unintentional part of your vocabulary. These
  include: "Better be careful of what you do around here."
  "You'd better, or else." "I'm warning you, and I don't want to
  have to say it again." "Don't ever do that again."

- *preach.* These are words that tend to "talk down" to subordinates: "You should do it this way." "Here's what you ought to
  do." "I say it is your duty." "Where is your loyalty?"

- *order and command.* Excellent suppressors of individuality,
  creativity, initiative, and communications are contained in sentences that begin with: "You must . . . You can-
  not . . . You will . . . You are expected to . . . You will
  stop it right now!"

- *give false praise.* The tendency to give a pat on the back with
  one hand rapidly becomes a slap in the face when a brief
  statement of praise is shortly followed by the potentially for-
  midable word "but." "You did the best you could, but . . ."
  "Everybody says you do good work, but . . ."

- *apply labels.* Exercise caution in the selection of adjectives and
  other modifiers that might be interpreted as ridicule. Examples

include: "You're a fuzzy thinker when it comes to . . ." "Wow, did you ever do a goof job!" "How can you be such a sloppy worker?" "Please, try not to be such a poor housekeeper."

- *spout proverbs and banalities.* Attempts at reassurance usually fall quite short of the intended mark when they take the form of overworked maxims. Look at these: "It's always darkest before the dawn." "There's a silver lining." "Things aren't ever as bad as they seem." Or one that translates from a foreign language as "The morning is brighter than the night." They have the sound of insincere solace, and usually only make matters worse.

- *minimize matters (nor overstate them).* Attempts at diverting the thoughts of the subordinate who has a problem and is in search of a solution are doomed to failure if the manager's approach becomes: "You think you've got it tough! This reminds me of the time I . . ." If humor is intended, it will probably fall quite flat when one of the two parties is feeling upset. At some other time, after a suitable solution has been suggested, the humor might come through. After all, your authority is based on knowledge, and on experience from which your subordinates will benefit if they are encouraged to engage in two-way communications.

Nine clues to successful group meetings

A meeting that is filled with arguments and interpersonal conflicts is destructive. A meeting that does not have an identified objective is not likely to accomplish anything. A meeting that does not give participants the feeling of "time well spent" is without value. A meeting that has no formal beginning and does not arrive at conclusions is unproductive, virtually meaningless. A dictionary definition of "meeting" is "an act or process of coming together as an assembly for a common purpose." When two or more people gather, as in a meeting, the incident must not be purely physical. In order to be successful, there must be a *meeting of the minds.*

Effective meetings may serve several purposes. Among other valuable purposes, they may be used to introduce new members to the group, review the status of a project against objectives, discuss administrative affairs, share knowledge of and information concerning technical developments in a field of common interest, and serve as preambles to planning for the future. Here are nine guidelines.

1. Meet at the right intervals.   There are guidelines that determine the frequency with which meetings should be held. There are *effective* managers who hold periodic meetings with staff members almost as a ritual, once a week or more often. On the other hand, there are *ineffective* managers who hold frequent, periodic staff meetings. Periodicity, regularly held staff meetings do not automatically make a manager *effective* or *ineffective*. Would that it were so simplistic. It is the *nature* of the meetings, the *conduct* of the meetings that produces effective results. Experience teaches the manager and his group the frequency-demand of meetings, and this is usually related to the subject or the objective of the meetings and, most critically, the productivity of the group meeting.

Status-report meetings relevant to a key project can only be successful when held with specific periodicity. The periodic interval may vary from daily, as among production personnel during the introduction into the system of a new product or assembly, to weekly or biweekly for a project team intent upon updating and exchanging information and data.

When there is a great deal of confusion over meetings, or there is resentment about holding periodic meetings, the manager who becomes sensitive to such feelings is wise to review the real value of the meetings or the manner in which the meetings are conducted.

Groups that are new, in the early stages of formation, will usually meet frequently because of the need to get to know each other's thought processes and articulation skills. As the group matures, it will evolve a meaningful schedule, determine for itself how frequently it should meet to exchange information and to resolve probelms.

There are rugged individualists who consider all meetings distracting from the true task and a waste of everyone's time. Such attitudes may conceal feelings of aggression, hostility, and lack of feelings of affiliation. When such attitudes are expressed, rather than condemn the individual the manager wisely attempts to probe, without threat, the thoughts the individual is harboring. From such "probes" may evolve a new and useful insight as to how to improve the effectiveness of the meetings.

Some feel that the "task force approach" to calling a meeting is the only way to go. That is, a meeting should be called only when there is something critical to discuss, and they believe the meetings should be entirely informal. This is well and good, when the "group" consists of the manager and one other person, or two others at the most. However, the moment there is the need for a group exchange of information, the need exists for planned meetings. Make certain that there are valid discussion topics for each meeting. This is one of the functions of an *agenda*.

2. Develop and publish an agenda. The function or task of putting together an agenda, an outline, a list of items to be covered during the meeting should be a group responsibility. The chairperson of the meeting is accountable for its planning and preparation, but the members of the group are responsible for the content. By giving each member an opportunity to contribute to the agenda, greater assurance develops that relevant and pertinent subjects will be considered during the meeting. Each member will develop a feeling of participation. Each will then "own" part of the meeting. It will not be the boss' or the manager's meeting.

One method for obtaining agenda items is to post a large sheet in the work area onto which subject entries can be made by anyone who so desires. If this is too public, one of the secretaries or administrators can keep a notebook, a three-ring binder with ruled sheets onto which the individual can make his entries or suggestions. If the chairperson for the meeting is someone other than the engineering manager, this person should keep the notebook or binder. Handwritten notes or memoranda can be passed to the keeper of the agenda in the same way. The chairperson for the meeting, whether engineering manager or designee, then is accountable and responsible for assembling the agenda topics, selecting and rejecting if necessary to fit the time frame, and then publishing and distributing the formal agenda prior to the start of the actual meeting. With respect to selection and rejection of topics, this must be done with great caution to avoid offending the sensitivities of any member of the group.

Having published the agenda, stick to it vigorously. With some exercise of judgment, other issues that appear suddenly during the meeting that are not revelant to other items on the agenda—usually prefaced with "I just thought of something!" or "That reminds me . . ."—should be scheduled into the next regular meeting or, if they merit such treatment, a special meeting should be scheduled involving only those whose presence is essential to the success of the "special meeting."

The intent is to completely cover all the agenda items, those that have been accepted as part of this meeting's agenda, within the alloted time frame.

3. Stick to the date and time.   Beware of postponements. When a meeting has been scheduled, its participants have been advised, and an agenda has been published, the time and date must be given the highest of priorities. Time conflicts may arise, but as much as it is within the control of the manager, the meeting schedule should be adhered to. Consider that those who are expected to attend, especially those who are a direct part of the published agenda, will have dedicated valuable thought and time to preparation of their materials, exhibits, reports, memoranda, and all aspects of their participation.

Last-minute cancellations, even postponements, tend to injure morale that has been stimulated by anticipation of the event. Those members of the group who have a *need for affiliation*, which need finds some measure of satisfaction in group meetings, will have feelings of rejection and some loss of esteem because some other event was "more important" to the manager. A cancellation or a postponement downgrades the significance of the meeting. It doesn't matter whether the meeting was scheduled to be short or long in duration. Make every effort to hold the meeting on time.

4. Rotate the chair.   Avoid the problems of boredom and ennui that a fixed routine can bring about. The same leader for each meeting, one whose style never varies the conduct or pace of the meeting, can prove quite fatal to any potential for productivity that the series of meetings could generate. "Here we go again" is a powerful indicator that members go to meetings because they are required to go rather than in expectation of a fruitful experience.

The manager should select and openly name the member of the group who is to assume responsibility for organizing the next meeting. If the meeting is entirely dedicated to a specific report or technology, the chairperson for this meeting is easily selected—the person whose report dominates the meeting should become the chairperson. Of course, this may be varied. A co-chairperson may be indicated if the preparatory work for the meeting demands a significant portion of time.

However it is done, the "ownership" of the meetings by each member of the group, as his turn is indicated, adds to the probability that the meetings will be effective. The vested interests become shared. Each member, knowing his time will surely come, becomes quite cooperative with the chairperson in expectation of reciprocal treatment. This may be called "manipulation" but it is entirely beneficial to the group.

As an added vote of confidence on the manager's part, the manager should excuse himself at several points during the meeting. Leaving the meeting room for five or ten minutes in the hands of the chairperson who is a subordinate is a silent-but-eloquent form of recognition. While attending the meeting, the manager must resist tendencies to control or direct the meeting. The manager has the authority of power and rank, A_p. It is never absent, but must always be under the manager's control. The manager's overt authority at the meeting should be entirely based on knowledge, A_k, nonthreatening, supportive.

5. Seek consensus. The Japanese have developed the practice of consensus, group solidarity in sentiment and belief, to a very fine science. The word "science" is used here quite deliberately. If you have had the experience of participating in a technical discussion with a group of Japanese engineers or scientists whose intent is to select from among alternative courses of action, you will have observed this science at work. It is an unhurried process. The lack of "speed" in decision-making tends to frustrate the eager-to-get-going American's approach to problem-solving. However, when the selection has been made, the course of action generally agreed upon and accepted by the members of the group, unanimity of sentiment and belief dominates and motivates the individuals. They attain a level of cooperation and commitment that results in exceptionally high productivity. Internal group communications become quite comprehensive among the peer members. The work environment becomes positive, morale and attitudes constructive. Identification and affiliation needs become satisfied and the members of the group may then move into a higher order in the search for need satisfaction. Motivation is enhanced. Commitment is assured. High productivity is quite probable.

It may not always be practicable to take time to achieve general consensus. Avoid a voting process. Although the right to vote is a democratic, constitutional right, it has little place in the departmental or project-group arena. It could create a formal environment for bad feelings, accomplish nothing of value. The chairperson should certainly be able to determine, without the need for an actual vote, how the members of the group are positioning themselves with respect to the specific situation under discussion. If some group members are not willing to defer to those members who have accepted responsibility for implementing a proposed solution to a problem, the chairperson may set up another problem-solving meeting between those who appear to be dissenting or preventing total consensus and those who have accepted the task that is expected to lead to a solution. Thus, the views of those who are part of the dissenting group will be given proper attention and ventilation. It is entirely possible they will make additional contributions to the solution process. Certainly they will be inclined to be cooperative. A potential for conflict will have been reduced or eliminated.

In the event that there is no clear consensus, no majority viewpoint is evident, the decision should be deferred to an ad hoc committee composed of representative members of the group, including those who will be expected to take responsibility for the work itself. Or if the group prefers, the decision may then be deferred to the manager. The manager, recognizing his leadership role, will vocally recognize the contributions each viewpoint has made to the search for a solution. He may decide the course of action at the end of the meeting, or promise a response by a specific date or time, which promise he will make every effort to keep.

6. Provide adequate facilities.   Engineers and scientists invariably use diagrams, sketches, statistics, and other forms of data to illustrate their findings or to reinforce their viewpoints. The meeting room should be equipped with a large scratch pad on an easel or wall mount, or a chalkboard or similar wallboard. Appropriate ink-markers, chalk, and erasers should be available for anyone to use. Writing tablets and pencils should be provided for those who did not come to the meeting so equipped. If overhead transparencies, slides, video, or audio tapes are to be used, the meeting room should have appropriate projection and transcription equipment. Of course one cannot have all sorts of audio-visual aids on hand for the presenters to use. Therefore there is a shared responsibility for seeing that it is available for the specific meeting. One share belongs to the presenter, who should make his need known prior to the meeting so that the facility can be acquired. The other share belongs to the meeting's chairperson, who should make appropriate and successful efforts to attend to the equipment acquisition.

7. Select the right location.   The purpose of the meeting is to accomplish one or more defined objectives. Unless the objective is a social one, such as introducing a new member to the group, announcing the award of an incentive, or a farewell to a departing member, the meeting place should not be in an environment as informal as a bar, cocktail lounge, or open area of a restaurant. Such places, although attractive for relaxation and esprit-de-corps chitchat, lack the privacy essential to creative expression, are not conducive to concentrated activities that enable problems to be explored and solutions developed. Stick to the conference room, either the company's or a similar facility that one might rent for the purpose that is away from the laboratory and offices.

8. Record the discussions.   Whatever medium is used, a tape recorder, dictation machine, or a stenographer, a record should be made of the subjects discussed during the meeting, the decisions made, accountabilities and responsibilities assigned, due dates, and any other information that might have to be reviewed or be questioned at a later date. By prearrangement, some member of the organization should be assigned the task of recording secretary for the meeting. The assignment should not be given to anyone who is expected to actively participate in the discussion for fear the "note-taking" process will interfere with the individual's ability to listen closely to what is being said or to engage in creative thinking without concern for accurately recording someone else's comments. Avoid assigning this relatively menial task to a member of the professional staff.

9. Distribute the minutes.   The same person who fulfills the recording secretary's function should also transcribe the recordings or notes, pass them to the chairperson of the revelant meeting for review, duplicate the transcription, and distribute copies to all who attended the session and to any others who have a "need to know." Thus all participants have an opportunity to review and refresh their memories of the discussion and decisions taken. Those to whom tasks have been delegated during the meeting are provided with a record of the description of the task, which they can check against their own notes. If they discover discrepancies between the minutes of the meeting and what is expected of them, they are enabled to correct the situation before much time has passed or work has been expended.

Brainstorming . . . the creative meeting

A warm feeling comes over everyone who is invited to a brainstorming meeting. Perhaps it is the use of the component "brain" that causes one to infer a compliment from the invitation. It's fun time! However, it often becomes waste time. The concept of brainstorming is valid as a technique for problem-solving through innovative and creative thinking. However, it is probably one of the least understood and overly abused expressions among those who spend much of their time in meetings with engineers and scientists. If rules are not established and *rigidly* observed during the actual meeting, creativity and novelty may very well be stifled rather than stimulated. The objective of the meeting can be easily frustrated by the absence of clearly defined rules or by ignoring the rules for such a meeting.

The first rule is to understand the objective of the brainstorming session. It always is to expose a specific problem or set of problems and to list *positive* alternative solutions. The word *positive* is emphatic. Here are a set of sixteen rules that, if closely followed, should improve the probabilities for successful outcomes of the time spent in *brainstorming*.

1. A chairperson is named.

2. The chairperson is given total authority, A_p, on the pure basis of rank and power. A_p is bestowed on him. It is inherent in the title "chairperson" and remains so for the duration of the session.

3. The chairperson starts the meeting promptly at the prearranged time. Having prepared himself for the role, he states the problem(s) the group will discuss.

4. A nonparticipating recording secretary is mandatory so that all participating minds will be enabled to concentrate on the problems.

5. All members of the group, with the exception of the chairperson, are considered to have equal authorities, A_k.

6. Small groups are more effective in this type of meeting than are large groups. The number of participants should be limited to a maximum of seven.

7. The mood is relaxed, as free as possible of tensions. The chairperson, by his manner, sets such a scene.

8. The location is such that outside interruptions are rigorously discouraged.

9. If more than one problem is to be considered, a discussion-time limit of fifteen minutes is established for each problem.

10. The entire meeting is short, limited to one-half hour if only one problem is to be discussed. If more than one problem is to be considered, the time should be the number of problems multiplied by the fifteen-minutes maximum time limit per unit. In no event should the session last more than one hour.

11. Positive thinking is mandatory. All negative criticisms, opinions, judgments, or doubts concerning any specific suggestions made during the session will certainly inhibit the creative process; they are forbidden, and must be withheld.

12. Quantity of ideas is stressed. Quality will automatically follow as a result of the mental stimulus.

13. Fantastic ideas, those that may seem superficially to be impractical, are encouraged. They can be reviewed later. Possibly a distillation process will render some elements of the ideas practical. The freewheeling mind is encouraged to function.

14. A thought expressed by one may be "hitchhiked" by another. A basic idea may be expanded upon by anyone who feels inclined to do so, as long as there is no negative implication or criticism of the original idea.

15. Comprehensive minutes of the session are to be transcribed, copied, and distributed to all participants.

16. A team of managers and section leaders is to be formed as an ad hoc committee to review the minutes. This committee does not necessarily have to have been part of the original brainstorming session. In fact, it is often better when they have not participated. Their function is to review the ideas that have been presented, analyzing, combining, evaluating, and finally selecting the best possible solution(s) to put into action.

There are a number of expressions and attitudes that may be vocalized by participants in the session. These must be instantly recognized by the chairperson as being counterproductive and therefore must be prudently suppressed. Here are typical statements that reflect a closed mind:

> "We tried that before."
>
> "It can't be done that way."
>
> "It just won't work in this company."
>
> "Management would never go for it."
>
> "Why change it? We've always done it this way before."
>
> "That's against company policy."
>
> "We don't have that much authority."
>
> "That's impossible!"
>
> "That's ridiculous!"
>
> "Now you're going too far!"
>
> "We don't have the space (or, the people, equipment)."
>
> "That would cost too much to do."
>
> "Who has time for that?"

These comments are invariably based on assumptions rather than knowledge. You may have heard them before and allowed them to become discussions. But there is no room for them during the brainstorming session. The only valid assumptions are: *new solutions must be found for new problems, or for those older ones that have, up to now, resisted solution.* Be aware of the possibility that people who make such comments may be avoiding the requirement of making a commitment to the group. This should be recognized by the manager and, if it reinforces the observation of negativism as an individual's trait, may provide important clues that can lead to a beneficial course of action on the manager's part—as we shall soon see. Meantime, consider carefully whether or not to invite that individual to any further brainstorming sessions.

7
Building team activity

Major projects are most often assigned to a task-fulfillment team, rather than to a single person. The old-world maxim, "If one is good, two is better" seems to be an accurate and dependable guideline for managers for the formation of project teams.

The engineer or scientist often works in concert with other professionals. It is usual to assign a junior to a senior, a lab assistant or technician to aid both, an administrator to coordinate the logistics of the project and to prepare reports concerning progress against budgets, and a technical secretary to support the whole.

The manager is faced with a broad test of his skills from the moment he assigns more than one person to the fulfillment of a single task or a series of closely related tasks. He must: (a) create the team through a people-selection progess, (b) delegate specific accountabilities and responsibilities, (c) obtain commitment from the individual members of the team, (d) define the team's objectives, (e) establish standards, (f) monitor and evaluate performance against objectives, and (g) take corrective action whenever it is indicated.

Selecting and assembling people with the appropriate skills and credentials is certainly the right place to start in creating the team. Hopefully, there will be no (or very little) conflict among the personalities. However, people behaving as people—imperfect organisms—will most likely encounter conflicts of concepts, ideas, approaches, philosophies, and needs. Through the skillful management of conflict, and through its constructive resolution, a positive ambience can be created and sustained. Although there will be peaks and valleys in the level of "ambience," also known as morale and attitude, the overall effect will be observed as forward movement toward task fulfillment.

We will discuss some of the more sophisticated elements of communications and interpersonal relationships. We will explore the impacts they can have on the work group as a team comprised of individuals.

Psychodynamism—human intercommunications

Each of us is made up of three significant *psychodynamic sets* that are mental processes and mental activities having an important effect on our ability and our willingness to communicate ideas and feelings to one another. The sets may be designated as: (a) *superficial*, the aspects of our appearance and behavior that are exposed, readily apparent, or obvious to others *and* to ourselves; (b) *discovered*, traits of our own character or of our personality of which others are aware but of which we are not necessarily aware; and (c) *concealed*, our personality and facts about ourselves that we try to hide, disguise, mask, camouflage, and of which we are very much aware but would prefer not to reveal to others.

The acquisition and processing of information about individuals is often made extremely complex and difficult by the willingness or unwillingness of each of us to expose ourselves to the view of those with whom we work or with whom we must have social contact. Our self-perceptions and the ways in which others perceive us are not always in consonance. Often there is inconsonance of perceptions. Similarly, our perceptions of others are not always in consonance with the ways others perceive themselves as individuals. The dynamics of personality and behavior are such that our mutual perceptions are usually in a state of flux, changing as we gain knowledge of each other's reactions to stress in particular. Our simplistic reactions are often stated as, "I never knew he was like that!" Or, "I was completely surprised by his behavior!" Or, "What do you suppose made him say (or do) that?"

The communiscope. The three sets of psychodynamics are states of awareness that are revealed to each member of a group about the individual. These "stages" occur between two people, a single person and a group, or between groups. They are not restricted to peers, subordinates, or superiors. They are separate from rank or authority. The sets and their progressions are diagrammed as Figures 4a, b, c, d, and e—our "communiscope."

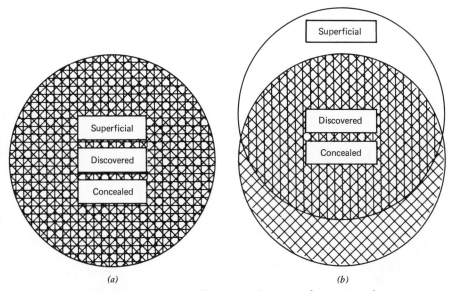

(a)   *(b)*

Figure 4(a) The *Communiscope* illustrates the state of awareness between two individuals, or an individual and a group. At the first encounter, the three states (Superficial, Discovered, and Concealed) are totally opaque; nothing at all is known about the individual. There is no awareness of identifying personality traits, or behavioral characteristics.

Figure 4(b) During the initial encounter, the obvious characteristics (Superficial) of the individual become known, while the "Discovered" and "Concealed" characteristics remain opaque; still unknown.

Figure 4a is an opaque circle. It contains all the knowledge and information about an individual or group that is known and that has not yet been exposed or whose existence has not yet been made known to another. It is the relationship that is nonexistent between two people who have not yet met. An example would be found in the circumstance of an engineering manager who is searching outside his company for a professional person to add to the department or project. Although a task or job description may exist, the specific individual is not yet known, not by name, culture, background, credentials, or physique. The three sets of psychodynamics are totally overlapped, causing opacity, non-identity.

In Figure 4b, we have learned something about the individual. Perhaps we have seen a resume. We know his name, age, education, credentials, perhaps something about his hobbies, age, height, weight, and family ties; limited data that is openly revealed by one individual to

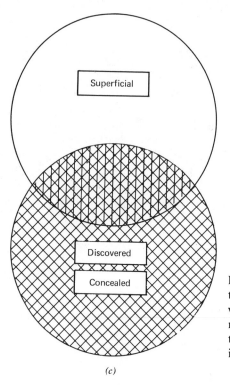

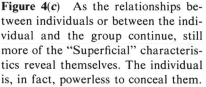

(c)

Figure 4(c) As the relationships between individuals or between the individual and the group continue, still more of the "Superficial" characteristics reveal themselves. The individual is, in fact, powerless to conceal them.

another. This is displayed as a clear, partially exposed circle of *superficial* information.

Perhaps we like what we have seen thus far, so we invite the candidate to an in-person meeting. As a result of this encounter, we have gained a greater insight, enhanced our knowledge of the individual. The *superficial* circle becomes larger and clearer, as in Figure 4c. But we have learned only that which the candidate has allowed us to learn; our perceptions are not yet profound.

Intercommunications implies a two-way situation. Therefore the same diagrams apply to ourselves. Each of us, in an encounter, is experiencing *psychodynamism*.

As we get to "know" each other, there is an ever-increasing series of perceptions. In Figure 4d we have accelerated the process. In the *discovered* circle, information is being communicated, being disclosed involuntarily. Returning to our example of the candidate being interviewed by the engineering manager, impressions are being gained

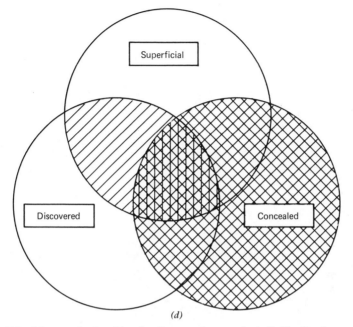

(d)

Figure 4(d)   Now, as depicted by the *Communiscope*, the individual's characteristics continue to reveal themselves. There is an involuntary revelation of personality traits, indicated by the increased clarity of the "Discovered" circle.

through nonverbal communications, such as an unwillingness to make eye contact. This may be received as a signal by the engineering manager that the candidate is not forthright, perhaps not quite honest in his responses to the questions, or evasive in the way he answers them. It may be transmitted through "body language." Perhaps the candidate is slouched in his seat with his arms folded tightly across his chest, his hands grasping his own biceps through his jacket. This might be taken as a signal that the candidate is uncomfortable, wishes he were elsewhere, or is on the defensive.

   We do not suggest that the so-called body language form of communication is a reliable technique for sending or receiving information; however, we do react to posture, body shifts, and other signs of "nervous energy" during an encounter or a situation in which two people are left to their own "ad lib" dialogues. Thus, one individual is being *discovered* by the other, almost involuntarily. This is also referred to as "drawing someone out," making discoveries, causing one person to reveal traits

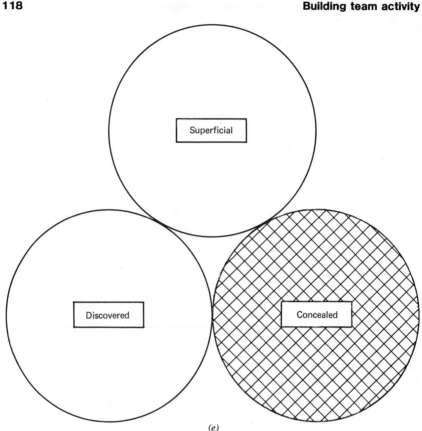

(e)

Figure 4(e)   In time, the individual reveals personal characteristics that he has tried to conceal, mask or camouflage from others. This effect is illustrated in the growing clarity of the "Concealed" circle.

and characteristics of which the person who possesses them has no conscious awareness.

Eventually we arrive at the third set of psychodynamics, those *concealed* personal facts, traits, and behavioral characteristics of which the individual is aware but does not want to reveal. This is the *disguise,* that which lies beneath the *superficial* and the *disclosed* circles. This contains the information and knowledge we have of ourselves but do not want to share. This circle, as in Figure 4e, remains a gray area because we strive to keep it so. If we should allow something secret, private, some *concealed* bit of information to "leak out" to another, this information becomes *discovered* or even *superifical* knowledge, no longer *concealed, masked,* or *camouflaged.*

The same series of circles in the *communiscope* can be applied to an individual as he enters a group. This novice progresses through the three circles as the group's members become more aware of the newcomer. Similarly, the novice's perception of the group and its members progresses through a *communiscope* situation, *psychodynamics*.

Groups, in encounters with other groups, progress through the communiscope.

Peers do so.

A superior and a subordinate do so.

The results of the perceptions play an important part in the acceptance or rejection of the individual by the group, and of the group by the individual, of one individual by another. If there is limited acceptance, there is limited productivity. If there if rejection, there is no "team" effort and the objective is in jeopardy.

Report-command theory of communications. Communication, as has been noted previously, means considerably more than people talking to or writing memoranda and letters to each other. It also means working together toward the attainment of common objectives. Some psychologists use the word "communication" to mean *behavior* in its widest sense, including words and their nonverbal accompaniments of posture and facial expressions. Silence, too, can be a form of communication. All of these convey messages to another person or to the persons to whom they are directed.

Information is the *report* aspect of an exchange or communication. "It is raining," is a *report*; whether true or false, it is a communication. "The investigation of liquid crystal technology is complex and challenging," is a communication that *reports*, makes a logical statement.

Of greater interest, perhaps, in the exploration of theory and practice of interpersonal communications is the observation that the *report* may also contain some elements of *command*, indicating how the information contained in the *report* is to be received. Every message, verbal or nonverbal, has a *report content* and a *command aspect*. The former transmits information about facts, opinions, feelings, experiences. The latter tends to define the nature of the relationship between the persons involved in the act of communicating.

As we participate in communications or exchanges of information, we attempt to define the relationships, seek to determine the nature of the relationship. The response each communicant gives to the other may confirm, refute, or attempt to modify the relationship. This process deserves close attention on the part of the manager, peers, superiors, and subordinates to assure that the intent or objective of an act of transferring information is clearly understood by the communicators.

For example, in the passing of the report, "It is raining," a relationship is attempted. Assume a parent has told his child, "It is raining." The implicit command that attempts to establish or confirm parental *control* is, "Be sure to put on your raincoat (or galoshes, or whatever)." It may be taken or received as an interference with the prerogative of the child to go out into the inclement weather without extra protection. Thus, the communication that has taken place combines the elements of a logical, factual statement with an order for action.

In the example of the comment on technology, such a statement from the engineering manager to one of his subordinates, however factual, even if it is an understatement or oversimplification of the complexity and challenge inherent in the technology, may be taken by the subordinate to contain a command to *solve the problem*, or to volunteer to accept the *challenge*. Or it may cause an inference of a question of intelligence such as, "What's your opinion concerning the facts?"

This brings to mind the story of the two psychologists who pass each other on the street, and each says to the other, "Good morning," and each asks himself, "What did he mean by that?"

Small talk, if there really is such a thing between peers, the manager and his superior, the manager and his subordinates, can contain elements of the *report-command* theory. In the exchange of small talk, the two participants may be attempting to establish a relationship, to determine the degree of separation or of togetherness in the work environment. One's daily life is filled with apparent *small* and *big* talk conversations from which one cannot escape, even if one wanted to. At the risk of sounding paranoid about the opportunities or risks inherent in human communications, the manager should maintain an awareness of the underlying objective of the *report* he may give or receive—to or from his superior, his peers, or his subordinates—and the *command* that may be implied or inferred.

Deliberate *struggles for power* are not implied in these exercises. Usually the actions and reactions are unconscious, intuitive. It is possible that, as a result of the *report-command* situation, one of the communicants may emerge in a position that is superior to the other's. However, such a relationship may prove to be temporary, indicating a dynamic state of equilibrium that is continuously changing and being unconsciously tested.

Self-perception and the team.   How one feels about himself, the level of self-esteem, is important to the survival of the individual as an element of the team or work group. Consider the hypothetical situation in which you, as the manager, ask two of your professionals to meet with you informally. You tell them you want their advice, and your request is quite sincere. Situation: you have been asked to act as chairman of a technical session during the forthcoming convention of your professional society. You are not expected to present a paper, but are expected to make cogent remarks as you introduce each of the people who will present papers. Of course, you want to present a good image of yourself and your company. Perhaps your professionals have some constructive thoughts.

You may not be aware that professional A actually has a low self-esteem, while professional B has a high self-esteem—in the context of the situation you presented to them at the same time. A sees this request as a threat because he believes he has a low sense of adequacy in such situations and is afraid he might reveal how little he knows about them. On the other hand, B sees this as a challenge and, because of his high sense of adequacy and self-esteem, readily provides suggestions and ideas at some length. Both A and B are behaving in ways that are logical within the arenas of their senses of adequacy and self-esteem. They are equally experienced (or inexperienced) in this situation. However, they have behaved, responded quite differently to the same set of circumstances occurring at the same time.

You, as the manager, recognize immediately that B has been more helpful at the moment. Even if his suggestions are not acted upon, they have triggered some original thoughts of your own, helped you find a direction. A has contributed less vocally, but has been part of the ambience that, at the least, provided a stimulus for thoughts and direction. It is important that you provide immediate recognition to both A and B, not to B alone. A gracious statement of thanks, expressed with equal emphasis to both professionals will avoid injury to A's self-esteem, while verifying B's. You are aware that the possibility exists that A might have responded differently, with strength and vigor equal to B if the same proposition had been put to him by another person, a peer member of the group for example. His silence (compared to B) in your presence does not indicate a lack of knowledge. It may indicate a latent fear of revealing less than complete knowledge on the subject in your presence. He knows and is afraid of the fact that you have the power to promote or dismiss him. A power that his peers do not have. Thus, A, when with his co-workers, may make vital contributions to the tasks that confront the group; yet he seems to withdraw, becomes somewhat introverted in your presence. You, as an effective manager, protect his self-esteem in the presence of others.

Feelings of adequacy and the team.   Consider the case of a highly reputed firm and the project manager who had five junior scientists reporting to him. Each of the "juniors" considered himself to be an individual capable of doing outstanding work and of advancing professionally. The fact that they worked for a firm with an exceptionally high reputation was regarded as a fine opportunity for career growth and self-advancement. Each of the five junior scientists put forth his best effort in order to assure that he would advance in the firm and that he would enhance his self-concept.

However, the project manager never offered positive feedback on individual or group performance. Instead, he frequently drew comparisons between the juniors and the seniors. Each time the project manager did this—no doubt in a mistaken effort to motivate by holding others up to view as role models—the juniors' sense of adequacy, the important concept of self, was diminished. The five kept these feelings to themselves. They did not share them with their supervisor, believing he was not a sensitive or empathetic person and would not understand the resentment they felt about the continuous comparisons. They began to believe they would not be able to advance within the firm, that they suffered severely in the light of the comparisons with the senior scientists. Even when asked whether or not there were any problems— apparently the supervisor did have some sensitivity, although it is more likely that he was concerned with the lack of productivity and its effect on his own career path—the juniors did not mention their concern and unhappiness. One should not have to ask for that which one had expected to be given, in this case, *recognition* that closely matched or enhanced the self-concepts of the individuals. Although they did work hard, they had gone unrewarded, unsatisfied. Morale and attitude were poor.

Some, but not all, of the five juniors shared their feelings of career frustration with each other. They decided they were at a dead end in the firm. Each of them quietly and privately sought a new affiliation. All of them did leave within a short span of time. Each joined another company, hoping to find reinforcement for their feelings of adequacy, hoping to become part of a team of high achievers.

The supervisor did not recognize the importance of the feelings of adequacy, the self-concept, among members of the group. In all likelihood he never will succeed in creating a team and, therefore, his own career path will take a serious detour.

Formation of the group

A "group" may be "formed" by the simple expedient of publishing a memorandum signed by an authority (A_p) figure whose instructions must be carried out. The memorandum may designate group members by name and title, and state the group's work objective. Thus, a number of individuals are collected, each with assorted and differentiated needs and desires. But somewhere after the identification of the group or the coming together of the collected individuals in order to perform work, the actual *development* of the *team* begins. As this development takes place, goals are defined, personal commitments to goal-attainment are made, and a structure is created that includes an appointed leader. And often, an informal leader emerges.

Goals must be relevant to needs.   One of the critical tasks of the formally appointed leader is to enable each individual member of the group to identify with the task the group has been formed to accomplish. For some, being part of the group provides satisfaction of the need for *affiliation*. To others it gives a sense of *recognition*: "I have been selected." Some see it as an opportunity to demonstrate their skills and knowledge, to advance and enhance their *self-concepts*. Others see it as an opportunity to do new, stimulating work, to satisfy a need for *self-actualization*.

The skillful manager, the leader of the group, rapidly perceives and identifies the needs of the individuals and makes certain to define the group's goals in terms of affording individual fulfillment.

The *psychodynamics*, as viewed through the communiscope, may be diagrammed for the individual group member as an aid to understanding and to effective intercommunications. The leader could actually list the *superficial* and the *discovered* sets of psychodynamics as an aid to improving his understanding and communications skills with his group members. Each new bit of information is added to the list, which is then used as a private means for providing appropriate leadership to the individuals, aiding in the *development* of the *group* as a *team*.

The open door.   It is possible to establish any of several communication channels and, by mandate, require each member of the group to follow the appropriate "channels." Two types of communication networks are found most often within organizational hierarchies: (a) directly upward, and (b) multipath.

In the instance of "directly upward communications," each member of the group may communicate his information to only one other member of the group, usually his supervisor, and with no other person. This channel may be faster for tasks in which a large quantity of information must be collected and transmitted from several different sources. Communications here are quite centralized, focused on one person. There is no formal, lateral exchange of information.

In the "multipath" network, anyone within the group may communicate information directly with any or all other members of the group, as well as with the supervisor or leader. This is a totally democratic process and, in the technical work group, it usually generates a higher morale, increased creativity, and a greater motivation toward higher quality of output than does the directly upward network. The multipath network is practiced by the manager and the leader whose approach to communications contains the statement, "My door is always open."

The prudent manager is able to make use of or apply the two networks at those times when each is appropriate to the need. Thus one network is not permanently more desirable than the other. Each is used or implemented in accordance with the task and the needs of the work group.

The informal leader emerges.   It is quite usual to find that soon after the group has been identified and the team had started to develop, an informal leader will emerge. It is not always practicable to predetermine who the informal leader will be, but it is important for the formal leader to recognize his existence, to observe his emergence, and to work with him.

The informal leader of a group will emerge quite rapidly if the formally appointed leader is not adequately effective in satisfying the needs of the members of the group. Some other member of the group, usually someone within the group, may be regarded as more powerful, motivational, inspirational, comprehending, and compassionate. There is no "formal" appointment of the informal leader; no election takes place. It is entirely an unspoken recognition of the influence of an individual who is highly regarded by the other members as being more capable of meeting and satisfying individual and collective goals than is the formal leader.

While it is ideal for the *formal leader* to also be the *informal leader* of the group, it is probably more usual than unusual for the formal and informal leaders to be *separate* persons. When an informal leader emerges, the formal leader who is prudent does not try to disable the informal leader. There is no need for the two leaders to be in competition with each other. The prudent formal leader may take the emergence of the informal leader as a signal that, in some areas, he is falling short of the role he has been designated to fulfill. With an open mind and a sincere desire to improve his own performance, he works with the informal leader to analyze his own performance. While engaging in this process of self-analysis he works through the informal leader, using the informal leader's power and influence to accomplish the task for which he is accountable.

The motives of the informal leader must, of course, be carefully examined. It is possible the intent of the informal leader is to undermine the formal leader's position, hoping to be appointed as the replacement for the formal leader in whose demise he may be assisting. Such an informal leader is better described as a "gang leader," one who foments and leads a rebellion against designated authority figures. Such people build *aggression* rather than *teams*. It is wishful thinking, perhaps, that such malevolence is eventually discovered and the wicked person is turned out. True or not, fact or wishful thinking, by that time such a *gang leader* can cause considerable damage to the reputation of the formal leader and can retard the development of the team.

It is easy to underestimate the power of the informal leader, whether he is sincerely dedicated to the development of the group or is fundamentally a rebel against authority other than his own. However, the informal leader who is in fact a gang leader may develop sufficient strength to create binding ties between members of the group to the extent that they would, without conscious thought, rather risk losing their jobs than to lose membership in the group and suffer the effects of isolation. A gang leader is usually a "natural" leader, operating purely on instinct, using force of personality to win the respect and allegiance of the group.

How does the formal leader know that a "gang" leader is emerging and that a "gang," rather than a task-oriented work group, is developing? Some of the indicators are that the members of the group are often evasive in their answers to your questions. They do not recognize the *command* aspects of your *reports*. You find that you must always be totally explicit, or nothing happens. Communications seem to be blocked, almost nonexistent. The formal leader searches for answers, explanations for these situations. He searches within his own actions for possible clues.

The formal leader tries to match his actions to a coincidence of the overt display of negative behavior by the group's members. Perhaps a new policy was initiated that was exceptionally unpopular. It might have brought about resistance instead of commitment. Or a punishment might have been inflicted on a member of the group in a manner, type, or severity that angered—a fear reaction—the members of the group. Instances such as these provide opportunities for the informal leader to emerge. Not all "informal" leaders are "gang" leaders, if we use the word *gang* in its evil connotation.

It is, above all, vital that the formal leader recognize the emergence of the informal leader, whether or not he is a constructive or negative person intent on undermining the formal leader. Certain specific actions are required on the part of the formal leader. He may take advantage of the existence of the informal leader, unofficially enlisting his aid in meeting the objective of the work group. Or he may elect to engage in attempts to dominate the informal leader. If the latter is his preferred option, the formal leader may find himself engaged in an undeclared state of "managerial warfare," a state from which only losers will emerge. There are several options available to the formal leader. After all, he does have the authority of power. What can he do?

He can fire the informal leader! This is an exercise of power that gets the malevolent gang leader out of sound and sight. It temporarily, at any rate, disrupts the gang, hopefully puts an end to the resistance to the formal leader. However, because this approach does not attack the basic root of the problem, it is entirely possible that a new informal leader will emerge and that the members of the group will unite even more strongly than before against the formal leader.

He can attempt to bribe the informal leader with promises of personal reward! If the gang leader succumbs to such enticements, he will lose his position as informal leader and enable another to emerge. And the game is likely to start all over again. This does not attack the problem.

He can have confrontations with the group! This is likely to lead to a debate, accusations, attacks and counterattacks. Feeling a sense of unity, even if the group gives in to the formal leader's urgings or commands, the members of the group feel absolved of any commitments spoken during the confrontation and very soon revert to the original state of silent rebellion.

He can confront individual members of the group! This becomes a divide-and-conquer approach that is doomed to failure because it too does not examine the root. The individual retains his commitment to the behavior of the group.

He can work through the informal leader, using him as a spokesman for the group! This may be construed as "if you can't lick them, join them." Not so. It is a wise approach to maintaining group identification while avoiding confrontation and bribery. It is a problem-identification approach that must lead to a problem-solving resolution. In this way there are no attacks, no counterattacks. Conflict is identified, alternatives examined, and a positive path is programmed.

The personal qualities that inspire confidence, faith, and trust, enabling the leader to provide a positive influence on the members of the group, assure that the formal and informal leaders will work together as one person. From this congruence of capabilities and roles, the *team* may emerge, mature, competent, and productive.

Hawthorne experiments—practice evolves into theory

The school of scientific management developed by F. W. Taylor was the major guide to management methods during the first quarter of the twentieth century. It held essentially that through a division of and specialization of labor to be rewarded through a series of financial incentives for work performed, maximum productivity might be obtained. However, a five-year study, approximately 1927–32, performed under the guidance and control of a group from the Harvard Business School, has become a classic among sociologists and is credited with being the actual beginning of the movement known today as "behavioral science." The name "Hawthorne" is derived from the Hawthorne Works of the Western Electric Company, near Chicago, Illinois, where the studies were conducted.

Hawthorne's management believed quite strongly that its workers were not realizing their full potential for productivity. With the cooperation of management and a group from Harvard under the leadership of Professor Elton Mayo, a sociologist and psychiatrist, a process was developed that, on the surface, appeared to be extremely simple.

A group of five people were placed in a room where their work environment in the assembly of telephone relays could be carefully controlled, where they could be closely observed, and their output could be measured.

At different intervals, specific changes in working conditions were effected and observations were made as to the impact these changes had on productivity. Records were kept of such environmental elements as room temperature and humidity, and of such individual elements as the number of hours each of the five workers slept at night, and the kind and amount of food each ate for breakfast, lunch, and dinner. Over the five-year period, vast amounts of data were collected and analyzed.

The workers operated with minimum supervision and were invited to participate in the making of decisions that affected their environment. They set their own production quotas, determined from choices given to them what their working hours would be, and were encouraged to offer opinions concerning their personal aspirations, hopes, fears, and work conditions. They were often invited into their supervisor's office for conversations concerning their views, and were allowed to chat and socialize at will on the job. They were made very much aware of the fact that they were participating in a long-term study.

Changes were periodically introduced into the environment. For example, the ambient light level of the workroom was gradually increased and records kept concerning relative output levels from the work group. Each time the light level was increased, the productivity of the group would increase. This continued for some time.

At one point, it was decided to reverse the environmental conditions. Light levels were reduced. Amazingly, productivity *increased*, again with each change.

This phenomenon led to the conclusion that the group was not actually responding to the changes in environmental conditions but was reacting to the *recognition* that was being given to it by management. The group was "something special." It was the fact that they, the members of the group, had been singled out as people, had been assembled as a team who would be separated from others at Hawthorne, be given special attention and notice: *recognition*. They were given opportunities for *affiliation* with other "special" people. They were given *responsibility*. Management, even those management people above their supervisor's level, was taking notice of their activities. Their *self-esteem*, their sense of *adequacy* as individuals and as members of a work group, were significantly supported by the unusual attention they received. Probably, their personal *aspirations* were dramatically raised to new heights with each new, periodic test. It was not the nature of the change to which they were reacting. It was the fact that their responses to change were being noted, and they wanted to prove their capabilities.

Thus *motivation to perform* was external to the environment. As Herzberg was to point out in later studies, the environment per se is a *hygiene factor*, a clinical consideration that may provide satisfaction, or dissatisfaction if inadequate; however, of themselves, *hygiene factors do not motivate performance*.

The current emphasis on human relations in management is said to rise from the Hawthorne Studies. There have been many reactions to the meaning of the Hawthorne Studies; however, since Hawthorne's time it has been difficult to view employees as pure economic beings. Today the training of managers and supervisors usually includes instruction concerning the identification and fulfillment of people's needs as the means to increasing productive performance and task attainment.

8
Analyzing verbal transactions (TA for the engineering manager)

When we make a statement or ask a question of someone, we usually are trying to provoke a specific response or reaction. For example, a hypothetical engineer makes a general comment to another hypothetical colleague, "Lab technicians aren't what they used to be!" The expected response is equally general: "You are so right and it sure works a hardship on us!" This is a *direct communication*. Even though it may be negative or inaccurate, the two participants in this dialogue are communicating with each other on a parallel plane. They are in direct contact with each other.

Another example of direct communications, with similar hypothetical people: "This photometric instrument is either unstable or I'm doing something wrong!" The expected response might be, "Yeah, isn't it a pain!" Either one of the two parties might continue the dialogue by adding, "Perhaps we should have the Calibration Lab check it out before we spend any more time with it." Note that the direct communication encourages further dialogue and discussion. It is designed or intended to bring about consensus between two participants.

On the other hand, a *crossed communication* discourages further discussion, signals an immediate discontinuation of the dialogue. As an example, take this simple exchange between an engineering manager and a secretary. Manager: "Where is the file on LCD technology?"

Secretary: "Right where you left it yesterday!" This is not insubordination, but it certainly is not the response the manager expected from his subordinate. The response terminated the exchange, probably created some irritation, and left both parties dissatisfied. They did not establish communications. This is an example of crossed communications.

Another example of crossed communications is in this dialogue between a lab technician and the engineer or scientist to whom he reports on a specific project. Lab technician: "It's next to impossible for me to get any work done around here with these miserable tools!" The expected response was for sympathy and commiseration on the order of "Yeah, ain't it awful!" However, the actual response was more constructive. Engineer or scientist: "Make up a list of replacement tools you need to do your job properly and I will requisition a purchase order for them." The engineer or scientist did not respond to the emotional content of the technician's statement. Instead, he moved several stages forward toward a recognition of the problem and proposed a solution. The response was quite positive. However, because the response was not that which the technician expected, a crossed communication occurred. The engineer or scientist was quick to recognize the "ain't it awful" invitation the technician's comment offered. The response might have been merely "ain't it awful" and a pointless nonconstructive dialogue might have ensued. This would have been a direct communication, each receiving exactly what he expected from the other despite the fact that the direction was meaningless. The engineer or scientist, obviously a productive person, evaded the "expected," and delivered an unexpected but, no doubt, welcome response. From this response it is very likely the dialogue was converted to a totally direct exchange as the technician "snapped out of" his negative mood and began a discussion of the specifics of the problem with his "tools."

It is extremely important that the manager be skilled in making an instantaneous analysis of the transaction that is taking place in such a brief moment of conversation. Learning to do this can become an interesting "game" from which the engineering manager, and all those with whom he communicates—subordinate, peer, superior—will certainly benefit. The "game" has become popularly known as *Transactional Analysis*, or by its initials: TA. Although it often is "fun and games," we will learn about TA primarily because an understanding of TA enables us to rapidly identify the directions from which we and others are coming. And as a result we can evaluate, appreciate, and comprehend the real significances of those rapid, short, and frequent exchanges of conversation we have with one another throughout the work period.

Transactional analysis is described in depth in numerous books, articles, academic classrooms, and seminars for clinical psychologists and the lay public. There are courses, writings, and lectures on TA for teachers, parents, children, and a plethora of other human and occupational categories. Here we describe the main concepts of TA—as they apply to and as they can be used by the manager of engineers and scientists. This can enable us to improve the effectiveness and value of short dialogue.

According to TA theory

It is held by those who support TA theories that each of us, without exception, has three parts to his personality. These "parts" are collectively called *ego states*. The names applied to the three ego states are: (a) *Parent*, (b) *Adult*, and (c) *Child*. At any given moment, we are operating from one of these three states. At any given instant, we may unconsciously, without deliberateness of thought, change from one state to another and back again, or back and forth. The reference to the Parent, Adult, and Child is entirely that of an emotional or intellectual rather than physical state. The words Parent, Adult, and Child are labels for the thoughts, feelings, and opinions that we harbor or express during the movement of an exchange of statements or questions between the manager and a subordinate, peer, or superior within the organizational hierarchy. They do not refer to chronological age, or physical or familial relationships between communicants.

As an analytical technique, the popular practice is to diagram the ego states that are operant and the transaction that is taking place between two individuals. Figure 5a is the basic diagram of the three ego states, invariably drawn as three circles, one above the other. The letter P within the circle indicates Parent. A indicates Adult, and C is Child.

The parent.   It is claimed that when we are operating in our Parent Ego State we are emulating the behavior of our actual parents, guardians, or other authority figures who made deeply indelible impressions upon us when we were forming our personalities. There are two types of

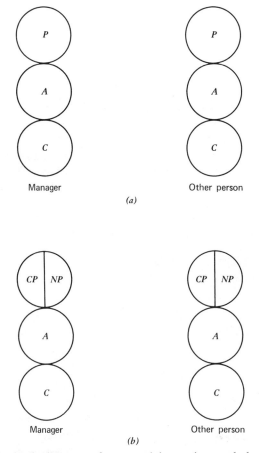

Figure 5(a) The basic diagram of two participants in a verbal transaction. The three ego states, *Parent, Adult,* and *Child* are depicted traditionally as two sets of stacked circles. **Figure 5(b)** The basic diagram is modified to indicate the two separate *Parent* characteristics. *Critical (CP)* and *Nurturing (NP)*.

Parent Ego State. One is the *Critical* or *Controlling Parent*. The other is the *Nurturing* or *Sympathetic Parent*. Thus Figure 5a is modified in Figure 5b to show two segments in the *P* circle, *CP* and *NP*.

The Critical or Controlling Parent is easily recognized from verbal and nonverbal communications. This parent makes demands and gives commands, often accompanied by a pointing or wagging finger and a stern or frowning expression.

Engineering manager: "The project status report is due this afternoon, in my office, at 3 o'clock. Don't be late!"

Engineer: "I know, but I have a supplier coming in this afternoon with some new data that might affect the report."

Engineering manager: "You heard me—3 o'clock!"

The Nurturing or Sympathetic Parent tends to be protective, non-judgmental.

Engineer: "I don't see how I can get the report to you by 3 o'clock today. I have a zillion things and details to attend to, including talking with a supplier this afternoon. He may have some new data for me that could seriously affect the report."

Engineering manager: "Yes, you certainly are carrying a heavy load. Do the best you can and I'll fill in the missing information for the report."

Is one Parent Ego State better than the other? The answer depends on the desired result. If the completion of the engineer's report by 3 o'clock is essential to the manager's function—perhaps it is required so that he can complete his report to his superior—it is more likely that the Critical or Controlling Parent is more effective in actually receiving the report at 3 o'clock. It is possible that the Nurturing Parent, in this example, is actually destructive, relieving the engineer of the responsibility of meeting the 3 o'clock deadline.

As we develop and continue the dialogue, we may move into and out of various ego states. We will observe how one ego state tends to "hook" the other, trying to achieve an expected response.

The adult.   The Adult demands facts, hard data, specific information. The thought process of the person operating at the *Adult Ego State* is organized, objective, apparently intelligent. It has nothing to do with chronological age, is concerned only with the nature of a transaction between the two individuals.

Let's continue the dialogue between the engineering manager who needs a 3 o'clock report from the harried engineer. When we last heard them, the manager had been "hooked" by the engineer's lament and had moved into the sympathetic Nurturing Parent Ego State. Recognizing that he had not solved a fundamental problem, and that he had better determine whether or not the engineer was carrying too heavy a work load, the manager moved into a fact-finding state, that of the Adult.

Manager: "I hear you saying that you are overloaded at the moment. Let's take a look at your assignments. I suggest we start with the PERT chart and isolate the individual tasks."

The engineer, moving into his own Adult Ego State, is now in direct communication with the manager, encourages the conversation to continue by responding:

Engineer: "That's a good idea. Perhaps we may have to reset our priorities and thereby hold the timetable."
Manager: "Makes sense. Shall we do it now?"

The child. Statements, responses, and questions that are emotionally charged usually come from the individual who is, at the moment, operating in the Child Ego State.

The *Natural Child* is characterized as being relatively free in spirit, doing just what he wants to do. He is aggressive, impulsive, rebellious, affectionate, curious, playful, selfish. When the Child stands up for his rights he usually does it emotionally rather than factually. If he attempts to state facts while in the Child mode, it is not done calmly; the emotions are evident.

The *Little Professor Child* is intuitive, creative, inventive, sometimes a "smart aleck," often manipulative. The engineer or scientist who has just made a discovery, for example, and comes excitedly to his supervisor's desk to tell him about it is operating in the *Little Professor Child*

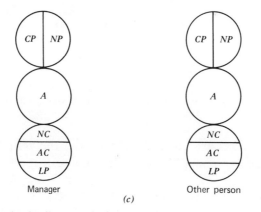

Manager   Other person
(c)

Figure 5(c) The basic diagram is further modified to indicate three separate sets of *Child* characteristics, *Natural Child* (*NC*), *Little Professor* (*LP*), and *Adapted Child* (*AC*)

Ego State. The conversation between the engineer and his manager may sound like this:

> *Engineer:* "Wow, did I just come up with something exciting! This really is a breakthrough! Fantastic!"
>
> *Engineering manager:* "I'm delighted to hear your enthusiasm. Tell me about the procedure you followed to verify the data."

The manager did not get "hooked" by the Child State of the engineer who expected the manager to respond with enthusiasm or excitement at least equal to his own. For a brief moment, the manager was a Nurturing Parent. Quite rapidly, however, he moved into the Adult State, searching for data and factual information. For a short while longer, the engineer continued as a Little Professor attempting to "hook" the manager's Little Professor State.

> *Engineer:* "What a feeling, after so many frustrations and blind alleys, to know I found the solution! Let me tell you—I feel great about it!"

The manager almost gets "hooked," but recovers quickly and finally gets the engineer into an Adult state.

> *Manager:* "Yes, we sure had a struggle. Now, let's review the setup in the lab. The original task was to determine the right combination of discrete and integrated components that would be both cost and performance effective. How did you approach the problem?"

The engineer responds from his Adult state.

> *Engineer:* "Okay. You will recall my initial proposal dated May 12th in which I established and defined several alternative approaches. I requisitioned appropriate samples of discrete and intergrated components. You approved the requisition and the first lab setup was completed on June 17th, as we had targeted."

Communications are quite direct now and the actual results of the project can be examined and evaluated by both the engineer and his manager.

The *Adapted Child* is well behaved, trained, and disciplined. He has highly developed awareness of social commitments and behavior. He is courteous, compliant, avoids confrontation; he is a procrastinator. The

Adapted Child often has a low self-esteem. He is not self-reliant, depending heavily on others and on his environment for support. The Adapted Child, when he is aware of his low self-esteem, tends to withdraw, to become introverted, to avoid interacting with others. Rather than be pointed out as an individual, he will go along with others in their actions, even though, in his thoughts, he may be in disagreement. The Adapted Child attempts to conform to the expectations of the Parent. It is possible for the manager to assume or to be endowed with the attributes of the Parent. The assumptions and endowments may be the result of the behavior of the manager, or they may be entirely within the mind of the subordinate who, having a low self-esteem acquired during his childhood, relates the words "boss" and "parent" as being one and the same. The Adapted Child can be depended upon to perform tasks in a routine, possibly adequate manner. He quietly seeks and needs approbation for his actions.

Let's assume the engineer in our example has possibly made a discovery and wants to report it to his manager. Operating in the Adapted Child State—instead of the Little Professor State—he approaches his manager.

> *Engineer:* "I'm not sure, but I think I may have come across something unusual. But could you check it with me? I followed the project plan to the letter."

The manager, feeling a bit uncomfortable, responds to the engineer's search for a Nurturing Parent.

> *Manager:* "I'm sure you did everything correctly. You always do. I can depend on you for that."

The manager, having given the expected response, moves the dialogue and the transaction into an Adult state.

> *Manager:* "Tell me about your approach, the procedure you followed, and the instrumentation you used."
> *Engineer:* "Here's the original project plan. The first thing I did was . . ."

Figure 5c diagrams the two Parent Ego States, the Adult, and the three Child Ego States.

direct and crossed communications

A diagram helps clarify the difference between a direct and a crossed verbal transaction. Note in Figure 5*d* that we have the usual vertical arrays of the Parent, Child, and Adult Ego States, one array for each of the communicants in the transaction.

Taking the example of the engineer's complaint to a colleague that "Lab technicians aren't what they used to be," we depict this an an unbroken arrow connecting his Child Ego State to the Child Ego State of his colleague. The colleague's response is shown as a returning dash-line arrow. The dialogue may continue this way until either there is an interruption that discontinues it or one of the communicants moves into another state. This "move" might be depicted in a statement that changes the mood, such as, "Perhaps we need a training program to upgrade our technicians' skills." This is coming from the Adult Ego State, directed to the Adult of his colleague. If the colleague responds with a continuation of the dialogue from his own Adult Ego State, we have continued the direct verbal transaction at a level that is different from the original statement and state that opened the verbal transaction. The unbroken and broken arrows are in parallel planes, although different throughout the dialogue, and are therefore identified as direct.

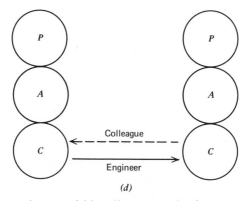

(d)

Figure 5(*d*)   The engineer and his colleague are in *direct* communication with each other. Their dialog could continue for some time, without necessarily being productive. If one or the other of the communicants moves into the *Adult* Ego State and succeeds in bringing the other to the same level, the dialog could very well achieve a positive objective.

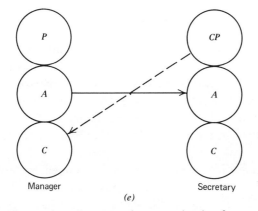

Manager   Secretary

(e)

Figure 5(e) An illustration of a *crossed* communication from an example given in the text. The manager's statement was directed from his *Adult* to the secretary's *Adult*. However, the secretary responded from her *Critical Parent*. The unexpected response terminated the dialog.

In Figure 5e we visualize a crossed transaction or communication set, using the example of the engineering manager who is frustrated by the response of his secretary. The engineering manager attempted a direct transaction in the Adult Ego State, shown by the unbroken arrow from the engineering manager to the secretary. The secretary's broken-arrow crossed communication came from her Critical Parent Ego State. She was implicitly criticizing the forgetfulness of the engineering manager and directed her response toward the engineering manager's Child. The diagonal nonparallel lines clearly indicate an unsuccessful verbal transaction, resulting in a rapid termination of the attempted dialogue. If the engineering manager had retorted with a direct communication based on power-authority, such as, "You should have filed it after I used it!" it is possible the secretary might have responded from her own Child Ego with, "I'm sorry and I'll certainly be more careful next time." His would have been Parent to Adapted Child, still crossed. On the other hand, if she had responded with a direct communication, answering Critical Parent with Critical Parent, the scene might have become quite unpleasant. The engineering manager would properly talk from his Adult Ego State with a response such as, "You are right. I did use it last and forgot to file it. I would appreciate your help next time, and thank you for helping to keep our place in order." The secretary would, most likely, respond with an Adult comment such as, "Yes, it is important that we be able to find documents rapidly and accurately. You can count on me." The direct communication at the Adult level can be continuous and positive, worth striving for.

It is vital for effective engineering management to operate as much as possible at the Adult Ego State. This does not mean that there should not be room for excitement such as the Little Professor can bring to the work environment. Creative people often operate in this ego state. However, in order to be productive, the demands of the Little Professor must be satisfied rapidly, and then the Ego State moved into the Adult.

A task or a project should always be defined in terms of specific objectives and goals. Reports and evaluations of results demand hard data, facts, and information. Only the *Adult Ego State* can deal with these.

Strokes

A "stroke" in transactional analysis is a unit of recognition. It takes many forms, including a pat on the back, a nod in a specific direction, a word of greeting, a statement of praise, a frown, or a negative criticism. A stroke may be verbal and formal, such as a toast or formal testimony. It may be nonverbal and informal, such as a wave of the arm, a pointing of the finger. There are two types of basic strokes: (a) *positive* and (b) *negative*. Within the positive, there is the *conditional* and the *nonconditional* stroke.

Positive strokes add warmth to the work day and generally improve the quality of self-esteem within the work environment. In the language of the transactional-analysis practitioner, they say, "you're OK, and so am I." While positive strokes by themselves are not necessarily motivating devices, they can have a significant effect on morale and attitude that sets the stage for achieving productivity through motivation. People need strokes. The total absence of strokes or stroking can be devastating to the ego. Rather than exist in an environment in which there is a total absence of strokes, people will accept a negative stroke. This is part of the *need for recognition* that must be satisfied—hopefully, satisfied with positive strokes.

When a project group or a technical department is small, it is relatively easy to send and receive strokes that are both verbal and nonverbal. The smallish group or department enables individuals to maintain close and constant contact with one another. Exchanges of informal expression, verbal and nonverbal, can be frequent. When the group or department becomes relatively large, such exchanges, or stroking, become more difficult. Communications become complex. Strokes are less frequently dispensed on an informal basis, are reserved for official pronouncements through awards, bulletin boards, company newsletters, and interoffice memoranda. The engineering manager can be hard-pressed to remember that an important role he plays is that of the satisfier-of-needs. His staff looks to him as the source of satisfaction. A brief comment is often all it takes to "make the day" for an individual. For example:

Manager: "You did a fine job of analysis, Joe. Your usual high-quality performance!"

You can very well imagine the boost this 5-second stroke gave to Joe. He received a positive stroke that was *nonconditional*, the very best kind.

Contrast the above nonconditional stroke with the probable effect of a similar compliment that carries a condition:

Manager: "You did a fine job of analysis, Joe. You can do good work *when you set your mind to it!*"

Joe was given a "yes, but" message, a *conditional positive stroke*. The first sentence of the manager's stroking statement was warm and gave positive recognition. The message said, "You're OK!" However, the message was rapidly diluted by the second sentence, which said in effect, "sometimes." The receiver, Joe, might actually perceive this as a negative stroke.

Negative strokes, whether delivered by design or without premeditation, tend to cause hurt feelings, are perceived by the receiver as "put downs." These carry the message, "You're not OK." This type of stroking can be verbal or nonverbal, formal or informal. Exasperated glances, pointing the thumb downward in a "death to the gladiator" gesture, rolling the eyes upward, deep sighs, and raised eyebrows are typical of the informal, nonverbal negative stroke. Keeping someone waiting ("cooling his heels"), looking at one's watch while appearing to be listening to someone who is talking, accepting telephone calls and other interruptions during a meeting—these too are nonverbal, informal negative strokes. They discount the importance of the other person or the value of the conversation. Formal negative strokes are given when an adverse, critical appraisal is put into writing, in a memorandum, a project progress report, or the periodic performance-appraisal form. Verbal negative strokes are built into such statements as:

> "You sure blew that one!"
> "Why do I have to repeat myself?"
> "When will you learn?"
> "This task may be too big for you."
> "There just isn't a spot for you in the project."
> "Sorry. Win some, lose some."

Each one of these sharply and unambiguously delivers a "You're not OK" message. It is not conceivable that they will have a positive effect on the recipient of the message. They come from the sender's Parent Ego State, the Critical Parent. And they are directed at the receiver's Child Ego State. They may generate anger and resentment against the sender, cause a deterioration in morale, and the development of a negative attitude.

We do not mean to imply that there is no place for a critical comment in the business environment. It is immature to expect a Pollyanna reaction to all situations without regard to the impact that the situation may have had on the progress of the project, the department, or of the manager himself. We do mean to indicate that if morale and attitude are to be maintained at a level that enables motivational efforts to be productive, a "top of the head" comment that comes from the Critical Parent Ego State will not have a desirable effect.

Instead of "You sure blew that one," try an Adult statement such as, "Let's you and me put our heads together and develop a plan that maximizes the probability for good results next time we take on a similar task." Short negative strokes can be devastating. The longer statement implies no criticism of the person, and points out appropriately that the manager (sender) owns the problem as much as does the engineer (receiver).

The manager of a group of engineers or scientists sets the pace, becomes the role model for individual behavior. He generates the ambience in which the individuals must function. An organization that is uptight and filled with tension breeds distrustful, defensive, and aggressive behavior. The manager can strengthen his ability in selecting people who will enter the department or the project, or who are to be promoted, by recognizing the Parent-Adult-Child ego strengths of the individual. If a manager needs a creative or innovative person for his team, he should be wary of the Parent-dominated individual and strongly consider the Child-dominated individual. On the other hand, if pure loyalty, integrity, and morality are the primary traits, a strong Parent may prove to be quite desirable. But if logic and rational thinking processes are essential characteristics, the manager should seek out individuals who are Adult-dominated, avoiding those who present Parent-Child profiles.

It is important to reiterate that each of us has all three ego states within our behavioral structures. It is equally important to note that each of us exhibits a dominant ego state that can be readily observed over a period of time. It does not take long for each of us to display the ego state that is dominant. Transactional analysis, TA, as a theory of personality and behavior that stems from our early environmental exposures, is empirical. Yet it may be used effectively to improve the interpersonal relationships that are essential between ourselves and our subordinates, peers, and superiors. Whether the communication is between the manager and one of his subordinates, or with his own direct supervisor, it is important to each of the communicants that regardless of the ego state from which the communication originates, the exchange must move rapidly into the Adult ego state. If this "move" is not achieved, one or both of the communicants may leave the dialogue with "not OK" feelings. If it is typical that we behave most often as the Critical Parent, we must maintain a conscious awareness of this tendency and make every effort to correct this behavioral pattern. If our typical behavior is that of the Child, seldom dealing in facts and logic, we must similarly learn to bring the Adult into dominance. The manager must feel "OK" about himself, and he must enable others to feel "OK" about themselves.

What is your dominant ego state?

It is possible to develop, empirically, an estimation of your own *dominant ego state*. You may come from one direction when dealing with your subordinates, and from another when dealing with your peers. And from still another when communicating with your superiors within the organization. The following are self-evaluation quizzes for each of the three levels within your organization: subordinate, peer, superior.

Each of the series of three quizzes contains 12 statements that might be made directly to you. Each of the statements has three optional responses from which you are to select the one that *most closely resembles* the way you feel about the situation that has been presented. Circle the letter that identifies your choice of options for each statement. At the end of the third quiz, we will describe the scoring method. Do not look ahead, but start directly with statement number 1 in the first quiz, which deals with you and your superior.

It is most beneficial to choose your response rapidly rather than to make a carefully studied selection. Your intuitive, impulsive reaction is what you want to examine through these quizzes. Do not try to "beat" the quizzes. Go along with them and learn more about yourself.

Your Superior Says	You Feel Like Saying
1 You are telling me I would be unwise to pass up the opportunity your plan proposes.	**A** I pay you a compliment and right away you take it as an insult. **B** Perhaps I was behaving presumptuously. May I suggest that we determine your level of interest in the project and whether or not it deserves your support? **C** I doubt you will ever get such an opportunity again!
2 I'm totally confused! You've given me so many inputs I can't make a sensible decision. What should we do to straighten this out?	**A** Quite easy. The right decision is the one that makes you look good. **B** How about starting with a discussion of the pros and cons of each of my inputs? **C** Sure is a tight spot! Do whatever you feel like doing. It'll probably work out somehow.
3 Do you realize how late you are for this meeting? Now I'm way off my schedule.	**A** Cool it for a moment! Getting so upset about it can't help you one bit. **B** Perhaps we should reschedule this meeting for a time when you don't feel so much pressure? **C** Relax! Relax! How about a cup of coffee? Then we'll both feel better.
4 Tell me again about the practical values of the task you propose. That's really all I want to know.	**A** Doesn't the fact that I feel it is important mean anything to you? **B** Can we concentrate on those specific areas about which you may have some doubts?

Your Superior Says	You Feel Like Saying
	C Look, all I need right now is your reaction. How does my idea grab you, personally?
5 I know you made the decision on priorities. But is it final? Not subject to change?	A We both know that if I didn't stick to my decisions I'd lose control of the department fast.
	B I don't mean to imply that. Certainly, if you feel differently about the priorities we should review them and implement any changes that are indicated.
	C Nobody has come up with anything better!
6 Why do I have to do everything myself? I'd like to see people with authority also take responsibility!	A Did you ever see me refuse to make a decision? When did I ever pass the buck?
	B Is there a particular situation I can help you with, or is this your general feeling?
	C Boy, that's the way people are around here. Afraid to stick their necks out!
7 I'd like to steer the project in that direction. But remember, last time we changed signals I took the blame all alone.	A Even the turtle sticks its neck out when it wants to go forward. You know you can count on my support.
	B Why not take time to consider the personal risks and the opportunities. Shall we meet again tomorrow?
	C Nothing is certain in this world, but think of all the fun we can have with this one.
8 This is a new technique. Seems quite logical. Can we review it in greater depth?	A This is a tough one. I'd like to review it alone and then come back to you for a discussion.
	B Let's isolate some specific points for detailed investigation, shall we?
	C It's really not that difficult. Are you stalling?
9 Right now I have the impression you are being different just for the sake of being different. You'll have to do a lot better to convince me.	A All I want to do is help you do a better job. My experience should mean a lot to you, personally.
	B I may have incorrectly said something that gave you the impression I was trying to "sell" you on my ideas. I do believe I have supportive data and would like to go over it with you.

Your Superior Says	You Feel Like Saying
	C You may be right. I do sometimes get bored with doing things in the same old way.
10 Have you heard the latest? Can you keep a secret? This is hot!	**A** You should know by now I can and do keep confidential information to myself. If it's gossip, please, I'd rather not hear it. **B** If it has some bearing on my work or on me, yes, I'd like to hear it. **C** Wow! I haven't heard a juicy bit in a long time. Tell me and my lips are sealed.
11 I want to keep an open mind. Describe the project and I promise to give you my honest reactions.	**A** After you've heard my description, I am sure you will agree this is the best of all alternatives. **B** Fair enough. Shall I start at the beginning, or are there some specific points you'd like to go over? **C** Well, I've written a summary of the project. Read it and give me a call when you've come to some kind of conclusion.
12 I believe I worked out a solution to that problem last night. Let's go over it right now and see how fast we can put it to work!	**A** Shouldn't we get full approval to go ahead before we commit ourselves to anything? **B** You certainly sound enthusiastic about it. If it seems feasible, we can discuss a plan of action on which we both agree. **C** Great! If we can put this one over we'll both be heroes!

Total the letters that you've circled. A= ___ . B= ___ . C= ___ .

Your Peer Says	You Feel Like Saying
1 For whatever it's worth, don't try too hard to be different around here. It doesn't pay.	**A** I hear you. However, I don't believe in staying in a rut unless you want to go nowhere. **B** I know you are not alone in that feeling around here. However, it is my observation that the reception to change might be good. **C** Are you ever right! That's the main reason why I double-check everything with everyone else.

Your Peer Says	You Feel Like Saying

2 My personal rule is never to wash dirty linen in public and I don't respect those who do.

   A Right. People who do can't have much self-respect.

   B I wonder about the value of judging others by your own personal rules?

   C My parents taught me the same thing. It's sure embarrassing when somebody does it.

3 It's a fact that you've never kept your promises to me. Why should I go along with you now?

   A After all the time I put into this project you're going to let the past influence your thinking? That's a cheap shot!

   B I'm sorry you feel that way about me. Honestly, I do not recall any broken promises. Can you give me some examples? I'd like to clear the air.

   C It was never intentional. Can't you back me one more time?

4 The whole argument is based on your belief I would be foolish to pass up this opportunity!

   A I mean it. There's no one better qualified for the job. It's a once-in-a-lifetime opportunity.

   B Perhaps I made too many assumptions. You should decide your level of interest and whether or not you have confidence in your skills as they relate to the situation.

   C Why get so upset about it? I thought I was paying you a compliment and you act insulted.

5 Why do we have so much trouble getting a management decision around here? Do you think it will ever get better?

   A Fear! That's the reason. They are afraid to take chances. They ought to take a course in decision-making.

   B Is there something in particular, or is this a general feeling about management?

   C Not likely. I bet they enjoy keeping us in the dark. Guess who gets blamed when things go wrong around here?

6 Stuff and nonsense! How can you swallow that crap?

   A Don't talk to me that way. Who do you think you are anyway?

   B I don't understand what you are really saying, but I do want to. Can we level with each other?

   C If you don't want to accept it, okay! Who cares!

Your Peer Says	You Feel Like Saying

7 That's not the normal procedure. It took us a long time to establish it. Why upset things now?

    A Don't you think it's about time for a change. I can name half a dozen reasons for changing procedures.

    B It is possible others are ready for change. My suggestion is based on what I see working well in other, similar companies.

    C You are absolutely right! That's a sure-fire way to get into trouble.

8 Amazing how a little bit of power can go to some people's heads! Makes you wonder who the grownups are in this place.

    A Yes, you'd think they'd know better than to behave like fascists just because of a title.

    B People do react differently to the same situation. I can't pretend to know why.

    C Hey. You're not referring to me, are you?

9 Sounds good, but the last time I went along with a project idea such as yours, it failed and I was blamed.

    A You can count on me, if the going gets tough. You won't be the only one blamed.

    B Think it over. No need to decide right now. It is possible the risk may not be worthwhile for you in this instance.

    C There you go again. Scared to stick your neck out and have some fun.

10 New ideas turn me on. Tell me about it. I promise an honest reaction.

    A I tell you there is no other way. You'll agree as soon as I describe it.

    B Let me start with a statement of the problem, the alternative approaches, and the reasons why I think I have selected the optimum path.

    C I've written it up. How about reading it and letting me have your reactions?

11 The value of the project proposal to the company escapes me.

    A Never mind the "value." How do you personally feel about my proposal?

    B Let me try to clear up some hazy points. Do you have some specific doubts we can discuss?

    C I know it will work and give a big payoff to the company!

12 Confused, that's what I am! What would you do in my position?

    A I'd do what makes me look good.

    B I can't really put myself in your place. Perhaps we can talk it over and clear up some of the confusion.

Your Peer Says	You Feel Like Saying
	C You're in a tight spot all right. I'd do whatever I feel like and let the chips fall where they may.
Total the letters you've circled.	A = ___ . B = ___ . C = ___ .

Your Subordinate Says	You Feel Like Saying
1 How do you expect anyone to work without proper test instruments?	**A** I expect you to do the best you can. **B** Develop a list of instruments you now have and what you feel you need additionally. **C** I know, but the front office says "tough!"
2 I'm not sure I should tell you this. But certain people in the group are not behaving properly.	**A** There'll be no carrying on in my department. Tell me and I'll put a stop to it. **B** You seem to be eager to tell me, whatever it is. If it has an effect on me and the project, I do want to know the facts. **C** You know you can trust me. What's the scoop?
3 Last night, at home, I suddenly found a solution to that problem we've been stuck on. I could hardly wait to get to the lab and test the idea.	**A** Slow down a bit. You may not get involved in a new test path without my prior approval! **B** Tell me about it and, if it sounds feasible, we can develop a program to test it. **C** Great! If we can make it work out we'll both look like heroes!
4 You seem to be trying to force your ideas on me. How about my own? Aren't they any good?	**A** I am, after all, the manager. And I am the manager because I have the best judgment skills. **B** That isn't my intent. Let's examine the pros and cons of your ideas and of mine and select those that offer the best probabilities. **C** Sure yours are good but mine are better!
5 Getting an approval around here is like pulling teeth! What do I have to do to get a go-ahead?	**A** You're all wrong, as far as I am concerned. Give me a good idea and you get approval pronto! **B** I wasn't aware of this difficulty. What spe-

Your Subordinate Says	You Feel Like Saying
	cific approval have you been searching for?
	C I know exactly what you mean. I have the same trouble with the front office!
6 I haven't got time for all these written reports. I'm an engineer, not a writer!	**A** Writing reports is part of the job. You have no choice. And I want them on time!
	C Written reports, bothersome though they may be, are an essential part of the professional's responsibilities. It might be beneficial to both of us to go over the functions and purposes they serve for you, me, the department, and the company.
	C I know exactly what you mean! I could get a lot more work done around here myself if I didn't have to take time to write all these reports.
7 I don't understand why my salary increase is less than average for my job classification.	**A** Do you really think you deserve more?
	B Let's review your performance appraisal form and discuss the strengths and weakness and how we graded your overall performance in comparison with the statistical average for our classification.
	C I can't help it! I have just so much money to work with and you know they won't give me more!
8 I've been waiting all morning to talk to you! Don't blame me for falling behind in my work.	**A** That's the wrong attitude to take with me!
	B I really am sorry I wasn't available this morning. It might be a good idea to get together at another time, when you don't feel so much pressure. Shall we set a firm time?
	C Oh, relax. You and I get paid by the week, not by the hour. Let's go get some coffee.
9 Do you mean your decision is final? You won't listen to alternative recommendations?	**A** That's exactly right! We don't have time to consider any alternatives now.
	B Not at all. I welcome all inputs as constructive. However, in the absence of such inputs, I must make the decisions on the basis of facts already in hand.
	C I haven't heard any ideas as good as mine!

Your Subordinate Says	You Feel Like Saying
10 Fact is you don't always keep your promises to the staff. Why should I accept one now?	**A** Aren't you being petty about the past? Remember, I have as much at stake in this project as you do! **B** Perhaps I am not aware of broken promises in the past. It would be helpful if you would fill me in so we can reestablish confidence in each other. **C** I never intentionally broke a promise. Try me this time!
11 You recall the last time we tried it this way the experiment failed and I took a lot of guff!	**A** But you aren't alone in this one. Don't you want to get ahead? You've got to stick your neck out to do so. **B** It seems we have to consider several points here: the probability for success and the consequences of failure. Take time to think it over and decide whether the opportunity is worth the possibility of failure. **C** Nothing is a sure thing in this world! Dare to succeed, and have fun while trying.
12 Frankly, I do not enjoy working with this group, although I do like the project per se.	**A** You will have to learn to get along with others if you want to stay in this company. **B** Are there specific, recurrent conflicts that we can identify and try to resolve one at a time? **C** There sure are some kooks in this operation! But don't they make the day go by quickly?

Total the letters that you've circled. A= ___ . B= ___ . C= ___ .

How to evaluate the scores. At this point you have developed totals for each of the three quizzes. For each statement given in the quizzes, there were three options from which to select the one most closely resembling your natural response. One of each of the three options reflected the Parent Ego State, one the Adult Ego State, and one the Child Ego State. In all situations given above, the letter *A* represented Parent, *B* the Adult, and *C* the Child.

For each of the three quizzes, Superior, Peer, and Subordinate, you arrived at a subtotal of the letters circled as indications of your own responses to the situations. The letter that has been circled most often in each of the quizzes identified your probable *dominant ego state* within the context of the situations with which you have been presented. It is entirely possible to respond to similar situations from totally different ego states, depending upon whether we are communicating with a superior, peer, or subordinate within the organization.

Add together the three subtotal scores, according to the letters *A, B,* and *C.* This provides you with a statistical average of your dominant ego state. Are you most often the Parent, Adult, or Child?

The PARENT is highly critical of himself and others; judgmental; moralistic; gives strong how-to instructions; rigid; prejudiced; authoritarian (Critical Parent) or permissive (Nurturing Parent); paternalistic; follows rules.

The ADULT is nonemotional; rational; logical; objective; deals with facts and data; considers probabilities; realtively a no-fun guy; concerned with realities of the moment.

The CHILD is curious; creative; impulsive; rebellious; stubborn; manipulative; griping; tends to sulk; dependent upon others; spontaneous; self-centered; self-pitying.

An understanding of transactional analysis can enable the manager of professional engineers and scientists to recognize the dynamics of interpersonal communications and therefore understand what is actually taking place between two communicants, or between himself and another person. An awareness of the operant ego state of the other person can help move a potentially destructive exchange into a positive arena wherein productivity and ego satisfaction can both be developed. An awareness of one's own operant ego state is valuable in assuring that positive communications do, in fact, take place during interpersonal exchanges with superior, peer, or subordinate. Two people who are knowledgeable and proficient in the practice of transactional analysis may not always have "fun and games" as they move themselves into their *Adult Ego States.* But they will most likely gain significant satisfaction from the fruits of their exchanges as they enhance each other's productivity and reinforce their attitudinal and motivational positions. Nonetheless, they are human beings. Therefore, they will, as will anyone else, expose their *Parent* and *Child Ego States* from time to time. They will enjoy an anecdote, spontaneously participate in a practical joke or other horseplay, feel sorry for themselves, criticize others, preach, and pass judgments. However, they will rarely allow a conversation to close without either a consensus of ideas or a specific direction for the participants to pursue.

9
Expectations and management styles

You have successfully presented a comprehensive proposal for an R&D project. It is satisfying to learn that the concept of the project and the request for a budget overlay have both been approved by general and financial management.

A new set of challenges is now presented to you. A new workgroup must be formed, its individual members selected, a formal leader appointed. Tasks and objectives have to be defined, standards of performance and measurement described, and commitment must be obtained.

All the elements of the set of challenges can be briefly stated. But this belies the complexity of the situation. How you, as the engineering manager, approach and deal with each of the elements seriously impacts the formation, development, effectiveness, and productivity of the work group. The "impact" will be either positive or negative. It cannot be defined as "neutral." For the life of the project, your skills as a manager will often be put to the test. Rarely will you have significant advance warnings of the sorts of problems that will test your skills.

If you are a power-based authoritative (A_p) manager, you may feel self-confident that you can easily handle or deal with any situation that may arise. People will work together because you have told them to. And they will avoid conflict and disagreement. They will work together as a *team*. Why? Because you have ordered them to—or else! What a neat, well-ordered world. People do as you bid them to do.

154

But we all know it doesn't actually work that way.

Ideas and concepts of leadership are going through a sequence of change. The humanistic view of management is becoming more dominant with each passing year. Recall the Hawthorne Studies of the 1920s. They produced some of the first scientific evidence that the way people feel and personally care about a work situation and about themselves can have a serious effect on the productivity of the individual and of the group to which he belongs or with which he identifies. Special and regular courses of study are offered in educational institutions that deal with the behavior of people within the work group. These are often referred to as "organizational behavior" or "human relations in management." One can even major in the subject as part of one's work toward a doctorate.

The term *organizational behavior* is somewhat misleading. Organizations do not "behave" in any manner. An organization, similar to a corporation, is a "thing," not a human being with all the sensitivities with which human beings are endowed. The term is more accurately restated as "behavior within the organization." The behavior of the organization is a composite, the result or product of the behavior of its individual members, which, for our purpose, is the specific *work group*. The manager is accountable for the performance of the *group*. And, since the group is actually an assembly of individuals, the most likely procedure for assuring group effectiveness and productivity is to recognize that the "manager" is in reality the manager of individuals. It may seem trite, but it is important to state that an *individual* is a particular human being as contrasted with a social group or institution; though he may work within a group, he has his own awareness and perception of the world that surrounds him.

The manager may have a preconceived notion of the ideal group that thinks, perceives, feels, and responds as though the entire group were a single being. Such a manager is assured of disappointment and a continuous series of surprises as his "group" demonstrates the individuality of its members. The manager must prepare his emotions and intelligence, therefore, for adaptability and flexibility in his *style of management*. No longer is there just one style of management that is to be considered *the best*. There are many so-called *styles*. They may not be considered, out of context of a situation, right or wrong.

Each *style* has its time and place, a set of human and physical conditions that make it "right"—at the moment. Under another set of conditions, the same *style* of management may be quite inappropriate, totally "wrong." The "right" style is the one that offers the greatest probability for achieving a desired result. Make the style fit the time, place, situation, and the individuals. The effective and productive manager is able to "switch gears," change his style. He is flexible and continuously as adaptable as he expects his superiors, peers, and subordinates to be in their relationships with him and with one another.

The Wheel of Interaction revisited

The challenge to the manager as he attempts to successfully interact with individuals and groups is illustrated in Figure 6.

The relative position of the manager is constantly changing from the central position, from which his influence radiates, to any one of the radial segments. The manager is, at various times, the focal point or one of the points toward whom a managerial action that has originated elsewhere within the Wheel is directed. The manager is the originator of a managerial action at one moment, and the recipient at another. All managers belong to several groups at the same time. This multiplicity is illustrated in Figures 7 and 8. The concept has sometimes been described in organizational behavior texts as the linking pin concept.

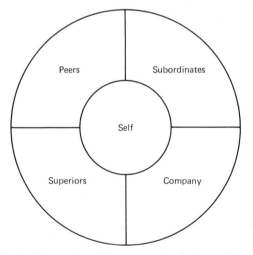

Figure 6 The Wheel of Interaction. The manager is shown at the center of the wheel. The outer segments directly connected to the "self" represent the entities of the company with which he must ineract effectively: peers, subordinates, superiors, and the company as a common objective.

Expectations and management styles

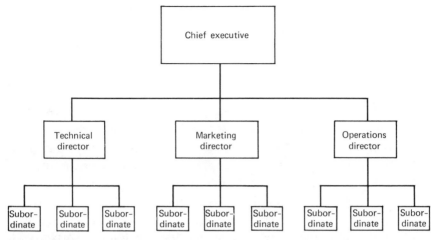

Figure 7 A typical but abbreviated organization chart. The intent is to display a hierarchy above and below and in parallel with the Technical Director who is accountable for engineers and scientists.

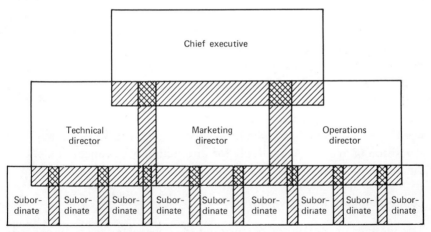

Figure 8 An illustration of the interlocking relationships of the hierarchy of Figure 7. Each member or unit of the hierarchy belongs to more than one group. For example, the technical director belongs to the group represented by his peers, his subordinates, and his superior. Each subordinate belongs to his peer group and that of his direct superior. By implication, each group is affected by the performance of its peers as well as by the style of its direct supervisor or manager.

The manager, the project leader, and the work supervisor are all members of at least four activity groups, linked together by a requirement for productive communications that will enable each of them to fulfill obligations and commitments to people, objectives, the company, and to himself. These activity groups include the following:

1   The work group, department, section, or project for which the manager, leader, or supervisor is officially accountable.

2   The group of colleagues recognized in the hierarchy of the organization as "peers" who report to the same superior, identified by name and title, as our engineering manager does.

3   The group of colleagues recognized in the hierarchy of the organization as "peers" who report to different superiors, but who are at the same staff or line level within the corporate organization chart.

4   The superior level within the hierarchy to which the supervisor or senior manager is directly accountable.

Thus each element in the Wheel of Interaction, each segment of the organization, has no choice but to develop an effective comprehension of the needs of each member of the several groups with which interaction is required. Individuals have needs. Groups have needs. No individual, no group may operate as an isolated entity and be effective. There are periods of time, of course, when the individual member of a group of professionals, or the group as a whole, may operate in relative seclusion as it or he pursues the objectives of the tasks.

However, the supervisor, leader, or manager rarely is able to place himself in isolation. He may act as a buffer between the relevant outside world and the group for which he is accountable. But he must maintain a position of access, be available for interaction with colleagues, subordinates, and superiors.

Leadership and management

The manner or method of performing that characterizes a manager is referred to as "style." Many managers deny that they have a style of management, preferring to convince themselves that they are "natural" leaders, some sort of Pied Piper whose slightest wish is reacted to as though it were a command. Subordinates follow him because they really want to do so. Such self-deluded managers generally have sufficient ego and drive to enable them to climb the organizational ladder to influential heights. Some may even become chief executive officers, or mount to the relatively secure (because of its personal isolation) post of chairman of the board. However, whether they own their own businesses with simple organizational structures or are part of complex multidivisional corporations, it becomes inevitable that they are one day rudely a-wakened to discover that their operations are at a crisis point, and their "natural leader" skills are not producing the desired effects. At some critical point, they cannot successfully resolve the situation, cannot cope.

Going back to transactional analysis for a moment, one of the games that some people play is called "firefighting." The person who plays the game is known as a "firefighter." It is played at all levels within the organizational hierarchy. Assembly-line workers, foremen, group leaders, department managers, even chief executive officers have been observed playing it. Most are unaware they are playing the role of the firefighter. There are no rules to such a game, merely common syndromes. The firefighter needs a "fire" to "fight." A "fire" is a *crisis* that is of such magnitude as to demand senior management intervention. If there is no "fire" readily available the "firefighter" will generate one. The objective of the firefighter is to call attention to his powerful skills at resolving important conflicts (conflagrations). The personal need is for attention and compliments. The firefighter, therefore, may start a "fire" in order to demonstrate his special talent for putting it "out," thereby focusing attention on himself as a leader, manager, problem-solver.

Such behavior and method of performance may be termed a *style*, undesirable and ineffective perhaps, but a style if it appears to be a continuing behavioral pattern.

Some label this style *management by crisis*, meaning that the manager either manages to create a crisis or allows a crisis to develop. At the point of apparent, impending disaster, the manager comes to the rescue and copes with the crisis, "fights the fire," once again demonstrating to his superiors, peers, and subordinates that he, indeed, is in control of the situation. This "control" is better called "manipulation," a dangerous sort of dramatic flourish that, sooner or later, may overtake the firefighter when he discovers to his complete dismay that his "fire extinguisher" has become impotent.

What is this manager, leader, supervisor to do now? He must recognize that his has been a nonstyle of management, *non*motivational, *non*productive, *non*functional, *non*effective.

Behavioral scientists have identified a dozen or so different styles of management. Some of the behaviorists have created names for the styles to enhance the memorability of the descriptions. The names are not important. The description, the value, the effectiveness or ineffectiveness of each of the styles is important.

The question is usually asked, "What style is the *best* style to use?" It is unrealistic to attempt a simple answer to this direct question. There is no such thing as a "best" style. There are only *effective* and *ineffective* styles. Of these two, the better style, the only valid style is the one that achieves the desired result. We will identify and describe twelve managerial styles. A defined style may be quite effective under one set of circumstances, totally ineffective or even capable of producing negative results under another.

The effective manager of engineers and scientists recognizes that the world, its people, and environment are complex structures. The people within it, for whose performance the manager is accountable, are individuals with sets of actions and reactions. Although a group of individuals responsible for the attainment of a common objective—the work assignment, the task—usually develops a distinguishing behavioral mode, a *personality* of its own, the individual members retain their singular characteristics and responses to outside stimuli such as the interaction with a manager, leader, or supervisor.

It is reported that groups with histories of repeated high achievement have leaders who understand their own needs as well as they do the needs of their groups. They also have a high comprehension of the needs of the individual members of their groups. This understanding of the operant human factors, when converted into appropriate styles of management, very probably accounts for the leaders' successes in nourishing and maintaining high levels of enthusiasm and motivation, resulting in the kind of productive output that also meets the needs of the companies or corporations to which the groups and leaders belong.

The power of expectations

High achievement, for the manager or the subordinate, is not an accident. It begins with *high expectations*, the expectations one has for one's self and the expectations the manager has for his subordinates. It is possible the manager's expectations for his subordiantes' perform-ances are in reality a means for implementing or fulfilling his own self-expectations for advancement.

The direct influence of the manager's expectations is often subtle; nonetheless it is there. Subordinates tend to do what they believe is expected of them with respect to levels of achievement and productivity. It is characteristic of a superior manager that he has the ability to create high performance expectations for his subordinates to fulfill. The manager must gain a perception of the expectations of the individual members of his work group. If they are lower than those essential to fulfillment of the objectives, the manager must devise means for elevat-ing those expectations. The manager may have the highest expectations for his own level of achievement but, because he delegates work respon-sibilities to his subordinates, he must ensure that his subordinates' expectations are at least as high as his own. The manager must ensure that his subordinates' expectations will remain high throughout the life of the organizational group or of the project for which he and they share responsibility.

A manager may be ineffective because he fails to develop the required level of self-expectations within his subordinates. As a conse-quence, the productivity of the individual, group, section, department, and the company may be lower than is desirable. Engineers and scien-tists who are treated as people of superior capabilities try to live up to the image of superiority in performance. However, there must be sub-stance to the expectations. Wishful thinking is part of the profile of those who are consistently high achievers. But they recognize the essentiality of going beyond dreaming of success. They work actively toward attainment.

The manager must be realistic in his expectations, those he holds for himself, and those he holds for his work group. Positive thinking con-tains power. The manager may persuade his people to pursue unattain-able goals. But when the "people" recognize and believe that the goal is not reachable, they may settle for a relatively low level of achievement. This "level" could very well be one that is lower than that which they are capable of achieving.

High achievers are usually moderate risk-takers. They require at least a 50-50 chance for success. Finding himself in a less than break-even situation, the high achiever tends to withdraw, back off from the challenge, settle for something that at least is face- and ego-saving, get the project out of the way so he can get on with the next and hopefully more rewarding challenge. The manager's, leader's, and superior's style of management can raise a subordinate's level of expectations within realistic limits, create positive feelings about the subordinate's self-esteem, help self-confidence to grow, develop his skills and capabilities, stimulate, motivate, and enhance productivity. Obviously, if the style is inappropriate to the people, the place, and the time, the effects on morale, attitude, motivation, and productivity can be destructive.

A catalog of management styles

Here are 12 managerial behaviors that have been identified as "styles." We have given each a label purely for identification. Also, we have listed some of the personality traits that characterize the individual while he is performing as a manager.

It is important to recognize that, although the style may reflect the early personality development of the individual manager, this manager may behave differently in a social or familial environment. The latter environments create series of stresses and strains, pleasures and displeasures that may force the "manager" who is out of his business environment for the moment to depend more heavily on his knowledge (A_k) and less on his rank (A_p). At the tennis club, the manager may have absolutely no A_p and, in order to assure pleasant experiences, must exercise his A_k. On the other hand, this same manager, in a familial situation may completely ignore his knowledge of how to be a parent and depend entirely on the responses he expects because of his A_p rank within the family.

Disappointment, the failure to achieve the desired result in either case may result from lack of knowledge or misuse of inherent authority. Ideally, this "manager," parent, and social being possesses knowledge as well as rank. He must be able to apply each of these with skill and wisdom as each becomes appropriate to the specific situation.

Conservative

This individual relies on published procedures, methods, organizational systems. The standard operating procedures (S.O.P.) manual is his working "bible." He prefers the paper-work aspects of his accountability over the interpersonal requirements. He does not interpret company policies; he follows and enforces them quite literally. Usually he maintains a very calm, patient demeanor in his dealings with his subordinates, peers, and superiors. He collects and iterates facts and data.

Basically, the Conservative manager may be insecure as a person. He has difficulty dealing with his environment. The published procedures become his book of rules of conduct, his sanctuary. He treats everyone equally and with fairness. Not necessarily because he is a fair-minded person but because this is one way to avoid involvement with crises and people, one way to dispose of problems impersonally and rapidly. He plays no favorites and is proud of this characteristic. Some view this as arrogance, indifference, or haughtiness. He is rarely guilty of being dictatorial. Yet some may view his adherence to the rules as a form of rigidity akin to acting as a dictator in his responses to situations involving people.

He is most comfortable when surrounded by people who are similarly conservative. When confronted with the need for change, he and his subordinates must be abundantly supplied with detailed procedures for making the change and with a directly relevant new set of rules, carefully written down.

The Conservative manager is most comfortable in a staff position in the organizational hierarchy. He is disposed toward working in finance, electronic data processing, administration, government, and other positions where there may be recognition for conservatism, accuracy, technical prudence, and little requirement for becoming involved with interpersonal relationships or creative performance. He works best in an assignment that contains much routine.

Captain

Recognizing the fact that productivity is related to effort, the Captain balances the relationships between the requirements for completing tasks and the requirements of people. He is a high achiever, and knows that expectations and results are correlated. His obvious commitments to the task and his understanding of the needs of people combine to motivate individuals and create a team effect.

Usually a good manager of conflict and disagreement, he recognizes that when such conditions exist they may be a sign of good health, an indicator that his people are thinking about the task and the interpersonal relationships. He has developed an expertise in resolving conflict;

therefore he does not try to disguise or ignore conflict. He does not avoid his role as the resolving catalyst. He has learned that when conflicts are resolved without winners or losers, the individuals or groups who have participated in the creation and in the resolution of the conflict or disagreement will develop stronger commitments to the completion of the task.

The Captain creates an environment that builds high morale and positive attitudes, both of which are essential to motivation. A hard worker, he expects his group and individual members to work hard. He is not status oriented, nor does he welcome power that comes with rank. His style makes strong use of A_k and tries to avoid A_p. Because he has enabled his subordinates to develop positive self-esteem, "I'm okay, you're okay" feelings, they are sincerely loyal to him. This fact sometimes disturbs the *Captain*. He does not necessarily want a social relationship with his subordinates. He prefers to have this loyalty or dedication directed toward the company's objectives rather than toward himself as an individual manager.

The Captain communicates and works best with peer-managers who have similar styles. He has serious difficulties in coping with power-oriented peers and, if forced into a competitive mode with such peers for advancement in the organization, he may lose. On the other hand, if his superior is also a Captain, he will maintain a high level of achievement and gain recognition on the basis of measurable completion of tasks.

Avoider

Cynically, we say this manager may not actually be a "manager." Perhaps he was a manager at one time, but something has happened to cause him to abdicate responsibility for tasks and for interpersonal relationships. He is viewed as a person who exercises neither rank nor knowledge. His low interest level has a negative effect on the morale of his subordinates. He doesn't communicate well and this may be mistaken as a tendency to keep things back from his subordinates, to conceal or withhold facts and data that they feel they need to do their jobs properly.

He follows the rules and is minimally productive, just enough to hold onto his job. His own morale is poor, although he may not be aware of this. Privately, if not openly, he engages in self-pity. He may feel his personal values and importance to the company have been unrecognized and unrewarded. Perhaps he was moved laterally into a position he felt was less important. Feels demoted. Thus he is holding on, hoping the situation will change. And in the meantime, he avoids involvement with tasks and people so as to avoid possible failures. He is adept at concealing his Avoider traits. Usually, only those who have seen him perform under other conditions can detect the subtle and negative changes in his style and behavior.

The Avoider avoids making decisions. Making a decision requires some involvement, which must not be allowed to happen. Nondecision may be accomplished by adhering to the letter of the law, the S.O.P., the rules and regulations published by top management. The intent of the S.O.P. may have been to guide, but the Avoider allows it to bind his actions, provides himself with a convenient reason for not being able to take any kind of action because of all the "red tape" thrown his way.

An engineering manager with Avoider tendencies, when presented with a proposal for a new project may search the proposal for reasons to delay or reject it. "I am not sure the project's objectives have been clearly defined," he may say, or, "The budget doesn't have enough detail." When the proposal is returned to the Avoider with additional information and detail, he will scrutinize it without revealing his feelings—neither rejection nor acceptance can be discerned—and then place it on the ever-increasing pile of papers in his "pending" basket with a weak promise to read it more carefully when time permits. This is the executive equivalent of a deliberate slowdown by labor at contract negotiation time. No rules are being broken. Enough work and attention is being paid to the situation to get by, barely.

Needless to say, the Avoider does not set a desirable example for others to follow. Unfortunately, it may set a standard for expectations of performance that others in the group try to emulate. Do as little as possible, no more than is necessary to keep your job. Do not excel because the reward for good work is more work.

Woe to the manager who may replace the Avoider as manager of the engineering and scientists professional group. His predecessor may have neatly concealed the lack of productivity, disguised the conflicts and problems. The new manager who takes his titular position more seriously and, thereby, uncovers a myriad of unresolved problems may be estimated as relatively incompetent because of the sudden rash of problems with which he has to cope. A naive management may not recognize the inheritance given to the new manager.

Ambivalent

He knows the importance of a well-balanced relationship between task and people. But, he is not willing to take a strong position on either task or people. He yields to pressure on a last-in first-out basis. Rarely doing things well, he does not escalate the expectations of his subordinates toward higher achievement. On the other hand, he does not applaud poor performance. He is content to believe that optimum productivity is never attainable and searching for techniques and methods that might optimize performance is a waste of time. Only those ideas and concepts that have been known to work in the past are acceptable.

The Ambivalent manager uses participation in decision-making only when the decision to be taken is quite obvious and there may not be any alternative courses that require decisions or the taking of sides. The Ambivalent manager does consider himself a participative manager, often asking his people to take part in the decision-making process. To the theorist or casual observer, this is a fine style. However, to the experienced pragmatist and close observer, all participants are participating in the obvious. The casual observer may marvel at the lack of conflict among the group's members. The experienced and close observer will marvel at the lack of creativity and initiative. At some point in time, conflict will come out into the open, to the surprise of the Ambivalent and to others outside the group, because it had lain dormant, unrecognized, suppressed, never released and resolved. Unfortunately (or fortunately, depending on one's relationship), this may be the beginning of the end for the Ambivalent.

Structured

This manager adheres rigidly to the rules and prescribed procedures. Actually, he doesn't have very strong feelings for either the task or the people involved. He is usually quite efficient. Busy with details, he communicates through channels, never intentionally by-passing anyone above or at his level in the hierarchy. Such a manager is valuable to the organization, if the organization has a mode of operation that must be maintained and is dependent upon a bureaucracy.

The Structured manager is not a problem-solver, not production or results oriented. He does not develop his subordinates, does not prepare them for advancement. While he is not an Avoider in his dealings with people, his style may be confused with an avoidance of responsibility.

He has not abdicated, as has the Avoider. But he must have rules and regulations to follow because he lacks initiative, creativity, and self-confidence.

Motivator

He has developed an extraordinary sense of the interrelationships between tasks and people. He has acquired an in-depth knowledge of motivational techniques that depend on participation and commitment to decisions. He manages change quite well, making certain that his subordinates understand the reasons why things are as they are, or are undergoing changes.

The Motivator often moves upward into the senior ranks of management where he has opportunities to develop enthusiasm among his subordinate managers. His knowledge of the needs of the individual tends to govern his own interpersonal relationships with his managers. Fortunately, he is in a position to exercise his knowledge. Possibly he is ahead of his time. Clearly he is an adherent, a firm believer in McGregor's Theory Y. Too often, the lot of one who may be "ahead of his time" is a lack of appreciation of the means used to achieve a desirable end.

Empathetic

The *Empathetic* manager places heavy emphasis on the importance of other people in the organization. He is people oriented and is sincerely concerned with interpersonal relations, actions, and reactions. Because of this orientation he is capable of establishing an environment that offers security and comfort.

This environment generally produced a high morale and a positive attitude among the subordinates in the manager's work group. However, as Herzberg theorizes, high morale and a positive attitude are not necessarily motivational of themselves. They do establish the base on which a motivational effect can be structured. Thus, the Empathetic manager, despite his ability to generate loyalty and a sense of affiliation among his subordinates who think he's a "great person," may not actually develop a highly effective group. A content group, yes.

And if the manager's personal needs are societal as compared with achievement, he may find satisfaction in the effect created by his Empathetic style. His subordinates know their Empathetic supervisor provides a supportive environment, a basic factor that should exist in all superior-subordinate relationships. However, the Empathetic manager may not be able to accomplish a meaningful balance between the individual, human side of the situation and the job, the task itself for which the individual subordinate is responsible.

At times, the Empathetic manager may become a manipulative person. Not that this is all bad. But he may be overly influenced by the societal or familial needs of his subordinates to the point where he may lose sight of the objective.

The management style and needs of his superior within the company can have a significant impact on the future advancement within the organization of this Empathetic manager. If there is a match, the Empathetic manager is in an okay position. However, nothing is forever. A change in superiors, a shift in organizational directions, a revision of the company's needs could occur as a result of economic changes, market-product demands and technological developments. This can leave the Empathetic manager with sympathetic subordinates who like working for this friendly, quiet, easy-to-talk-with supervisor who stands quite alone among his peers and superiors. His ability to communicate warmth may have been recognized. So may his difficulties in creating an achievement-oriented work group.

Driver

A line manager, seldom a staff manager, he has a strong touch of the self-made entrepreneur. The Driver is aggressive, determined to get the job done. He may have found his niche in the production or field sales department of his company, wherein many important decisions must be made throughout the work day. And such an environment will test the mettle and self-confidence of the manager.

The Driver is interested in results, measurable and quantifiable output that can be verified. He is not intuitively interested in participative or group approaches to decision-making. However, he is aware of the fact that some technical aspects of the task may be better defined by some among his subordinates and will, therefore, be influenced by their inputs and viewpoints, not as much because they are people but because they might very well influence the productivity of the tasks for which he is the accountable manager. They just might have a good idea once in a while.

He drives himself as hard as he drives others. This characteristic separates him from the purely autocratic manager who may attempt to transfer all the pressures to his subordinates, who maintains a close watch but does not necessarily pitch in to do the work itself.

On the other hand, the manager who drives himself but pays little attention to his subordinates may not be considered a Driver. He is usually more closely in tune with the Avoider or the Structured manager.

The Driver is often considered to be an aggressive person who can operate only when environmental pressures are high. He is usually most effective when a task must be completed within an unusually short time span and strong direction and rapid decision-making are essential. Although he is not necessarily popular, his subordinates, peers, and others in the company know where they stand at all times in their relationships with the Driver.

The Driver style is not all bad. Some people work best or at their maximum personal capabilities when directed strongly by a Driver, and therefore they do not feel threatened by the Driver. Where there is a need for dramatic change within a company or within the direction of a task or project, the Driver will usually prove his value to the company. Unfortunately, in the process of implementing the change, restructuring the task or the group, he is not likely to win many friends among his subordinates. Those among his peers who may not be totally familiar with the situation may deplore the Driver's personality and behavior as a manager. The Driver may be totally insensitive to these feelings or, if he is aware of them, may rationalize his behavior as essential to getting the job done.

The Driver is not usually successful in retaining professional people on his staff while opportunities exist in other departments, divisions, or in other companies that consider the importance of good interpersonal relationships as well as the measured completion of the tasks.

Laissez-Faire

Conflict or disagreements among or with his subordinates are strictly avoided, not necessarily prevented, but carefully avoided by the Laissez-Faire manager. He believes the concept of good management and the way to make people do their jobs is to provide them with good companionship, warmth, feelings of fellowship, an easy-to-take environment.

The Laissez-Faire sees himself as a "good guy," a very good guy for whom people will do anything. He confuses his own kindnesses and pleasant behavior with the equally kind and pleasant responses of his subordinates. Unfortunately, this does not always lead to adequate productivity. Usually the Laissez-Faire leads a group of subordinates who are mediocre in expectations and in effectiveness. They equate their social-club work style with good management, a nice place to be.

The Laissez-Faire fails to be effective because of a total lack of balance between people and task. In fact, he believes that people come first. This may be philosophically correct; however, in some situations this may not be appropriate. At times, if the task fails, the people who are associated with the "failure" may be swept away. If total priority is given to the feelings of the people, without regard for the need to properly complete the objectives of the task, the Laissez-Faire manager may prove to be ineffective and could be charged, by behavioral scientists, with the responsibility for having injured rather than helped his people.

This manager will go to extremes to avoid conflict. When made aware of a potential or actual conflict, he will become overly concerned with the feelings and sensivities of the individuals involved in the disagreement. He will make every effort to smooth ruffled feathers, calm tempers, and restore what really is a superficial kind of harmony. The basic cause of the conflict will not be resolved. It can lie dormant. But it may surface at some other moment with even more serious consequences and effects that may be still further beyond the capabilities—or the desires—of the Laissez-Faire manager to cope with.

This manager is totally without a direction of his own beyond the social aspects of relationships. Thus, he generates the effect of being something other than a manager. He'd rather switch decisions than argue with any of his people who may speak out in disagreement. Very few people enjoy or want to work for such a manager. Few are able to find challenge, growth, advancement, or opportunity under a Laissez-Faire manager. Those subordinates who welcome and seek challenges as a means for growth and advancement will quickly seek transfers out and away from the frustration of working for this do-nothing, leave-them-alone manager.

Achiever

Self-confidence and deep trust in his own abilities to make the correct and appropriate decisions characterize the Achiever. He is a highly productive person with high expectations for himself and for his people. He knows how to be a "driver" without creating resentment. His energy level is high. Never leaves a job unfinished.

While others may measure output that results from input, the Achiever also measures wasted or lost time as lessons from which he expects to learn self-improvement. He is ambitious for himself and for his subordinates. The Achiever is a team captain who does not necessarily involve his "players" in the decision-making process for each move in the game. He may ask for inputs, as he feels the need or, more likely, as he believes some good ideas may be generated from participation. He may not use the ideas that are proposed by his "team," preferring to follow his own guidelines based on personal experience, intuition, or a combination of both.

The professional members of the team who possess a high level of competence may find personal rewards and satisfaction in working for and with the Achiever. The expectation is that suitable rewards will be distributed for task completions to those who have earned them. And appropriate punishments or nonrewards will be delivered equitably to those who deserve them. He's tough, but knows how to bring out the best from among the strongest of those among his professional people.

Dictator

He is punitive, threatening, action oriented, and demands results. He doesn't really understand why people fear and dislike him. Some of his people would like to tell him why—or "tell him off." But his manner is so overwhelming at times that few can screw up the courage, fearing that to do so is tantamount to resigning. And it often may work out this way. To tell the Dictator that he is not quite correct is to challenge his authority, A_p. This is rebellious in the mind of the Dictator, and because rebellious people are "bad apples" they must be removed from the "barrel."

His orientation is strictly that of McGregor's Theory X. And he perceives that his role is to coerce, induce, or seduce the workers to "work." Conflict is seen as a challenge to his authority and, therefore, he suppresses conflict quite ruthlessly. Transferring or terminating people is his response to challenges of this sort.

The Dictator has no patience with the theories put forth by behavioral scientists and writers on management techniques. Ask him how to motivate people and the answer is—although the words may vary—

threaten them with an "or else" option. The Dictator may conceal (poorly) his belief in Theory X as describing his own belief in the natural behavior of his subordinates. One of his favorite lines is, "If you complete this assignment, you get to keep your job!" He usually has and uses several similar clichés that, on close review, communicate his feelings of superiority and dominance.

His behavior alienates him from his professionals. He may want to develop close relationships with his people, but is usually unable to find the way to do so. Out of frustration and impatience, when confounded by an inability to achieve a desired effect—such as overcome an alienation—he resorts to increased agressiveness and thinly veiled threats. These only result in making matters worse, increasing the distances to which his people will withdraw from him.

Supporter

This is the manager for whom creative professionals will do their best work. Those who seek growth, development of their talents and skills, advancement into and through management levels are fortunate indeed when they are accountable to the Supporter manager. This manager sees his primary function as that of providing an environment and interpersonal relationship that generates motivation of the individual and the group.

The Supporter believes totally in McGregor's Theory Y description of human behavior; that work is as natural and as welcome as play; that, given the opportunity, people will exercise self-direction and self-discipline; that imagination, intelligence, creativity, and the ability to innovate exist in abundance among professional engineers and scientists and that they are not solely found in senior managers.

Due in part to his ability to communicate his ideas, concepts, and feelings, and in part to his willingness to give credit to those who deserve it while keeping his own profile quite low in visibility, he obtains high commitment from his people. This sense of commitment is to the manager as well as to the task or project at hand. Engineers and scientists consider themselves to be working *with* not merely *for* their Supporter manager. This manager is highly receptive to new ideas and innovations. His professionals respond to this combination of human and job relationships by being highly productive, effective, and motivated to consistently high performance for the long term.

The Supporter manager develops the skills and talents, latent or active, of his people. He fosters two-way communications. He creates a nonthreatening environment in which his people readily come to him to exchange or express their thoughts, which, stimulated by an aura of trust, are always honest and constructive. He trusts others and is trusted in turn. When the time comes for his professionals to move on to other assignments or companies, they will often maintain contact with him because of the good feelings they take with them. The Supporter is most likely responsible for many engineers and scientists moving into the ranks of management, either because of his direct efforts or because he makes the role of the manager most attractive.

Characteristics of management styles

Style	Concern for People	Concern for Task	Remarks
Conservative	Avoids involvement. Calm and impersonal. Seems haughty; indifferent	Prefers paperwork. Guided by "policies"	Likes routine. Is insecure
Captain	Understands people's needs. Enables his subordinates to build high self-esteem	Committed to tasks but knows technical work is done through people	High achiever. Good manager of conflict. Uses authority based on knowledge
Avoider	Does not want to get involved with his people	Does not want to get involved with decision-making requirements of the task	Low interest level in his environment. Poor morale. Sticks to rules for sources of decision and strength
Ambivalent	Yields to pressure from his subordinates	Appears unwilling or unable to take a strong position	Rarely does things well. Accepts only ideas that have worked before. Rarely takes sides

Style	Concern for People	Concern for Task	Remarks
Structured	No strong feelings about people	Not results oriented	Stickler for rules. Communicates only through channels. Not adept at solving problems. Lacks initiative
Motivator	Understands theories of motivation. May know the practice	Understands the interrelationships of people and task	Adheres to McGregor's Theory Y
Empathetic	Provides secure and comfortable environment for his people	May lose sight of the objectives of the tasks	Has difficulty creating an achievement-oriented work group
Driver	Insensitive to the feelings of his people. Not very much interest in group decision making	Interested only in measurable results	Entrepreneurial. Drives himself as hard as he drives others. Operates effectively under pressure
Laissez-Faire	Overly concerned with creature comforts. Usually unaware of conflict. Believes in leaving people to their own ways	Gives low priority to tasks. Would rather change than defend a task-related decision	Subordinates may be frustrated by unmet needs. Subordinates' expectations and effectiveness are poor
Achiever	Appears to seek ideas from his subordinates but makes his own decisions	Success in the task is most important. People are important but only for technical work completion	Very self-confident; great faith in his own decisions. High energy. High expectations, but may not be able to fulfill them because of inability to motivate his subordinates to meet his expectations

Style	Concern for People	Concern for Task	Remarks
Dictator	Punitive and quite threatening. Creates fear and insecurity	Demands measureable results and action	Doesn't understand why so many fear and dislike him. Questions may be interpreted by him as challenge and insubordination. Adheres to McGregor's Theory X
Supporter	Provides an environment that stimulates and motivates. Gives credit for good performance and behavior on the job. Gives trust. Is trusted	Subordinates have commitment to this manager as well as to the task. The productivity of his group is high	Good communicator. Receptive to new ideas. Definitely, he is Theory Y

Although a diversity of management "styles" is displayed, one must be aware of the danger of assuming that some styles are "right" and that others therefore are "wrong." A "style," or a manager's behavior as "manager," may be appropriate or inappropriate to the occasion, the time, and the needs of the people and the tasks at a finite point in time. To achieve the desired results—to be effective as a manager—the manager must be able to adapt, to modify his behavior (or "style") to suit the need.

10
Effective use of management styles

Names and labels are devices that help us recall, identify, and associate concepts, ideas, and practices. In the previous chapter we labeled a dozen management styles and provided descriptive phrases to enhance our understanding of the practice. However, the *application* of the management style is what really counts. This leads us into the question: "Which style is best?"

As with most questions that appear to be simple and brief, the answer is necessarily lengthy and complex. We can say up front that there is no such thing as a style that is *always* best or correct. There is also no style that is *always* wrong. Let the punishment fit the crime, in management technology, translates into "Let the style fit the need." There are sets of conditions—emotional, environmental, and physical—wherein one style will be more effective than any other. "More effective" means having the greatest probability for achieving a desired result. It is absolutely important to learn from this statement that the effective manager is not rigid in his style of management, that the effective manager has considerable adaptability. The effective manager is able to adjust his own behavior to the fundamental consistency or congruity of people and situations, even though incompatible with his own needs. This manager is able to rapidly revise, modify his own styles and practices of management. He enables himself to suit the dynamics of his role as communicator, satisfier of needs, achiever of objectives; he is capable of developing and guiding a group toward the fulfillment of defined tasks and common goals.

Rigidity is out. Flexibility is in.

The effective manager of professionals, engineers and scientists, recognizes that the balance between people and tasks is dynamic. His orientation is continuously flexing, adjusting among the needs of the individuals, the group, and the company. And, of course, he is attempting in the midst of all this turbulence to satisfy some of his own very human needs. When all needs of the sectors of the Wheel of Interaction are satisfied, managerial effectiveness is assured.

The dynamics of management style requires smooth yet rapid transitions from one mode to another. One does not say, "At this minute I am using the Captain style . . . at this moment I have shifted to a Conservative style . . . next, I will become a Driver." The manager must adopt a style that is best suited to the needs of the moment, adapting to the psychodynamics of the environment, shifting imperceptibly but quickly to another definable style.

The adjustments are more often than not made intuitively by the manager. Yet when intuition alone is the controlling influence—that is to say, external learning, training, or education have not played a specific part in the development of the person as a manager—fortune or misfortune may take control of the situation. If the needs of the situation fit the intuitive style of the manager, the people may be fortunate and find satisfaction; the outcome of the task may be acceptable, even positive. On the other hand, the manager who has learned the values of various styles knows how to apply them. He has developed his own adaptability to assure the exercise of a style that is quite appropriate to the situation. Thus, he reduces the risk element in achieving a desired effect.

As with all technical situations (and we may consider the theory and practice of management to be a technical matter because it can be defined in specific terms), a sound basis of theory improves the probability for successful practice. And with continuing practice, the responses to the dynamics of people and environment can become both instantaneous and appropriate. As the success rate of the practice of the manager increases, the speed with which he makes decisions and responses becomes even greater. In fact the ability of the competent manager to make the correct decision and to take the most appropriate action can become so rapid that observers will often make the comment that "Joe is a fine manager; outstanding intuition and instincts!" More likely, Joe has a solid foundation in theory and a great knowledge of interpersonal relationships. He has sharpened his K so that he acts consistently from authority sub-K (A_k), rather than an authority sub-P (A_p). Joe appears to be intuitive; he is also, really, quite knowledgeable. He is not necessarily a "born" or "natural" leader. He is most likely a person who has honed and sharpened his managerial skills. There is no evidence that any person is a "born," "natural," or "instinctive" leader. While such a person may exist as a possibility, the probability is that the absorptions of theory and opportunities to practice leadership roles began at an early age and it is these nurtured capabilities that have been recognized by his superiors. Thus because of this recognition, new and additional opportunities to practice his managerial skills have been given to Joe.

Those who have been less fortunate than Joe, who have not had or who may have rejected similar opportunities and exposures, may not move into the managerial ranks. Or if they have been given such opportunities or exposures, they may not have enjoyed them or they may not have been successful in terms of satisfying the needs of the Wheel of Interaction, including themselves at the center of the Wheel. It is not unusual to find that, in large R&D organizations that have been divided and subdivided into task units, those who have been appointed as the formal managers of work groups will request downward transfers into project work rather than retain administrative/managerial duties. This may result from an inability to satisfy the needs of all sectors within the Wheel of Interaction. Usually their own needs are those that are most frustrated. It may result from an inability to practice the theories of good management. This "inability to practice" may be caused by an inadequate foundation of the knowledge of theories of human behavior, needs, and personality development.

Not everyone wants to be a manager. Too often, the reward for outstanding performance as an engineer or scientist is promotion to a management level position. Too often, the new manager, although outstanding as an engineer or scientist, has never had either time or opportunity to acquire knowledge or to sharpen his skills in the role of a manager. Suddenly he is endowed with a new level of authority with an inherent power base (A_p). If he is lacking in the theoretical and practical base (A_k), he may rise or descend to managerial methods (I hesitate to call them "styles") that will predominantly reflect those movements and decisions that tend to satisfy his own personal needs. These "personal needs" will not have been thought through. The instinct is to provide good self-feelings. When these self-feelings cease to be "good," the titular manager will recognize his own shortcomings and seek to reenter the ranks of the work group from which he was "plucked" and in which he feels more comfortable. Or he may become more and more aggressive in attempting to find satisfaction and role fulfillment, as he perceives his role. This action or reaction is doomed to failure and defeat. When the failure becomes evident, he may voluntarily terminate his position within the company, or be involuntarily terminated. Whether he recognizes the situation as his own failure, tries to blame external events and personalities for his failure, seeks to reeducate himself as a manager, or returns to technical work is a matter of individual conjecture and reaction.

As we have said, "Being an effective manager is not easy." And we have also said, "Not everybody wants to be a manager." Have you ever heard a senior manager say, "I've taken many good engineers and scientists and made poor managers out of them?"

At no time does the manager have the right to play the role of the "dealer at a blackjack table." The effective manager stacks the deck of cards so that the "game" does not have a *winner-loser* result. He skillfully directs the situation and the people in a way that assures there are no identifiable *winners* or *losers*. The result of his efforts must be *no-lose*. When there are no *losers*, the inference is that all participants are *winners*. Well, nobody ever told you that being an *effective* manager is easy!

Vector analysis of style

You will have noted that characteristics overlap among the twelve managerial styles described in the previous chapter. Because the lines of demarcation may not always be immediately apparent, we will reduce the twelve-count to five styles and use these five to illustrate their applications, their appropriateness under defined conditions. As one becomes more familiar with the characteristics that clearly differentiate the five exemplary styles, one may review the twelve styles for a sophisticated elaboration of managerial behavior.

At one point in time, the effective manager's thoughts and actions are dominated by a concern for human relationships, people. At another, his responses are dominated by the task at hand, the meeting of objectives, the completion of an assignment.

Figure 9 graphically depicts five of the most significant management styles, those that are most often requisite to effectiveness under widely different circumstances. The Y-axis represents *concern for people* as the dominant influence upon the manager. The X-axis is the manager's *concern for task* as having precedence over the needs of his people. The five managerial styles are depicted as vectors moving upward in amplitude from the junction of the two axes. The junction represents non-

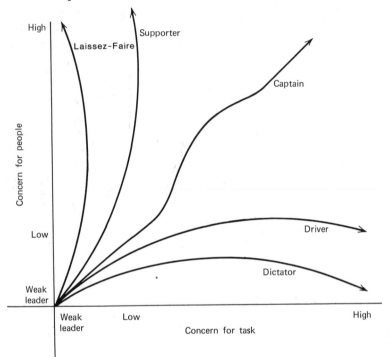

Figure 9 Style vectors. Five dominant managerial styles are indicated in direction and amplitude relative to their concern for people (Y-axis) and concern for task (X-axis). The greater the amplitude of the vector, the stronger the inclination toward the Y- or the X-axis. At some point in strength the manager who expresses and practices these styles becomes totally concerned with either *people* or *tasks*. The *Captain* tends to waiver from one axis toward the other. As this style matures and becomes dominant, as indicated by the vector for *Captain*, an extraordinary balance is found between the *concern for people* and the *concern for task*. Even though the manager may find this idealistic balance, the dynamics of individuals and the group will usually require the manager to move toward or directly into the mode of one or more of the other vectored styles. The effective manager is able to make such transitions smoothly and rapidly in accordance with the needs of the sectors of the *Wheel of Interaction*. Abandonment of one style for another is always temporary.

style, zero effectiveness, total abdication of the role of the manager.

The individual vectors move upward in amplitude to indicate increasing expression and identification of the manager's style. An individual style, however, does not move in a straight line with the same balance of concerns for people and task throughout its expression or application. Therefore, the vector line tends to curve or flex toward or away from the X- or Y-axis, indicating that there is variation even within a defined style. This is also intended to indicate that even the most task-dedicated of dictatorial managers will, at times and to the surprise of his subordinates, demonstrate a sensitivity or concern for his people. It also indicates that the Laissez-Faire, leave-them-alone manager who doesn't seem to care whether or not the job gets done (he may be planning to leave the company or retire, anyway) will briefly take an interest in the progress of the task, as well as how his subordinates are doing as people. Thus the vectors swing moderately away from one axis and toward the other and back again.

One may correctly assume from the arc of these vectors that there are moments in time when each of the styles is totally dedicated to one or the other of the two axes. The exception might be found in the Captain's style. When one perceives that a manager whose style is dominantly that of the Captain is showing a relatively strong concern for people or task, one to the virtual exclusion of the other, simple study of the "style" will usually reveal a change, adaptation, flexing, or modification of the dominant style. Thus in Figure 9 the Captain vector is not precisely a straight line but demonstrates variances, a tendency toward *people* or toward *task*. But the Captain never allows concern for one to exclude concern for the other.

Ideally, the effective manager of scientists and engineers is always able to and succeeds in maintaining a proper balance between people and tasks. The reality demands that this "balance" cannot be statically equal, perfectly balanced. In the case of managerial technique, balance does not necessarily mean 50–50, equal distribution. In order to be effective and totally responsive to the needs of the individual sectors of the Wheel of Interaction, the manager must demonstrate his skill at modifying and adapting his position.

The individual vectors represent five styles that provide an adequate cross section of managerial behavior: (a) Laissez-Faire, (b) Supporter, (c) Captain, (d) Driver, and (e) Dictator. To illustrate the values of each style and the appropriateness of their uses, let's establish a hypothetical situation with you, the reader, as the manager.

You are the manager of the professional staff. You have been given approval, budget, physical resources, and a choice of personnel (human resources) for the purpose of implementing a major project. Project specifications exist in writing and have been "signed off." But you are not really concerned with details of the *technical* specifications at this moment. Your initial overview is for the timetable, the critical path and the identified events with reference to time and output. These are among the standards of performance by which you, the accountable manager, will be appraised as an individual.

Let's make important assumptions. These include the fact that you are familiar with theories of personality development (Freud), needs (Maslow), motivators and dissatisfiers (Herzberg), theories X and Y (McGregor). You have learned them well and are beginning to successfully practice two-way communication and the management of conflict. We do not forget for one moment that you, too, are an individual with a personality and a set of needs. However, as the Wheel of Interaction illustrates, you cannot indulge yourself, your ego needs and defense mechanisms. You are a member of several organizations that are linked together in the hierarchy within the company. You are not able to insulate or isolate yourself from your environment. You must share your environment with other complex organisms—people who look to you for direction, controls, and standards.

The project is important. Its outcome will have a significant effect on the future growth of the company. Implicit in this outcome is your personal growth and advancement within the company's hierarchy, perhaps even within your industry. You want to do things right. You have accepted your role as a manager with all it implies, especially the implication that you are accountable for the work performance of others as the means for achieving the end—completion of the project in accordance with specifications, time, and costs.

You start at the vertex of the axes. Although your reputation precedes you, accurate or not, you have not yet demonstated your leadership skills with respect to the use of A_k or A_p, concern for people or task. You are at the beginning of the relationships. You have the option of moving outward and upward in amplitude in any one of the five directions, or leadership styles, that are indicated by the five vectors of Figure 9.

The staff has been identified. The individual tasks have been identified and standards have been published. Tasks are known but not yet assigned. At this point, you need the participation, commitment, ownership of the project on a shared basis with all members of the work group. Which style should immediately be adopted to obtain commitments? Captain, of course.

You are a high achiever. We accurately assume that your self-expectations have been fruitful. For this primary reason you have been named manager of the project, or even of the department or section. You are dedicated to your project. But you know full well that you can only complete the task, meet the specifications and the objectives, through the productive performances of your people. You sincerely believe this. You believe in your people and want them to believe in the task.

Under the style of Captain you provide full opportunities for participation and expression of ideas. You are positive and constructive, always maintaining a neat balance between your concern for the task and for the people. You help your people build high expectations and self-confidence. Your positive attitude helps them believe in you as well as in the project. You have *knowledge* as well as *power*. You assign tasks or obtain agreements from individuals for the performance of specific aspects of the task. You provide "okay" feelings.

Conflicts, arising in the form of doubts or disagreements, are a continuous challenge to your management skills. You do not ignore these conflicts. You resolve them as they occur in the *no-lose* manner that is essential to the maintenance of high morale and positive attitudes. It isn't easy but, again, nobody ever told you it was going to be "easy."

Now, task assignments have been accepted and you do believe each member of the group knows his role and accepts ownership. Materials, work areas, documents, and people are in place. Work begins. Do you remain statically in the role of the Captain? You may, of course. The option is yours. But what really happens now? What are the dynamics?

Would you move to the Driver's seat? Or become a Dictator, whipping everyone to a frenzy of activity? You could take the position that says, Okay, gang. You know what you have to do. I want to see you doing it!" But would you or should you?

Would you move to the Laissez-Faire position, the opposite of Dictator? "Okay, gang. You know what you have to do. I'll be around somewhere, if you need me—and I hope you don't." You could. But should you?

Suppose you were to become the Dictator? In the beginning, your people are orienting themselves, thinking through the environmental, technical, and procedural approaches to solving the problems related to the tasks. They certainly do not need the tough and threatening pressures of the *Dictator* right now. No. Not likely to succeed.

Suppose you were to move to the Laissez-Faire posture? While your people are in their start-up phases they don't really want to be left alone. They have some concerns for selecting the best directions to pursue. They want, may need guidance, someone with whom to discuss their options, the alternative approaches. A sounding board, if you will, for new ideas. They want to know that they have the support of their leader. That's you. They need to communicate with you on a two-way basis. Openly and honestly. Without fear. The creative processes are starting and they want encouragement. Also, they want to test—not consciously—the extent of the support they can depend on from you, the manager. Obviously, then, the *Supporter* style is appropriate to the time and the situation.

The work group has formed. Alternative courses of action or investigation have been agreed upon and support is recognized. What now? The heck with McGregor and his Theory Y? You are the boss, the manager, after all. You are the one who is accountable for the productivity of the group! Unfortunately, the tendency is to become impatient, even frustrated. Because everyone else is doing exciting hands-on work, exploring, creating, or at least being ingenious. While you, the manager, are saddled with reports and paper work, administrative duties. Nobody told you it was going to be easy; now you are learning firsthand how hard it is to be a *manager*.

What mode now? Try Laissez-Faire—in short intervals. Laissez-Faire in the direct translation form of "let them do." For a while, a short while, test the theory that an individual is most productive when he is allowed to pursue his own interests without external restrictions. Allow the individual to develop his self-confidence. Do not go so far as to ignore the development of conflict. Do not abdicate your accountability. But for a while "let them do," let go of the reins. You have chosen your people well, haven't you? They are professionals, engineers and scientists, aren't they?

Thus, as the group is formed into a task-oriented team you have moved from Captain, to Supporter, to Laissez-Faire. And you have moved back and forth from among these three styles as each seemed most appropriate.

Time passes. Your team is moving right along. The project is advancing toward its completion dates. By prudent use of management sytles you have demonstrated your leadership skills, maintained high morale, positive attitudes. These have generated motivation, and the payoff is in productivity. You are effective. Your peers and superiors recognize your skillful use of authority, A_k and A_p.

Now the project is nearing completion. Your superiors are beginning to apply pressures. Staff meetings with your peers and hierarchal superiors focus on your status reports. The questions probe more deeply. Are you on time? Are you on budget? What about the technology; has it been developed? The prototype that was to be one of the objectives of the project—is it meeting cost targets as a product? If not, why not? If yes, what can be done to exceed the objectives? Can't you make your people more productive?

Do you sometimes get the feeling you are being put on the defensive? Is it just your feeling? Are your peers and superiors playing with your human feelings of inadequacy? After all, nobody's perfect. Imagine saying at a status-report informational meeting: "Nobody's perfect, after all."

Next manager, please!

Nobody told you it was going to be easy.

The fact remains that time is getting short. What style should you adopt (or, adapt to) now? You can't really transfer the pressures you feel from above to your subordinates. You can't openly expect them to "own" this part of your problem. However, because you have skillfully demonstrated your abilities (and adaptabilities) by moving from Captain to Supporter to Laissez-Faire as was appropriate to the time and the need, you will competently make yet another adaptation of your leadership style.

Perhaps it is time to demonstrate your ability to adapt the positive aspects of the Driver to the situation of increased demands for performance and measurable output. In our earlier description of leaders we said the Driver style "is not all bad." In fact, some people actually work best or at maximum productivity when strongly directed by a manager whose dominant style is that of the Driver. Used judiciously, and temporarily, as the need for quantifiable progress becomes pronounced, the manager may inject himself quite deeply into specific aspects of the project that may represent bottlenecks or can potentially affect the overall performance of the work group. Now, you, the manager, may make use of your technical skills, become involved in the actual work, design, analysis, data collection, or whatever is needed and would be expected from the engineer or scientist who is responsible for the specific activity. Now you join those who have *responsibility for work*, temporarily appearing to abdicate *accountability for the people*.

You drive yourself as hard as you drive anyone else. Yes, you appear to be more aggressive than usual, but you are handling interpersonal relationships so well that you never threaten or challenge the self-esteem of those among your work group who have the assigned responsibility for the task in which you have become directly involved. You do not "cry" on anyone's shoulders about the "hard time" your own boss and peers are giving you. This is one of the characteristics that separates you from the autocrat, the Dictator. Another of the characteristics that distinguishes your Driver style from that of the Dictator is in the fact that you are willing to physically participate in and share the responsibility for work. Well-done or otherwise, you are willing to be counted along with your own people. They know you are not searching for a scapegoat, protecting yourself in the event of failure. They admire the fact that you will not accept failure and are willing to "roll up your sleeves" and pitch in when it is for the good of the individual and the group.

As a Driver, however, be aware that you do risk your popularity and there is an inherent challenge of the capabilities of the professionals with whose specific work you have become involved. (Note: "popularity" rarely, if ever, appears as an element of a job description or as an appraisal item for managers of engineers and scientists.) Although you are not concerned with winning a popularity contest, you certainly do not want to become "unpopular." So, prudently you enter and exit the role of the Driver. Tactful, but forceful. Concerned primarily with the task. But sensitive to the people. In part the Captain, as well as the Driver.

Assuming the professional staff is competent, well credentialed and highly experienced, the use of the Dictator style can prove to be counterproductive; it can generate results that are destructive and undesirable. Under special conditions, as we will illustrate later, the Dictator style may be used. But very carefully!

The Dictator is entirely oriented toward the task, a Theory X person. He believes that people do not perform without intense external pressures from the boss. Money is the only motivator he recognizes and, when extra effort is needed, he resorts to bonuses, prizes, and other material elements that are supposed to excite people, turn them on to greater effort. He calls these *incentives*. He cannot understand, however, why this type of incentive has such a short-term effect, why it has to be reinstated, renewed each time a new level of quantified output is needed. Such an incentive is much like feeding a person a sumptuous dinner and being astonished to learn that this same person some short period of time later is hungry all over again; just as "hungry," if not hungrier. The Dictator, observing this phenomenon, takes this to be proof of his belief that people only respond to repeated material rewards.

He deplores those who preach participation, sharing, consensus, and the motivations created by the search for satisfaction of secondary needs. He may allow himself, this Dictator manager, some brief moments of concern for his people but, perhaps because of the brevity of his interest or the perceived lack of sincerity of his interest, he moves back to his primary concern, for the task. He does not consider that he has retreated from his concern for people. He considers that he had "retreated" earlier from his native concern for the task. And "see where it got me!"

If the Dictator style of leadership of management is so undesirable, why include it in our descriptions and in the diagram at Figure 9? Because it would be totally unrealistic to ignore the existence and practice of this style. The Dictator exists as a common phenomenon. Ignoring it won't make it go away. Recognizing it, when one observes it, avoiding it when one is tempted to exercise pure A_p is important to one's effectiveness as a manager of engineers and scientists.

We all recognize that we do not live or work in an idyllic society. Although some behavioral scientists may generalize that the ratio of managers who practice a style based on Theory Y to those who practice a style based on Theory X is increasing, it is unlikely that the Theory X manager will diminish to insignificance in this last quarter of the twentieth century. He is real. He is numerous. Threatening, ruthless, impersonal, but real. No discussion of management styles can ignore his reality.

Style must match need

Let's examine another set of circumstances. Hypothetically, we create a short-term situation involving three work groups. Each has the same assignment as does the others. Each works in isolation with respect to the other two groups. And we have carefully coached each manager or group leader in a different style of management. These are our basic parameters:

1. The task is defined in writing. Each member of the work groups is allowed to query and discuss the task until each totally understands what is expected of the individual and of the group.

2. The results of the completion of the task are measurable, in product units. Thus, the results of performance are quite visible. No ambiguities.

3. Time and productivity are the keys to successful attainment of the objectives established for the task. It is important to note that *very little time* has been allocated to result in a *large output of units*. (Are not the engineers' and scientists' worlds continuously confronted with this apparent set of conditions?) Pressure. High pressure and large demands.

4. The leaders are identified, but their nominal styles are not revealed to the work group. They are:
   a. Laissez-Faire.
   b. Captain.
   c. Dictator.

5. The relationship of manager and subordinate is intended to be temporary, only for the duration of the project. We are quite unconcerned with any long-lasting effects or interpersonal impacts.

6. Each individual and the work group is given the same physical environment, materials, tools, and instruments with which to complete the tasks.

7. There is no recourse, nor is there time for personnel matters, disagreements, or conflicts to be resolved by anyone outside the work group and its manager.

8. Go! Time is short (as it would be in the final wrap-up phase of a project). The winner is the group with the greatest measurable output of units.

This is a hypothetical situation, but it is typical of the environment and demands placed on the manager of the work group. What are the probable results? Who is the probable winner, from the style perspective?

Let's take the groups one at a time and examine their effectiveness. We are dealing in terms of most-likely or probable results.

1. Laissez-Faire. This leader's style (if he can be called a "leader") was totally hands off. He had absolutely no concern for the task. He wanted everyone to feel each could do his own thing. His attitude was: "You all read the objectives and a description of the task. You had ample opportunity to discuss your role in it. We answered all your questions. Okay. Go ahead." Then he became invisible. He provided no further direction. Made no decisions. Provided no bouncing-board for ideas for the expression of problems, or of ingenuity. Result: although his group members liked the manager as a person (he was very popular), they became argumentative, frustrated, confused, fearful, insecure, nonproductive. They felt like losers. Output: probably minimum.

2. Captain. No question asked of him was unimportant. No personal problem was ignored, especially if it might have an impact on the group's output or productivity. He balanced the concern for people with concern for the task. Actions depended upon the decisions of the group. Everybody "owned" the total situation. You might describe his approach as holistic. But the group ran out of time. Productivity was a respectable quantity of units. Almost, but not quite on target. Too bad. An effective work group did develop in a short period of time. They could have taken on the world—if they'd had a bit more time! They formed a cohesive view of themselves as being strong and effective. They would welcome an opportunity to work together again on a difficult task, one that would challenge their technical skills (and, of course, the capabilities and adaptabilities of the manager). They found satisfaction for their needs for affiliation and identification. Next time, they would have to be reckoned with in a competitive environment that would be based on a quantifiable measurement of productivity. They did not feel like losers. Next time they would satisfy their need for status and recognition through quantified achievement.

3. Dictator. In the presence of time restraints, this manager pushed and pressured. He was a skillful technician and recognized good technical performance when he saw it. He threatened punishment, banishment from the group, if he felt it would result in increased output. He had no time for thoughts of popularity. He was totally dedicated to the task. His group members? He did not consider the long-term impacts on interpersonal relationships. He had a task to do—and he would do it! His group members almost despised him, but they produced the greatest number of units in the short period of time allotted for the performance of the task. This group "won." It was the group with the greatest measurable output in units. No matter that the group members hope they never have to work with this *Dictator* again! He shook them. Created fears for their security, a primary need. They were motivated by the need to "keep their jobs," not by the need to achieve, excel, win, attain status or recognition. They did not identify with the group. They did not feel like winners.

The conclusion that one should draw is that *all styles* have elements that may be described as *good and bad*. It depends entirely on the situation. The onus is on the manager to recognize the situation, the needs of the individual, the work group, and the company. The burden rests entirely with the manager to develop his awareness of the options available to him as a manager accountable for the performance of his subordinates. He must learn to adapt, flex, bend, curve, and twist his *style* of leadership as is appropriate to the time, place, personalities, expectations, and pressures. He may validly move through the spectrum of styles illustrated in Figure 9. The amplitude as well as the direction of his style must be well within his control. He must practice each with deliberateness. Eventually, he exercises them intuitively, correctly, appropriately, always increasing his effectiveness as a manager.

11

Twelve management problems and how to solve them

The manager who is totally task-oriented may *believe* he has found a workable solution for dealing with people who express or try to satisfy their personal and professional needs. He may consider these people to be "troublemakers." That is, they make "trouble" for him. His solution? Order them to "shape up or ship out!" Therefore, individuals who do not conform instantly to his way are out! This is, of course, the supreme *Dictator*, king of all he surveys, master of everyone's fate. But not always his own fate because, sooner or later, he will run out of energy, people; conditions will not prevail that favor his style of management. Conscienceless, perhaps. But it sure makes this manager's job appear easier. It can also make his job tenure shorter.

The manager who is totally people-oriented may have found a different solution for dealing with people who express or try to satisfy their personal or professional needs. These people never become troublemakers, per se. This *Laissez-Faire* manager just gives in. No argument. Hardly even a discussion. "Whatever you want to do is okay with me," he tells his people. Just imagine this "manager" as leader of a ship's crew. The sea is rough and the winds are strong. The ship is heading for the rocks! The crew, his professional staff, can't agree on who should grab the wheel, manipulate the ship's direction. The skipper doesn't want to do it. He doesn't want to make decisions. Will the ship hit the rocks? Will it go under? Will somebody come to the rescue? The rescuer might be the admiral of the fleet, the manager's own manager.

Neither one of these two extremes is oriented toward constructive problem-solving as far as people are concerned. The effective manager of engineers and scientists is managing human resources who, in turn, are managing physical resources. Yes, somewhere between these two extremes is the real world of the *effective* manager.

In this chapter, twelve specific types of managerial problems are described that are people-related and are impeding the completion of the task. Some may be the products of managers who preceded you in your present role of manager. They goofed and you inherited the problem. Now it is up to you to find the best solution. Some of the situations we will describe may be new problems, as far as the organization or the work group is concerned. They may also be new to you. In time, as you continue to grow in your role of manager of engineers and scientists, you will have encountered virtually every conceivable combination of problems—call them challenges. You will deal with some of them quite neatly, constructively and positively. Others may not be readily solvable or may never be solved without the most drastic action on your part. "Drastic action" is defined here as involuntary termination, firing the person you consider to be an inseparable part of the "problem."

Each of twelve "problem people" will be identified and described. Courses of action will be proposed as optional solutions. Any one of the options will probably work for the short term. But one is best for long-term results that are positive. In no case do we offer terminating, firing, or transferring the problem person as a workable option. We will assume that there are restraints on such drastic actions. For example: there may be difficulties in finding a replacement. There may be budgetary controls that consider any reductions in staff are a desirable attrition and a requisition for a replacement will not be approved. The individual may be grabbed up by a competitor, and that is not the way to maintain technological leadership. This particular individual may have special knowledge that is hard to find elsewhere and you require this knowledge. Or he or she may be related by blood or marriage to your boss (or to his boss) and, politically, it would not be prudent to do anything drastic at this time.

Without exception, the people who may appear to be troublemakers are competent professionals. You sincerely want to have the benefit of their potential productivity. You do not want to lose them. Whatever the basic reason, you do not have the option of letting the person go as a way out of your dilemma. This is not far-fetched as a limitation on your managerial skills. Termination or involuntary transfer is always a last-resort action. Often, the manager who resorts to this option casts an unofficial gray mark on his own reputation.

No, let's not even consider anything other than working it out with the individual "troublemaker" so that neither you nor he losses. You must develop a *no-lose* resolution to the problem, thereby converting a negative to a positive.

Following each of the twelve "challenges" are several optional courses of action. You must select the specific course of action that offers the greatest probabilities for long-term success. It is inherent in the long-term success that neither you nor the hypothetical "challenger" loses in self-esteem or need satisfaction. It is entirely possible that more than one of the options is a desirable course of action. However, you must select only one. It is not practicable, obviously, to pursue two courses simultaneously.

On a sheet of paper or a scratch pad note the following:

1 The course of action you would pursue.
2 The reasons why you choose it.
3 The probable results of pursuing the other options.

Do not read ahead of the "problem" on which you are working. Immediately following the pages dedicated to the descriptions and options of each of the twelve situations we offer our viewpoints for comparison with your own. It is fair to point out that none of the options should be described as "wrong." We are dealing in probabilities for success, a qualitative effect that always contains some gray areas. This serves to emphasize what we know: that the human mind is an exceptionally complex organism and the technology of dealing with interpersonal relationships is still in the developmental stages.

You may recognize some or all of the situations described below. You may have observed other managers who have been confronted by these challenges, and had the opportunity of learning from your observations. You may have already had some experiences with these "problem-people." If so, you will profit from a review of the optional courses of

action that were avilable to you. Did you deliberately consider all of
your options and their unique advantages and disadvantages, or did you
intuitively and immediately take action? How well did it work for you?
For the so-called problem-person? Perhaps you decided to "let nature
take its course." There are reasons to believe that engineers and scientists are not gamblers. If so, this tends to support the probability that
you did select and pursue a course of action rather than "let nature take
its course."

Joe Cool

Of course you do not underestimate the influence and power of the
"informal group." The informal group tends to develop almost immediately after the formal group has been identified. You are the leader or
manager of the *formal* work group. There are memos and organization
charts that are written proof of this fact. Channels of communication
are explicit. However, you begin to sense (or for concrete reasons know)
that most of your instructions to your group members are being ignored
or modified. When the group does act, there is a cohesiveness of action;
but the action doesn't seem to be a response to your direction. "Direction" is coming from somewhere else within the work group. An "informal leader" has emerged. He is easily identified. He's a real cool person,
this "Joe Cool."

He seems to be operating as a gang leader, fomenting a sort of
rebellion against your instructions and directions as the formal leader of
the group. How do you know there's a "Joe Cool" in the group? What
caused this gang leader to emerge? Something you did, or should have
done but didn't do? How do you deal with the situation, especially with
Joe Cool, the leader of what has become a "gang" that seems to operate
either counter to or despite your directions? First order of importance is
the relationship between you and Joe Cool, whom you have now identified as the informal leader of the group, the gang leader. Which option
is most likely to have the most constructive effect over the long term, at
least for the life of the group assigned to the project?

a   Call a meeting of the work group, including Joe Cool. Have a
    discussion. Of course you will keep it from exploding into an
    argument with the entire group. Tell them again who the real
    leader is. (That's you, like it or not.) Make it clear that this
    resistance to you must stop at once!

b Take Joe Cool aside, privately. Let him know you recognize his influence with the group and you believe that, together, you can make this thing really work. On a confidential basis of course, promise some special reward for his cooperation with you. After all, you both have the company's best interests at heart!

c Be "cool" yourself. Joe Cool will probably trip himself up and control will return to you. Hold on. Don't get discouraged. Time is on your side!

d Without resentment or aggression, get to know the informal leader, Joe Cool, better than you think you do. Assume that he doesn't actually want your job, that he satisfies his need for recognition and status by dominating the group. He may also be aware that he is walking a tightrope strung between his ability to maintain his dominance over his peers and not pushing far enough to lose his job. Enlist his cooperation by making certain that he thoroughly understands the reason, the logic that supports your decisions and managerial style. He might make a better supporter, "Joe Friend," than opponent, "Joe Cool."

e Have private and individual sessions with each of the members of your work group, your subordinates. This could be the appropriate time for a confrontation. Use your persuasive powers to convince each of them they are making a mistake by siding with Joe Cool. Remind them who their leader is, who will appraise them, give them their performance reviews and recommendations for raises and promotions. After all, participating in an organized resistance to the accountable manager is insubordination. Morally, functionally, and even legally, this is wrong. Even if they have an employment contract or union membership, insubordination is often considered reasonable cause for termination. This approach may take time because you have to get around to each of your subordinates individually. But *if it works,* it's a worthwhile use of your time and energies to get the organization back on the track it was designed to ride!

Discussion. One of the primary reasons for the emergence of a Joe Cool, an informal and rebellious leader, is the existence of dissatisfaction within the group. It is entirely possible that the sheer dynamics of an exciting personality can bring an individual member of the work group to the position of informal leader. But this informal leader, Joe Cool, is not a positive force as far as your role is concerned. Joe Cool is in effect competing with you for a sort of control of the individual members of your group. Why does he come into being? What forces are at work, negative forces that produce a Joe Cool? This emergence of a counterproductive personality is generally symptomatic of a troubled relationship between the formal leader and his work group. Things have gone wrong, or they were not right to begin with. Among the worst of all aspects of the situation, Joe Cool is a guerrilla fighter. He rarely comes out into the open for a one-on-one confrontation with the formal leader.

When faced with a Joe Cool, the manager should examine the situation quite closely. Ask for an outside and objective viewpoint. The possibility is quite strong that the manager's style has not been appropriate to the situation, or to the people and the task. If the manager has been weak, the work group may seek strength and leadership from an informal leader—Joe Cool. If the manager has been too overwhelming, unrelentingly dictatorial, the members of the work group may seek reinforcement of the need for security and recognition through an informal leader who establishes norms of behavior that are acceptable to the group but not necessarily conforming to those set by the formal leader.

Thus while reestablishing his own identity and role, the formal leader is examining his own managerial behavior and introducing corrections where indicated. In fact, this very action of correcting his own behavior will tend to make the role of the informal leader less meaningful to the individual members of the group. But the problem is alive and a course of actions must be selected. Which is probably best? Let's consider them individually.

Option a.   This completely ignores the possible existence of a basic problem in interpersonal relationships between the formal manager and his subordinates. If the manager has been weak, this sudden show of strength will probably not be very convincing; possibly the manager will not be able to sustain this "strength" and will soon revert to his normally weak behavior. All the members have to do is agree with the manager and bide their time. Joe Cool may even gain new strength for his position as informal leader. If the manager has been dictatorial, the exercise of this option may serve only to drive the subordinates further away from the formal manager and toward Joe Cool. If such a confrontation as this option proposes does not erupt into an open argument between the manager and his subordinates, it may be greeted with exactly the opposite—complete silence. The manager discovers that he is talking to himself in a room full of subordinates. Obviously, you reject this course of action.

Option b. Joe Cool likes his position. He really thinks you are a loser. Why should he cooperate with you? In fact, why should he even admit he is the leader of a group of "rebels"? Suppose you are in a position to "sweeten the pot," increase the size of the special reward to the point where he can't resist, and you do make a generous proposition? As soon as Joe Cool detaches himself from his control of the group he loses his influence as the informal leader. You've bought him out. But you haven't automatically obtained the support of the individual members of the work group, your other subordinates. You've only converted Joe Cool, now a *former* mutineer. You may have opened the way for a new informal leader to emerge. For the short term, the group is without a rebel leader. But the prognosis for long-term solution is poor. The environment that allowed morale and attitudes to foster a Joe Cool informal leader is still there.

Option c. You may be placing too much faith in the "spin of a wheel," gambling that time will heal the situation all by itself. Gambling is not in the makeup of an effective manager of engineers and scientists. You do not believe in letting nature take its course—not without some trimming and tweaking from you. Joe Cool may trip up and lose control. But, unfortunately, there could be another Joe Cool lurking in the background. This is a high risk. While waiting for time to come to your aid the project may be slipping away from its targets. You have a task to do. Without your people on your side, the task will falter. This is not an attractive option.

Option d. You like this option. You like it very much because you are aware that you've got to learn more about the environment that enabled an informal leader to emerge. Joe Cool would probably prefer to obtain his recognition and status on the basis of his effectiveness as a productive engineer or scientist. His motivation, fundamentally, is to help the members of the group satisfy their needs. He can do this to some extent because he understands their needs. Even though he may not be able to articulate the needs of the individuals and the group in glorious technical detail, with encouragement from you he can become a critical and valuable link in the chain of communications between you and your subordinates. Non-threatening discussions with you, at your invitation, may help articulate the basic problem that exists between you and your subordinates. And because you are knowledgeable about needs, dissatisfiers, and motivators, you recognize the human factors that are operational. You modify and adapt your managerial behavior and style. In effect you bring your subordinates back into the *Wheel of Interaction.* You move now to function as the hub of the Wheel, applying your authority based on knowledge as well as power. You gain the cooperation of Joe Cool in defining the environment, morale, and attitudes. You use him as a sounding board, a communications vehicle. "Joe Cool" becomes "Joe Friend." Soon, "Joe" concentrates on productive professionalism and leaves management to you. His role as leader of a subtle rebellion disappears because it becomes unneeded. As with all organizations, there will be perturbations in the calmness-curve of human behavior viewed over a long base of time. But each time you become aware of the potential emergence of a new Joe Cool you investigate the situation and look inward at your own style. You know that the option of converting "Joe" to a "Friend" is best for the long term. And nobody loses.

Option e. Theory X of human behavior would indicate that this is a workable option. However, assuming it does work, perhaps it would work with unskilled laborers; rarely with professional staff. Choosing this option may also necessitate a long-term contract with employment agencies for a perpetual search for replacements for those who have either been fired or have quit because they can't tolerate the environment and the personnel practices. This is neither a short-term nor a long-term solution.

   Option d is preferred.

Superstar

An outstanding engineer or scientist, this professional is convinced he can do just about anything better than most other people can. Fact is, he's not too far from the truth. He is an outstanding performer, as an individual. You have some doubts about his ability to identify with a team or a group. Nonetheless, he believes his time has come to take on managerial duties. He's not subtle about it, as his memorandum to you clearly indicates:

> For the past three years I have worked for you as a member of your professional staff. I have never failed to meet the objectives of every one of my assignments. My reviews have been excellent. Three of my original designs now have patents applied for through the company's legal department. I have delivered technical papers at several meetings of our technical society. You and others have often told me I have unusual skills and you have given me appropriate salary increases and bonuses. I feel I am ready to take on more responsibility as a manager of a major project, section, or department. If this company is unable to make correct use of my skills I will have to look elsewhere for a company that recognizes my true value.

You have immediate reactions to this memorandum. Is the writer resigning? He doesn't really say that but does seem to imply an ultimatum of sorts . . . promote me, or else! True, he is an unusually competent professional and has made significant technical contributions. You'd hate to lose him to the competition. Also, you'd rather not have to explain to your own supervisor if this staff member should decide to resign or ask for a transfer. Sometimes you think good professionals are harder to find than good managers are. Sometimes you think your supervisor thinks the same thing. He may not be right when he blames one of his managers for losing a good man; there often are extenuating circumstances over which a manager has little if any control. Yet your supervisor does hold his managers accountable for keeping the staff happy and productive. And that is part of each manager's task.

"Superstar's" memorandum calls for and deserves a reply. And you are the one who must make that reply. For good internal reasons and because you do have good two-way communications with your supervisor, you bring the memorandum to him for discussion. But you can't just "lay it on him." He expects you to describe the problem and propose an appropriate solution. You list your options for discussion with your supervisor and recommend the one that is most likely to succeed; that is, prevent Superstar from resigning and keep him in a productive mode. You make special and accurate note of two important facts: (a) there are no openings at this time or in the immediate future for a suitable promotion to managerial level, and (b) he really isn't ready to perform as a manager of a professional staff.

a   Make a promise to Superstar, one you mean to keep. As soon as an opening occurs, you will see that he is promoted to manager. This might keep him happy, pacified.

b   Consider the memorandum a letter of resignation. Accept it as a signal to him and to others on the staff that an ultimatum just doesn't work. Promotions go only to those who are willing to go along with the company's growth, and pressure doesn't sway you. Of course, you will handle this as a voluntary termination and see that there are no hard feelings that might give the company a bad name.

c   You feel the budget can handle a significant salary increase, also some special perquisites such as a week's trip to the convention he said he'd sure like to attend. Make the offer. This is a measurable form of recognition.

d   Propose a comprehensive training program at company expense that is specifically directed toward the objective of developing his management skills. This could include seminars on several management disciplines such as marketing, manu- facturing, and operations. These will broaden his perspective of how engineers and scientists must interface with other depart- ments within the company. It could include selected courses of study at a nearby educational institution. Recommend specific books and publications for him to read. Expenses would be borne by the company, of course. Offer to provide counseling and guidance periodically concerning his progress toward a managerial responsibility. Without making a commitment or promise of a promotion, point out that if and when a manager's spot opens in the department, his credentials and progress would most likely be influential in the selection process. Point out also that you have an obligation to offer the same benefits for training, education, and counseling to all members of the group, although not everyone wants to become or is capable of becoming a manager.

Discussion.   Superstar may not have thought about all of the tasks that a manager has to deal with. Thus, regardless of the option you choose, it would be time well spent to review with him some of the tasks (outside of engineering and scientific project work) that become the responsibil- ity of the manager. For example, this list can serve as an outline of peripheral but important tasks:

- Identify and recruit new professionals.
- Interview candidates for staff positions.
- Check references and make the selection.
- Indoctrinate new staff members with reference to company and departmental policies and procedures.
- Communicate with other departments within the company: finance, marketing, sales, manufacturing, operations, procurement, general administration.
- Make periodic written and oral progress reports to management.
- Resolve interdepartment (and intradepartment) conflicts.
- Deliver special presentations to marketing and sales meetings.
- Meet with the technical staffs of the company's customers to discuss specifications, concepts, and problems.
- Attend weekly, monthly, quarterly, and annual staff meetings with senior managers.
- Review marketing's statements, publications, advertising, and brochures for technical accuracy.
- Do the same for public relations releases.
- Assist in the development of marketing forecasts, especially where the introduction or phase-out of a product is involved during the forecast period.
- Explain a new program to a group: stockholders, securities analysts, investors, senior managers, and board members.
- Analyze reports and publications on technology.
- Analyze and critique technical statements made by competitors about their products' capabilities.
- Review and appraise the performance of subordinates.
- Make decisions concerning the disposition of human resources (staff members).
- Fire someone, if necessary.
- Conduct an exit interview.
- Keep track of a multiple number of projects, people, progress, and budgets.
- Solve problems.
- Recognize the strengths and weaknesses of subordinates in

ways that protect their self-esteem, and that enable them to meet their personal needs and the needs of the company.

This sets the stage for what follows, the option you will choose and explain to your supervisor and to Superstar.

Option a.   Superstar may believe your promise and take it as a commitment. It is possible an opening will occur. It is also possible that someone else in your department or in another department will be better suited to the new opportunity in management. If he, Superstar, is turned down or not promoted, he will probably resign to save face. He might get tired of waiting for an "opportunity." Or he may start a search for a new job elsewhere and, in the meantime, lose his motivation, creativity, ingenuity and productivity—the result of negative morale and a defeated attitude.

Option b.   Accept the memo as a resignation. It will be difficult to find a replacement for him, you know. However, it is important to let him and your staff know, by example, that an ultimatum is the wrong approach to use with you. Unfortunately, the company loses a valuable employee. The cost in time and project delays can be considerable while you attempt to backstop the loss of this professional staff member. It is also possible that the company will have lost a potentially strong and effective manager with this professional's departure. The effect on the other engineers and scientists on your staff can be quite severe if this course of action is adopted. You could be "branded" as a person who is "on an ego trip": you versus your subordinates. Your subordinates will probably develop some fears, uncertainties, and insecure feelings about working for you. Without a doubt, two-way communications will be damaged. Your subordinates will be somewhat afraid to speak their minds openly to you for fear of triggering a drastic and undesirable response. Reject this course of action as bad for morale and having no positive aspects.

Option c.   This is industrial "bribery." Promises of material reward will be recognized for what they are: evasions, putting off things, attempts at distraction. Superstar will be insulted by this response to his statement of a need. Reread his memorandum and you will see that he isn't complaining about material rewards. In fact, he says he has received "appropriate salary increases and bonuses." So money won't "buy" him. He has a need for ego satisfaction, possibly approaching the highest order of need: self-actualization. *He wants to be a manager,* preferably in your company. If he can't make the grade in your company he will search for another company that will give him the position. This course of action has no redeeming features.

Option d. In his memo to you, Superstar didn't say he wanted to be a soloist or even chairman of the board. He stated a need that requires satisfaction. He didn't say "make me a manager immediately, or else." As an engineer and scientist he is probably quite logical in his approach to problem-solving. You must ignore the emotion that has crept into his memorandum and recognize that Superstar is good and he knows it. He has self-confidence, a high level of self-esteem that is important to those who are or will become achievers. He is asking for help, guidance, steering in the direction of management. You can give it to him. With your supervisor's support, you can implement the type of events and programs outlined in *d.* You will have presented him with a challenge within which lies opportunity for advancement and growth. His attitude will most likely be positive, constructively matching yours. His morale will be high. Thus, you will have established the elements for Superstar to move to new levels or productivity, creativity, and ingenuity in his work as a member of the professional staff. The long-term effect quite probably will be that Superstar will wait for and earn the opportunity to move into management in your company. Both he and the company will benefit. You will be credited as having brought him along, having developed Superstar as a fine asset to the company.

Option d is preferred.

Mister Miserable

Every department, section, and group has at least one. No matter how vigorously you may try to avoid such people, especially among your subordinates, at some time or another you will meet "Mister Miserable." He's the unhappy one. Always unhappy about something. A positive thought so rarely passes his lips that you can even remember the last time one did. Always "down," hardly ever "up" about anything, he is the classic malcontent. A complainer. Mister Miserable may realize that he appears to be a malcontent but he rationalizes his manner by saying: "I am not a robot. I have the right and I exercise the right to question things around here. Am I supposed to accept things just as they are?"

However, most malcontent people—people who are always unhappy and seem to resist happiness—are almost always angry about something or other. They do not want to or cannot articulate their real feelings. They usually do not understand why they are so unhappy. Many are not even aware of their behavior and would be quite shocked to discover they are referred to as "malcontents." The root of the unhappiness might very well be outside the control or influence of you or the company. He may have personal family problems, a health problem, or may be reflecting his childhood environment and its influence on his personality. Not much you can do to change the past. But the present can be quite trying for everyone.

You have become immediately aware of Mister Miserable. His negativism is more than random. It typifies his behavior and personality. Should you deal with him at the first signs of this malcontent behavior? Or should you wait until a crisis develops that forces you into action? He is an excellent professional. Despite his comments and complaints, he does produce and makes valuable contributions to the group and the project. You decide that you must deal with him quickly to avoid escalation. Quite correct. Mister Miserable usually contaminates the environment, pollutes the ambience that promotes good morale and attitudes. He's intelligent. But you are aware that he can also be emotional about relatively insignificant matters. Which course of action, which option holds the greatest promise for long-term benefits?

    a   Be especially considerate of him. After all, he is a human being and he's probably hurting inside. Give him extra attention. Spend more time with him. By getting close to him you will be able to come to a reconciliation of ideas and opinions. Be sympathetic.

    b   Perhaps it's time to get help from the personnel department. Maybe one or more of Mister Miserable's peers can get through to him and make him aware of the effect he is having on others, especially on you. Personnel might be able to get to the root of the problem because they are supposed to be impersonal and deal with people situations, employee relations.

c   Put pressure on him. Without using words like "shape up or ship out," lean on him. Perhaps he just needs a critical parent for a boss who will let him behave like the natural child. You feel that eventually he will respond with a change in behavior.

d   Is it Mister Miserable who is wrong or is it the company? Find the right opportunity to get him to talk to you about what's bugging him. Take it from there.

e   Job enrichment might be the thing to do. Not job enlargement, but *enrichment*. Assign him to tasks that are challenging and that clearly imply you have confidence in his professional skills and talents. This is a form of recognition and status to which professional staff members usually respond quite positively.

Discussion.   You are really on the spot with a habitual malcontent. You are not a trained psychologist. Nor are you expected to be a minister, priest, or rabbi. Mister Miserable will put you to the test. Again, he is hard to replace, as far as his engineering and scientific talents are concerned. He makes you angry, but you must resist the temptation to fire or transfer him out of your group. Let's examine each of the options available to you and see if we can choose a course that holds the greatest promise for a no-lose resolution.

Option a.   There are some very positive values in getting close enough to Mister Miserable to enable you to talk openly with him. Even if you do not develop a good relationship, at least you will have an opportunity to debate your differences or those he may have with his peers. You know this is a time-consuming course of action. It may not even work. His ego defense mechanisms will very likely give you distorted impressions. You may never get to the bottom of his misery barrel. On the other hand, he might just talk himself out of his discontented attitude. It's not likely, but who knows until you try it? There's a big risk here. Can you really spare all the time it might take? What about the project? You can become heavily split between your concern for a person and your concern for the task. If the project slips while you are taking time to develop a relationship, the explanation might not be acceptable to the company. Your attention to him might just stop the escalation of Mister Miserable as a disturbing influence within the group. However, what about the other members of your work group? Will they accept your attention to Mister Miserable's needs, probably at *their* expense? Probably not. Too much risk here. Try another option.

Option b.   This means calling in a translator. And you know how much can get lost in the translation. Also, this tends to put others in the position of psychologist, minister, priest, or rabbi. Amateurs in these areas might just make matters worse. Further, if Mister Miserable becomes aware that you needed outside assistance to deal with him, the situation could escalate instead of ameliorate. No, this has too many "backfire" possibilities.

Option c.   You could be right. Strong pressure might work. He needs a "parent-child" relationship. But you don't really know how he has responded in the past to such relationships. He might consider your assumption of the role of "critical parent" to be a painful reminder of his childhood environment. His reaction could be compliance. But consider your own experiences with children who appear to comply. They find a way to resume their original behavior. In fact, Mister Miserable may just go underground, disguising his native feelings. He will remain a malcontent fundamentally. There is a strong possibility he will change his tactics, try to get others to work against you, even go to your superior and complain about how "you mistreat your people." Another possible response to your strong pressure on him: a big blowup! What happens if he loses his temper, or you lose yours, and you tell each other off? This has to become a *no-win* situation. If you "win" such a confrontation you'll probably have to fire him. If you "lose," your position as manager and resolver of this conflict will be significantly weakened. Wrong course.

Option d.   Mister Miserable could be right and it might be his manner of criticizing things that bothers everyone. Watch for the opportunity to get him to open up, to privately tell you about his view of things. Consider this to be a research phase of correcting this interpersonal situation. He is intelligent, as everyone agrees. He might make a contribution to the improvement of a defective situation. At the same time, you might recheck references to determine whether or not he has a reputation for being continuously discontented, a long-term "Mister Miserable." Suppose he *does* tell you about those things within the company, with his peers, or with you that bother him so much? Suppose you even agree with him, but are not in a position to either make concessions or correct the situation within a reasonable period of time? You tell him "You'll just have to live with things and people as they are!" This brings you back to ground zero, corrects nothing. Mister Miserable may consider it justification for his outspoken behavior. This could be a *lose-lose* condition. Nothing resolved. Nothing gained. Time lost. Escalation probably.

Option e. This is the nurturing parent attempting to move the natural child into an adult position. Enriching his job, carefully done so that no favoritism is interpreted, could improve his self-esteem and his confidence in you. This appeal to the higher order of needs for ego satisfaction and self-actualization is always in good order where a highly competent professional is involved. Few people who are finding satisfaction with their tasks and responsibilities will spend time being Mister Miserable. With the support of your supervisor and the understanding of your logic by the personnel manager, this could be your "best shot" for preventing escalation and improving the ambience for the members of the work group. Certainly worth trying.

Option e is preferred.

Answerman

He has an answer to every situation and problem. On the surface this sounds fine. However, he is inflexible. His answer is "the only one that can work." His way is the only way. Answerman is highly opinionated. He doesn't ask questions. He just gives answers. He's outstanding as an engineer or scientist. Even though his answers to questions and problems often turn out to be correct, his manners are offensive to the other members of the professional staff. His personality is strong,but not likable. He overwhelms his peers through sheer self-granted power. Even when his peers recognize that he is right, they resent him and his argumentative disposition. Much time is spent by you and others persuading him to try things that are not "his" ways. How can you get him to recognize the rights of others?

a   Is this the time to assume the *Dictator* style of management? Possibly. Briefly, order Answerman to change his ways. You insist on it. As the manager of the group, it is your duty to enforce team cooperation and he must be told that he is countering your efforts to develop the team spirit. Prohibit, by directive, this opinionated behavior and rudeness. You require, for the good of the project and the group, an open mind. You can't believe that any one person has all the answers all of the time.

b   Let the other members of your work group know that you are aware of Answerman and how aggravating he can be. Enlist their cooperation in the form of reporting to you each time Answerman engages in his abhorrent conduct. Then, you promise to confront Answerman as in option a above.

c   Send Answerman to personnel for a good talking to. This will let him know he is "on thin ice." Possibly this implication of threat coming for someone outside the department will change Answerman to an open-minded team member.

d   Assume he isn't fully aware of the unpleasant effect he has on others. Without threatening or implying that this is an "or else" condition, treat the situation as a conflict. Follow the steps to *no-lose* conflict resolution. Tell him how highly his professional skills are regarded by you and his peers and that his effectiveness will be advanced if he will listen more closely to the views of others, evaluating their content and respecting the rights of his peers. Obtain agreement that you will privately let him know when he is coming across too strongly as the group's "Answerman." Together you will improve the relationships toward team development.

Discussion.   The Answerman developed his behavior, or it was allowed to develop through the influence of a parent, a relative, early-stage schoolteacher, or a supervisor he had some time in the past. Answerman probably welcomes guidance given at the right time and place. He lacks self-discipline and his self-esteem could use a boost concerning how to interact with other people.

Option a.   Answerman is quite likely the product of too many Dictators and not enough Captains in his past. Direct orders will be heard but not necessarily followed. If his childhood and young adulthood have been filled with critical parents (as is indicated), the last thing he wants or will welcome is another such "parent." He may hear your orders and understand what you mean by them. He is really interested in the growth of the team but just doesn't know how to express this interest. His ego defenses will discount your orders. Results of this option may be positive for a very short term. But, in the long run, things will return to the original state.

Option b. This is merely a twist that modifies *option a.* It also can make you, the manager, appear weak and unable to cope with conflict. It is doubtful that your subordinates would welcome your invitation to report to you behind Answerman's back. Some of your subordinates may report to you as you ask them to do; however, be suspicious of the accuracy of the reports, which may contain distortions and exaggerations.

Option c. We can reject this one quickly. It contains all the undesirable elements of *options a* and *b.* The threat to "Answerman's" job and the fact that his personality have become a subject for official discussion will probably demotivate Answerman and start him on a search for a new job elsewhere. These are in opposition to the direction or result you sincerely want.

Option d. Your assumptions are probably correct. "Answerman" may know that he doesn't have the best rapport with his colleagues. But he may not be aware of the exact reasons. He knows he has strong ideas and has no fear of expressing them. But he may not be consciously or deliberately ill-mannered, interruptive, argumentative, or rude. A private session with him at the office, called at a time when tempers are cool and reason and logic seem to be prevalent in your relationship with Answerman, can become quite beneficial to everyone. The first step is to describe his behavior to him as you perceive it. This defines the existence of a problem. Help him recognize it and agree that it does exist. This is a confrontation that is free of hostility. Then you move through the stages of conflict resolution that include alternatives, evaluations of alternatives, selection of a corrective course of action, bench marks for monitoring progress through feedback from you to him. You and Answerman will probably develop a new relationship that will prove quite satisfying to both of you. Just as important, you will probably see a gradual, long-lasting modification of Answerman's behavior, with all members of the team participating in growth.

Option d is preferred.

Sprinter

He's intelligent, likable, articulate, works effectively and without peer-conflicts. Your problem is that he is totally inconsistent in his productivity. He works in spurts, short bursts of superbly effective energy. He's like a sprinter at a field meet. Lopes along, then shoots ahead, seems not to be trying hard, then suddenly sprints for the finish line. But this is not a solo field event. This "Sprinter" is out of step, too often, with the rest of the team. Give him a task and he might develop a brilliant solution path, even lead the group in creativity, which proves his value to the total effort. But, you can't depend on him to produce exactly when you and his colleagues need his capabilities.

Is he afraid to reach for high goals for fear of failure? Possibly. Such people generally work at levels that are significantly below their real capabilities; a problem with self-esteem, perhaps. Risk implies failure, rather than success—in his mind. He plays it safe. Well, that may be acceptable for him. It's not acceptable for you and the project. You know he has unusual capabilities for performance. You can't put up with his "sprints" and "works-in-spurts" approach to his tasks. The other team members are beginning to grumble and his "sprinting" is hardly an acceptable explanation to senior management for the imbalance in progress toward on-time on-budget completion of the project. You've got to take action right away. Things are not getting better by themselves. What to do?

a   Guide him out of his negative work habits. He has to do it himself, but it is possible that he is not entirely aware of the negative effects his works-in-spurts conduct has on the others as well as on the project's progress. After all, the solution to any problem, with people or with things, begins with developing an awareness. That you can do, appealing to his high level of intelligence and friendly disposition.

b   Pressure. Apply pressure when he slows down. Gently, of course. But strong enough to push him out of his pattern and back onto the track of the project and the group's needs. Praise, genuine praise should be given to Sprinter when he is performing as expected. Bear down on him when he starts to lag behind.

c Probe. Probe gently to discover what's bugging him. He may be unhappy with something. Who knows? This approach might disclose an unknown condition that, if ameliorated, will make a consistent performer out of Sprinter. Let him know he can depend on you for support. Your knowledge and experience are there for him to use. You can make suggestions, give him specific pointers. He can lean on you for support any time he feels the need. After all, isn't this one of the manager's functions? Support for subordinates.

d He needs a disciplinarian and, recognizing this need, you will help fill it. Start with a moderate confrontation. Tell him quite clearly and explicitly about his work habits and how you and the others feel about it. Establish defined rules of conduct and performance that clarify exactly what you expect from him. Set up benchmarks of time for periodic meetings with him to review his progress away from his habit of working in spurts. You could use others in the group as examples of desirably consistent productive output. It appears to you that he needs a role model and, proud of your staff of professionals, you have no difficulty naming others who are good examples to follow.

Discussion. Is Sprinter an underachiever? Are you placing too much faith in his past performance? It is possible that his previous performance(s) were more luck than talent? On the other hand, creativity cannot be delivered on demand. Few people are continuously creative. Regardless of the past, he is intelligent beyond the apparent norm, and the possibility exists that the expectations you have for him have not been clearly communicated to him. Are you sure he really understands what is expected of him? Don't take his intelligence for granted. People with high intelligence capabilities often need more thorough explanations than do others in the group. Their minds seem to work faster, looking far ahead into the project, visualizing situations and challenges about which others may not have prescient capabilities. Out of concern for appearing to be less than gung ho, he may keep these questions to himself. The unanswered (unasked) questions could keep him from going all out consistently. This is a possibility that you must consider. Make certain that you have taken elaborate care to communicate the company's and your expectations for performance from each member of the team as well as from the team as a whole. Do not assume that expectations are equally clear to everyone.

Option a.   Make the assumption that Sprinter is not totally aware of how he is affecting the group, his peers, and the project. If he is not aware, he cannot be expected to make corrections in his behavior. Your skill as a communicator is most helpful in this situation. You engage in *responsive listening*, giving him "I" messages and questions that are intended to evoke an open-minded discussion that will provide Sprinter with insights, a basis for self-evaluation. He may have personal home-life problems that distract and disturb him. Although you can't solve these for him and should not get too heavily involved in the details, he should be made conscious of the fact that his inconsistent performance on the job might be related to the timing of each crisis occurring at home. These distractions may not be readily solvable but, when they do occur, he must take stronger control of himself on the job.

The same distractions can be caused by overindulgence in an outside hobby, sports, participation in local civic and political organizations. Perhaps this "overindulgence" is caused by an incomplete satisfaction from his work. It may be possible that he is working on tasks that are not sufficiently demanding and he feels he can complete them easily with a burst of effort. Thus, he does his work in spurts, "sprinting" down the home stretch. After all, he never had let you down; just created considerable concern on the way, especially as critical events on the flow chart are approached. The appeal to his intelligence and a restatement of expectations hold a strong promise for long-term effectiveness.

Option b.   Pressure is easy to apply. You have the rank. If you can't use your rank to demand obeisance your title is just a couple of words strung together, not much more. Applying pressure will work. No doubt about it. But the duration is very much like flipping the power switch on an electric motor on and off. "On" (pressure applied) and the motor runs. "Off" (pressure removed) and the motor stops. If you are willing to keep your hand on the switch all the time (pressure applied continuously), the motor will run continuously. However, a circuit overload or motor fatigue might set in if you have not taken the entire system into consideration. Your "Sprinter" and his behavior are part of a complex system. This use of pressure is not a long-term solution by any means. Also, you do have other people and tasks to tend to. Overall, not a desirable course of action.

Option c. You have broad shoulders. You offer them to Sprinter. However, he may not like to lean on anyone for support. Also, if he does reveal his problems to you and the solution, or even the evaluation, is beyond your technical skills, you may wind up indicating that he can't really lean on you for support. You may not be able to (even if you want to) advise him on problems he has with his wife, children, girl friend or other very personal situations. "How did I ever get involved in this?" You'll ask yourself. Another risk factor for you: people sometimes develop resentment toward others on whom they become dependent. This is the human paradox of the crib. The child depends on his parents for food, sustenance, and safety. Yet, he severely resents this dependence. The crib and the playpen are sometimes perceived by the child as prisons rather than as secure places. The child tries to climb out of (get away from) the confines of the crib or playpen. When he succeeds, and most do, in climbing over and out, the parents are faced with a new dilemma: how to provide a new level of security and support for the child. This becomes an ongoing game, a contest between parents and child. You don't want to get involved in such "games." You don't want to trade one type of conflict for another. You want to find a long-term solution. This is not the way.

Option d. This is not too remote from *option b*. Just a bit more complicated and may be done in conjunction with *b*. You assume he needs a disciplinarian. This is the critical parent in transactional analysis. This is open confrontation between you and Sprinter. You may have misinterpreted his need. Enforcing a discipline could arouse fears for his security that could disable him. This could cause his beneficial spurts of work to diminish. He could move from what appears to be an underachieving status to a nonachieving status. It is possible Sprinter's native intelligence and sense of independence will seriously resent your exercise of discipline and arouse very strong feelings of antagonism toward you. The effect could be a reversal of productivity—underperformance that could seriously impede the performance of his peers and the progress of the project. No, you don't want to be the *parent* in this transaction. He's not really feeling such a need. He's logical. Responds to an *adult*. You certainly don't want to go this route.

Option a, the adult approach, is preferred.

Writer's Cramp

He's a productive member of the staff, inventive, creative, a superb problem-solver, and very popular with his colleagues. You wish everyone would be as cooperative and agreeable as he is. But there's a critical flaw in his performance. He's invariably late with his written reports. His notebook is a mess. You feel if you didn't nag him about reports and the notebook they would never be done at all. Also, when he finally does a report or makes an entry in his notebook, it is usually cryptically short, illegible, incomprehensible. All this is terribly frustrating to you and a severe hindrance to the administrative and progress reports you have to deliver, and which you accept as part of your responsibilities. Your supervisor and the system require that you file or deliver detailed reports on time. You may not like the chore of writing, but you stopped fighting and accepted the concept long ago. "Writer's Cramp" could be one of your subordinate managers, project leader, section leader, or report directly to you.

You've had it! Nagging is embarrassing and seems to have had no lasting effect at all. Strange that others in the group who are less intelligent and not as effective as engineers or scientists don't fight this task. Something has to be done about Writer's Cramp. Something that could produce a long-term behavior modification. Here are your options. Only one has a strong promise for success.

a   Learn to live with it. He is a producer. Maybe you are being too much of a perfectionist, a conformist. Creative people are individualists who find it difficult to conform to what might be the accepted norm for everyone else. After all, he does have other attributes you wish would rub off onto his colleagues. Such is the burden of being a manager. Accept the situation as it exists.

b   Find a compromise. Do you really need the reports in writing? Perhaps he could make them to you orally and you could put them into the written format. Why not suggest he do only some of the reports in writing? Those that you and he agree are most important. And his notebook? Important for potential legal situations as well as for a documented resource on which the company may draw in the future. Give some thought to having him dictate the entries to your secretary who could then enter them into the notebook. Maybe this isn't a bad idea. After all, he signs them and she becomes the witness-signature.

c Issue an ultimatum. He doesn't have any choice in the matter. The reports will be done properly and on time. His notebook will be kept up to date and legible. If he doesn't follow your very specific orders and do as all the other staff members do, Writer's Cramp will not get good reviews at performance-appraisal time, which could affect his raises and promotions. Tell him he is on probation from this moment on. This quite clearly means he has just so much time to do exactly what you expect of him. Although it is really the last thing you want to do, you might just have to fire him for insubordination and incomplete competence.

d Consider this a conflict situation. You will try to determine with whom or with what Writer's Cramp has a conflict. Is it you, or is it the system? He knows he is especially productive and, because he is essentially a nonconformist, he opposes symbols and actual procedures that he interprets as "controls."

Discussion. Writer's Cramp may be rebelling against your symbols of authority and control. Paper reports addressed to you by him are an acknowledgment of your power. So perhaps he does all he can to resist, forgetting or delaying his reports. He may be opposed to the system, the corporation's demands, which he thinks are insatiable for paperwork. Why should he write down those things you already know concerning the status of his task? Genuine or not, this may be his rationale. Also, he never gets feedback on the reports and therefore assumes they are serving no useful purpose; they take time from his work on the project where he knows he excels.

Writer's Cramp may have a low esteem of his ability to put things accurately, concisely, and intelligently in writing. Maybe he just can't express himself well in this medium. He became aware of that in his university days when every thesis or term paper was a fiercely traumatic experience. Another possibility: he may not really know what is supposed to go into his reports. The guidelines may not be clear to him. His notebook? He's always had a problem with his handwriting: slow, a scrawl, a painful experience. His schoolteachers gave up on him long ago. No diagnostic work or special training was ever offered to him during his entire school experience. All he ever heard were criticisms, and threats of poor grades if he didn't improve his writing. He always got excellent grades and compliments for his concepts and originality of ideas. These talents pulled him through, but he still gets hassled about his writing—or his lack of writing. Writer's Cramp may be fighting himself, the system, or you. Well, whatever. You need his professional talents. What are the pros and cons of each of the options open to you and that you will discuss with your supervisor?

Option a.   This institutes a double standard. The other professionals on the staff may not like all the paper work either. They do it. Some do it well while others are just adequate in this area. If you should ignore the problem, which is what you are doing by "learning to live with it," you risk irritating the staff members who do meet this paper work obligation. Isn't this favoritism, whatever the rationalization for the situation? Where do special concessions stop? How do you excuse others, who will most probably test you by being late with their reports or by asking you to let them off the hook this week because they are deeply involved with the other demands of their tasks? Writer's Cramp himself might escalate this special consideration you will have given him to an entire series of special treatments and waivers.

Option b.   You are the one who is making the compromise; an 80–20 situation with you giving up 80 to his 20. If you are to do his writing for him, why shouldn't you do it for the other staff members? How can you explain this so all will accept it? This is just like the double standard proposed in *option a.* If your secretary, or the department's secretary can take time to transcribe his notes you may have some difficulties getting other work done. No. If the policy exists concerning reports, there can be no compromise. If the policy is incorrect or unenforceable, it should be changed. This doesn't seem to solve anything.

Option c.   As we have learned from other experiences, an ultimatum given or received is a *no-win, win-lose,* or *lose-lose* situation. If the ultimatum is a bluff, Writer's Cramp might just call it and continue his part of the game. If he sees your ultimatum as a challenge to his individuality, he might just accept the challenge and choose to protect himself by doing battle with you, refusing to comply. In fact, his productivity might fall off as a result of the development of a negative attitude toward you, now on a personal level. He might choose to engage you in an open, public battle, blowing up in the middle of the next meeting when you ask for reports by a specific date. Your pride as well as your leadership could be tested on a very personal level by such an incident. Usually, such engagements end in a firing or a quitting. Writer's Cramp may lose, or he may win if your competitors race to pick him up. You and the company lose a productive professional. You also are diminished in the eyes of your staff (possibly in your supervisor's view, also) as a problem-solver, as a manager who has failed to resolve a conflict with an important and popular member of the staff. Very little probability for success of any kind with this option. You do not choose this one.

Option d. This course of action calls on your authority sub-K, your knowledge. Under this option you will make serious nonthreatening attempts, well thought through, at diagnosing the reasons behind the behavior of Writer's Cramp. You would endeavor to draw him out through responsive listening, enable him to articulate (and he is an articulate person), to verbalize what he perceives as the reasons for treating paper work with such apparent scorn. "Scorn" may be a strong word to use in a friendly conversation, so you avoid any use of adjectives to describe his conduct. Beware of taking a judgmental position by trying to describe in a word or two that which you perceive. Making and pronouncing judgments is one of the sure ways to kill two-way communications. And what you need more than almost anything else at this point in your relationship with this subordinate is wide-open two-way communications. He must be encouraged to verbalize his feelings.

If he feels he must resist your authority, or the system, he must be allowed freedom from threats while he expresses the views he had not been invited to give up to this time. It is entirely possible this creative and original thinker has some very constructive ideas to offer concerning improvements in your managerial conduct and in making the system more effective and supportable.

If he is fighting himself, you might help him develop courses of action—entirely of his own choosing—that will improve his personal situation.

Above all in importance, you will have established a strong line of communications with Writer's Cramp. Both of you will have gone a long way toward correcting your mutual positions. With the recognition that a conflict exists and having defined the conflict, the next steps are those of *no-lose* conflict resolution: listing alternative courses of action, evaluating the alternatives, selection, implementation, monitoring, and reviewing progress.

During your contacts in which you develop the courses of action, you will explain the meanings and values of each of the reports you ask your staff to write; why they must be done by specific time intervals; how they are used; what their distribution is; and how they serve the objectives of the individual, the group, and the company.

Option d is preferred.

Panic Man

Up to this point, "Panic Man" has appeared to have all the makings of an effective manager. You've given him an opportunity to learn by doing, named him leader of a section or group of engineers and scientists on an important project. He is quite intelligent, a brilliant and productive professional, articulate. He has always communicated well with you, told you about his progress and problems without having to be queried. His paper work is always well done, on time, and exemplary in format and content. You've given this leader primary responsibility for the staff (concern for people) who would complete the task for which you feel primary concern. Now there are signs of trouble. The task is slipping. You are feeling some anxiety. Your man seems to have made several panicky decisions.

You sense that the members of the group have had a change of attitude. You knew them to be cheerful and enthusiastic. Lately they are quiet, withdrawn, almost sullen. Not like them, really. Absenteeism has grown to such a magnitude as to affect the progress of the project. There have been several requests for transfers, leaves of absence for "personal reasons," one voluntary termination, and one involuntary termination. You've had some uneasy feelings about the situation. Didn't really have a good feel for what might be developing.

You have had some informal feedback that tends to support your feelings that all is not quite right with the relationship between your protegé and the staff. Relationships have become emotionally charged, negative. You tried to ignore the feedback as operating at the normal gripe level. However, the information being given to you has taken on a pattern. Decisions are being delayed by this group leader. He shifts back and forth unpredictably in making up his mind about directions that affect the members of the group. Questions put to him in the regular course of events by his subordinates usually lead to verbal battles and elevated tempers. The only time the leader will make a decision (so you are hearing) is when it is too late to argue any further. By that time the leader is in such a state of panic that it rubs off on all the members of the group. *Panic* seems to be the general state of this group's operation. The leader in whom you had so much faith is referred to as "Panic Man!" This collection of symptoms, slippage, overruns, stress, and strain—*this state of panic*—cannot be ignored or shrugged off any longer. Overtly calm and unruffled, you ask for a status report from your appointed leader. This time you will go somewhat further than the usual discussion of the progress toward completion of the task per se.

A review of memoranda concerning the requests for transfers, reasons for the terminations, the status reports all clearly show your perception of attitudinal changes among the subordinates was accurate. You realize it is essential for you to intervene, diagnose, evaluate, and resolve the situation; prove or disprove your fears for the worst.

You sit in on some of the group's meetings and note there is virtually no participation, no enthusiasm at all. Much too businesslike for these professionals with whom you have worked on other tasks. The leader is obviously undergoing stress and strain. Among the quotations you read for transfer requests and terminations are several disturbing statements:

"I need greater opportunity for growth."

"I don't see the possibility for advancement."

"I need more money and had to look elsewhere."

"The company no longer seems to care about its people."

"This engineer was terminated because his performance was below our standards."

"He was continually insubordinate and disturbed his colleagues with his constant complaining."

Everything you observe, all dependable feedback indicates the root of the trouble is with the leader for whom you've had great hope and expectations. You've also noticed a steadily changing behavioral pattern on the part of this leader. His oral reports to you have taken on a mood of high emotion, a sense of panic and finger-pointing. He has few good things to say about his people and you wonder if he is engaging in projection, an ego defense mechanism, trying to blame others for his own shortcomings rather than trying self-improvement. Skimming his status reports, too, bears this out. The trouble is always with someone else. His solutions seem to be as charged with emotion as are his analyses. He has earned the nickname "Panic Man." He has been depending entirely on his A_p, the rank and power you gave to him. Where is the A_k you know he is capable of practicing?

You don't want to fire him. You do want to develop a *no-lose* resolution that restores the use of the skills and talents you honestly know he has but has not been applying. What to do?

a   Review the problems with the leader and put him on probation. He is responsible for results and you are accountable for his effectiveness. You do have other things to do, which is why you named him "leader," but others have named him "Panic Man." Give him a finite period of time to show change and improvement.

b   Show Panic Man your collection of facts that point to him as the root of the problem. Ask penetrating questions. Make him face up to reality, abandon his emotional ego defenses. Deep down he knows exactly what's wrong. If he wants to stay with you and the company he will have to explain his actions in full detail. Also, he will have to describe to your satisfaction what he intends to do about correcting the situation and preventing a recurrence in the future.

c   Call in the employee relations department. Have them do an attitude study; anonymous responses, of course. This will tell you what the subordinates think about the situation and their immediate supervisor, Panic Man. Employee relations could also talk privately with him to find out what his own problems are. Sounds like he is mixing personal and business affairs together. If he has some personal problems outside the job that are affecting his job performance, let employee relations take on the role of psychological, philosophical, marital, and religious counselor; whatever is called for in this case. Managers at your level are not supposed to get involved with these matters. If employee relations says it can't get to this for some time, call in an outside consultant to do the same task. Time is important. Too much has been lost already. Emotions are running high.

d Concentrate on the problems rather than make any assumptions about the person. Talk with Panic Man. Keep your cool. Beware of emotional build-ups and tension between you during the discussion. Help him keep his own "cool" so that you and he can openly discuss the things you perceive and the physical status of the project and his subordinates. When he agrees that there is a problem, move toward an agreement of the definition of the problem and how you and he can implement a program that will convert a "panic" style to Captain.

e Tell him he is too emotional, panics on the job. Suggest he talk with a psychiatrist or psychologist as soon as possible, for everyone's good.

Discussion. When the manager is removed from the action by one or more "layers" within the hierarchy of the organization, he often has difficulty separating facts and fictions. Rumors and gossip drift back to him from all directions. People seem to be more eager to say uncomplimentary things than nice things about another person. The very words "rumor" and "gossip" have negative connotations. But there does come a time when you have to step in, with obvious caution, intervene and diagnose to your own complete satisfaction. When quantitative information reports that a project is behind time and/or over budget (being under budget can also be a cause for concern—when staff members succeed in getting transfers or terminate, the labor costs are reduced), things have gone beyond dependence upon rumor and gossip to tell you there is a problem that may be out of control. Your attention is mandatory. It is clear to you that the reputation "Panic Man" is well deserved. What are the probable effects, the pros and cons of the options you have defined and must present to your own supervisor for discussion and support?

Option a. This seems quite abrupt, the kind of response to a situation that has characterized Panic Man himself. If it took him a long time to get into this undesirable position and reputation, it may not be reasonable to expect him to get out of it in a short time span. This will probably cause Panic Man to withdraw into himself as a defense mechanism, protecting his ego. Or he might resign, considering you to be unreasonable in your expectations and demands, and you will have a new notch added to your own reputation: "He took a good engineer and made a lousy manager out of him!"

Option b.   You would be acting judgmentally, prosecuting by interrogation. This is certain to counter your basic intention to develop two way communications. The short-term effect will be the same as in *option a*. The long-term effects are negative.

Option c.   Very threatening, whether or not you intend to be so. While there is nothing wrong in admitting to yourself that you need outside intervention and diagnosis, this usually puts Panic Man on the defensive. There are few consultants, probably few employee relations people who should be expected to succeed when placed in the role of counsel in personal affairs. Purely out of self defense—the position he may feel you have put him in—Panic Man might panic again and try to point fingers at his subordinates, or even at you. It is quite "normal," to the dismay and perplexity of most consultants, to encounter resistance to their efforts at problem-solving through intervention and diagnosis. Very few managers, regardless of their levels within the organization, line supervisor or chairman of the board, have the experience or skill that introduces the consultant as an objective person. The perception on the part of the person, such as Panic Man, is that the consultant has been brought in to either prove the person is wrong or find out why the person is wrong. The assumption here is that "the person is wrong." Very risky for everyone as an effective course of action.

Option d.   This course of action reduces the pressure on Panic Man, demonstrates that you feel this is just as much your situation as it is his, and that you certainly have not reached any preconclusions. He still has your complete support. Your nonthreatening approach clearly states that you and he are going to define and solve any problems together as a common need and objective. You have not judged him. He is not on the defensive. He does want to do a better job. His need for recognition, ego status, has been frustrated. His motivation is to satisfy this need. He will very likely recognize at once that you are going to help him satisfy this need by guiding him toward an appropriate management style, redirecting his energies and improving his interpersonal relationships. You are empathetic and strong. Prognosis is excellent for long-term benefits from this course of action.

Option e. Expect his resignation to follow shortly after you have made this very personal suggestion. It will be interpreted as: (a) you think I am all wrong, or (b) mentally ill, or (c) just who do you think you are? Don't touch this one, no matter how long you have been personally or professionally associated with Panic Man.

Option d is preferred.

Obfuscator

You selected him as project leader because of his outstanding knowledge of technology and practice. He had always produced outstanding results when he worked as part of a project team. He is intelligent, likable, and asked for a promotion. You groomed him for leadership and, when this opportunity presented itself, you offered it to him. He was elated. He organized the project and the staff. Got off to a rapid start. Almost the perfect person for the position of project leader.

But something's gone wrong. Something that can't be overlooked. The response of the group to your directives, instructions, feedback, and informational reports—all made through channels, through your project leader—seem to have no meaning to the members of the work group. Are they being ignored? Is the project leader being ignored? Is he really leading the group? Is the project leader ignoring your supervisory actions? Does he misinterpret them?

You discuss the situation with him. You admit you are puzzled. He shows you his file of the memos he has published to his staff. Sure enough, every one of your instructions has been relayed to the group. Not one omission. His complaint is that people just don't listen to him (or to anyone else, he adds in self-defense). They do just as they please, despite his written instructions that are based entirely on your directives. However, you see the key to the problem very quickly.

He's telling the truth about his comprehensive efforts at communication. But hardly a single one of his memos is free of contradictions, ambiguities, or totally obscure language. He confuses the reader. Not deliberately, you realize. He doesn't know how to communicate ideas, principles, and policies in writing. Now you are not so sure he can do it accurately verbally. You had no idea that this specific problem existed before you named him project leader. Just one of those important things about people you may learn after the fact. He's an "Obfuscator." He isn't aware of this shortcoming, this inability to develop two-way communications with his staff. You want to help this high achiever over-come his and the group's frustrations and, as a result, improve productivity. There are six options that you can think of, but only one stands out as optimum.

a Determine, with Obfuscator's help, the reasons why communications are not working. You know why and you will help him see his shortcomings, see how he unknowingly confuses people. The next step is to design a program that will help Obfuscator become "Mr. Clarity." This may include seminars on written communications skills, possibly guidance in how to change some of his concepts of how to develop two-way communications.

b Run an in-house seminar for "Mr. Obfuscator" on communications skills. Do it yourself. You have an exceptional reputation as an effective communicator. You might include in these sessions the whole staff, all your subordinates, managers, and workers who do written reports.

c Seminars take too much time away from the project. Order the best books you can find, at department expense, on the subject of communicating and give them to Obfuscator. He is certain to get your message. There's a lot of knowledge to be gained from reading the works of good writers who have been published.

d Write a communications how-to manual directed specifically at Obfuscator. Explain the essentials and the reasons why good communications skills are so important to effective management. Instruct the staff, especially Obfuscator, to read and practice your teachings.

e Take on the communications detail yourself. When you issue a directive, address it and distribute it to everyone concerned. Don't depend on others to carry your messages for you. By communicating directly with the staff members, the work groups, you know the information will be transmitted accurately and promptly, without confusion. This could be one of those areas often described by the cliché: "If you want to get things done right you have to do them yourself."

f Accept it, this situation with Obfuscator, for what it is—part of the burden of being a manager of a staff of professional people. Learn to live with it. Any efforts to correct the situation will probably fail.

Discussion. In varying degrees, this could very well be one of the most common problems in interpersonal communications, whether one-on-one or among a group. People do tend to hear those things they want to hear, or to interpret what they hear in a way that is meaningful or that will not cause "pain" to them. Man is a pleasure-loving animal, will go to great lengths to avoid pain.

However, the manager's job description does not call for the inflicting of either pain or pleasure. It calls for good communication skills, usually quite explicitly. The difficulty is that one cannot always tell with any degree of certainty the level of an individual's skills in communication without putting them to the test. That's what you did. Nothing wrong at all with your method of selection. Nobody's perfect. But the fact remains that Obfuscator, for whom you are accountable, is having difficulties communicating with his work group of engineers and scientists. Let's examine your options to determine which one is most likely to remove or reduce the obfuscation. This time, let's take the last option first.

Option f. Accept the situation? Of course, you have to consider this, but you know it cannot be accepted. As a scientist and engineer yourself you cannot accept the premise that "any efforts to correct the situation will probably fail." You must take action. This one is obviously not acceptable.

Option a. Make this a joint program for analyzing and remedying the defects in communications. By giving the project leader nonthreatening opportunities to verbalize the situation, he will very likely come to recognize without having to be told that he has a deficiency in this area, that he has been causing some confusion that has had a negative effect on his people. He will probably make several suggestions on his own on how to correct this problem. Together, then, you will arrive at a suitable course of action that, because of his recognition of the problem and proposals for solution, has a very high probability for success. This seems outstanding for the long run. There are some short-term benefits you will observe. Obfuscator's morale and attitude will improve. He will complain less, if at all, during this adjustment period, about his people not listening to him. His "people" will respond to Obfuscator's change in attitude toward them with improved morale and attitude. Here we see the environment being cultivated so that motivators may take effect.

Option b.   In-house seminars are beneficial, if prepared and presented by experts on the subject. You are an exceptionally good communicator, no doubt. But what are your credentials and experience as a teacher of communication? Sure, running an in-house seminar by yourself sounds like fun. Probably will be—for you. But if you are not experienced as a seminar leader, you might do little more than waste time, get a feeling that things are happening. Not much more. Change is unlikely. In-house seminars, as we said, are beneficial. If you've "locked" onto this course of action, do call in an expert, either from the company's training department or from an outside consultant source.

Option c.   Nothing subtle about this approach. Hand Obfuscator some how-to books with a strong suggestion he read them. Sure he'll get a message from you. But *you* may be guilty of obfuscation by taking this approach to the problem. Yes, there is a lot of knowledge one can get from reading. But one has to have a defined objective for the search for specific knowledge. Otherwise the reading may prove interesting but not useful. Does Obfuscator know he has this problem? Guidance is needed in exactly how to apply the knowledge gained from this reading directly to the condition, the Obfuscator's problem, which is also your problem. Long-term benefits? Doubtful.

Option d.   A sound idea, if done in conjunction with some other more definitive effort. Even if you are a good writer of instruction handbooks, the same deficiencies that pertain to *option c* apply here. Also, do you really have the time to research, write, and produce such a manual on effective communications? Your time is valuable and could probably be invested in more productive directions.

Option e.   Short lines of communications may appear to be most effective in speed and, sometimes, in clarity (fewer middlemen could mean fewer opportunities for losing something in the translations). This places an extra heavy burden on you. Without the pyramid of the organizational structure, everybody tends to report directly to you. This could create an intolerably horizontal organization, probably unmanageable, uncontrollable. You could tell everybody that you will communicate directly with them but that they cannot communicate directly with you, they must communicate upwards through their leader, Obfuscator. This is patently absurd. Obfuscator might confuse you, if he hasn't been doing so all along, just as he has been confusing his subordinates. You would be by-passing, disabling your project leader, the person you appointed to the position. You would not be correcting the problem, just adding to your own work load. Not an option you would propose to your supervisor as a desirable course of action.

Option a is clearly the course that *holds the greatest long-term benefits* for the project leader, his work group, the project, you, and the company.

Day-at-a-time

Perhaps you started as a technician, or worked in a lab or a shop during summer vacations to gain some hands-on experience. You might have been fortunate and started as a junior engineer right out of school. When you were on your way up, gaining solid experience in how a company or organization functions, you learned that one of the essential elements in the makeup of any effective manager resides in his ability to plan ahead—*short-term plans* measured in weeks or months, *medium-term plans* measured in semiannual slices of time, and *long-term plans* measured in reference to the duration of a major project, or in years.

Before anything could happen or gain management approvals, you learned there had to be a master plan that defined objectives, strategies, tactics, and standards of performance by which accomplishment would be evaluated. You learned your lessons well and have been practicing them consistently.

Now you have a situation in which one of your new subordinate managers, an outstanding engineer or scientist, creative and productive when at work on a complex phase of a project, seems to be hard to pin down to specific objectives. For example, you ask for estimates of progress, bench marks for his group's task so you can develop a comprehensive PERT diagram that will display critical events and critical paths, leading toward a meaningful forecast for completion of the master project. What do you get? Sometimes it seems to be evasion, indirect responses. At other times, you get promises for delivery of estimates that you never receive. Further, you discover from experience, bad experience, that his estimates are not reliable forecasts of events. Not that he comes in late all the time. He may even bring his tasks to completion ahead of time. You are aware that he does not set meeting dates with advance notice. Tasks are assigned at the last minute. Supplies are always inadequate, running short. You need reliable inputs, not just dates and estimates done as though they were a ritual intended merely to satisfy "the boss." You conclude quite accurately that your man does not plan his group's activity. Nor does he plan his own. He "flies by the seat of his pants." He does things a "day at a time!"

"Day-at-a-time" may feel comfortable with this approach to his work. (You're not even sure of that.) Certainly, such behavior cannot be tolerated in an organization containing groups that must interact; peers, superiors, subordinates must pull together toward a master plan. "Day-at-a-time" *must* know this. Or do you assume too much? The important and urgent thing with which you are concerned is getting Day-at-a-time to plan, to estimate with greater reliability. It's not just for "the boss." There's a lot at stake, including your own performance reviews. You are alerted. What's your appropriate action, selected from among these options?

a Reassign him to another position as a staff engineer or scientist. He was a top performer in that role. You had no problems then, as far as this individual was concerned. Put him back where he performs best. Accept this as another example of "I took a good engineer and made a lousy manager out of him!"

b Do his planning for him. After all, except for this shortcoming, he is about as close to perfect as a professional staff member can get to be. Take control during his staff meetings. Assign specific segments of the development of forecasts and time estimates to his subordinates. This assures you of getting what you need to do your job of assembling the overall paths to completion of the master project.

c A better idea might be to assign the role of forecaster-estimator to one of the members of the group in whom you have very special confidence. This might get the planning data such as bench-marks-to-completion in your hands when you need them and with great accuracy.

d Take time to discuss the importance of the planning function with Day-at-a-time. Maybe he doesn't appreciate its importance. Perhaps if he did gain an appreciation of the need and how it fits into the master plan he would change his ways—with your coaching, of course. There is a possibility, too, that this type of planning is new to him. No one showed him how to do it. His self-confidence is low in this area. So he is not comfortable with it; avoids it for fear of revealing his lack of knowledge in this area of management. You will be his coach and mentor to make certain his "day-at-a-time" approach to task completion isn't merely rebellion against the system or your authority.

Discussion. Day-at-a-time's problem(s) may be difficult to identify. Planning ahead may be a difficult process to prove beneficial to him. After all, he is popular, productive, knowledgeable. Perhaps he doesn't totally identify with the company and is, in effect, operating as a soloist with a private "gang," the subordinates who report to him with your approval. Let's look into the probable effects, short- and long-term, of each of the options.

Option a. A reassignment might be viewed as the demotion you intend it to be. You would have to consider the individual's responses to such a move; ego effects could be quite demotivating, not to mention the potential embarrassment within the organization. However, don't discard this too quickly as an option. Day-at-a-time may actually be pleased to get back to a hands-on status and be rid of the administrative details. If there is an opening better suited to his skills and talents, discuss this possibility with him. Give him an option. If he elects to move back into the lab on a full-time basis, make certain you have an alternative choice for promotion as his replacement as the project leader. If he chooses to stay in his managerial role, move onto the other options for a selection of alternative course.

Option b. Some companies do separate the planning function from the line-staff operation. There are pluses and minuses, of course, concerning this type of organizational structure. Our assumption is that in your organization each manager is required to contribute to the plan with specific data, even if he is not the sole author of the "plan." Obviously, such is your responsibility and you must share it with your subordinate managers who are closer to the specifics of the project. Again, the problem with Day-at-a-time is that he either doesn't feed you data at all or, when he does, the confidence level is very low. No. You must have subordinate managers, project leaders who will do their planning, forecasting, and estimating when required and with as much accuracy as possible in this difficult task of forecasting the development of technology, products, components, and systems. No, you may not do it for him. Planning ahead is his task, too.

Option c.   This sounds attractive. But, isn't it "band-aiding" a wound? Planning involves the development and analysis of options leading to decision-making. You want the project leader's decisions and commitments. If the planning is done by someone else, Day-at-a-time may not feel strong ownership of the forecast and estimates, meaning a low commitment level. There can only be one project leader, one decision-maker for the group who makes decisions on the basis of the options developed and reviewed by his subordinates. Assigning the planning process to one of the members of the group other than the leader creates two leaders for the same group. This could create a new set of problems, even if the problem of timely and accurate planning is solved.

Option d.   Self-confidence, belief in one's own skills and talents is essential to individual effectiveness. Most of us tend to concentrate on those work areas in which we feel comfortable because of our self-esteem, our knowledge of how to approach and dominate a situation. A nonthreatening discussion of how he feels about the planning process with responsive listening on your part could enable him to open up his thoughts and reveal how he feels. If he doesn't believe in the process, you can educate him about how it fits into the master plan of the company. Explain why it is done by every leader and manager throughout the company's hierarchy and how it minimizes risk and maximizes opportunity. You might tactfully cite some examples of how the lack of planning affected a project or company program, offset by examples of how commitment to written plans have been beneficial to the company and its people. If he does recognize the value of planning but considers it a miserable chore that causes him to procrastinate, perhaps he needs guidance and instruction in how to do it so that the task becomes less onerous and more acceptable. You've done it many times and expect to do planning as long as you are employed by this company, any other company, or become self-employed. Yes, this is well worth your time as a course of action to pursue. There are no losers here.

Option d is preferred.

Mind-set

This member of your group has fixations! No matter what the task, no matter the previous history of failure or success, he takes the same approach to each task and its problems as he has done before. He becomes most persistent and tenacious when he is confronted with a problem in technology that resembles one he has had to deal with before; this is especially unfortunate if he has failed at this task before. His mind is set, fixed. He refuses to look at alternative approaches to the problem. "No. I'm going to make it work this time!" He has a mind-set. He behaves like the boxer who is getting his face bloodied by his opponent and, despite his predictable defeat, ignores his manager-coach's advice to lead with his left instead of his right because "what you're doing just isn't working!"

He's got a mind-set that narrows his vision, blinds him to the fact that there must be a better, more promising way. Few companies and not many task-oriented teams can afford a person who has a single, over-powering obsession to prove his way is right and who displays no regard for the probable costs of his persistence. Mind-set is a superb engineer or scientist, from a technical standpoint. He has outstanding credentials, academic and experiential. He has proven that he is dedicated to task completion. He does excel. However, you do recall Freud's person-ality theory, the Repetition Compulsion Principle, which contends that man is a habit-following animal, tending to repeat whatever is success-ful. In fact, Freud held that repetition of a practice can become a part of man's daily habit, so fixed that he may compulsively and repeatedly follow a habit as a method of coping with each new problem. Okay so far. But man may repeat the method even though he comes upon a series of failures. He is compulsive about pursuing the same habit-formed method. He has a mind-set. And that's what you have to deal with on the pragmatic level with no time for psychoanalysis, even if you want to or were skilled in this area. You have to get the job done, the task completed on schedule, within budget, and according to specifications. How do you cope with mind-set?

a   If he is going to carry his childhood-developed habits over into your department or section, treat the situation by assuming the role of the *parent*. Tell him that in no way are you going to support the same approach that has failed before. He must find another method, a different way to handle this new situation. The project must be given every possible chance to succeed and you don't want to risk the same kind of failure you and he had the last time he tried this method. He just has to take off his "blinders" and search the technology for a different, more promising method.

b   Develop an incentive system for the team members. The one who comes up with the most novel approach to a solution to the problem wins the prize: a dinner for two, theater tickets, a trip to a convention, or some similar material award. Dangling a "carrot" works in the sales department, you hear; why not try it on your professional staff. Mind-set enjoys the good life as much as anyone does. This might help him broaden his vision.

c   Keep a close tab on Mind-set. If you notice that he is going to repeat his compulsive approach to this problem (and probably fail as he has done before under the same set of conditions), step in and demonstrate your knowledge of the technical problem and propose alternative solutions. Of course "propose" really means: *insist*! Remind him of his responsibilities to the team and the company and that he has no right to risk failure by beating a dead horse. Perhaps if he realizes you are aware of his compulsion to repeat the method, even if it is an admirably stubborn persistence, he may stop this sort of thing or get better control of his habit.

d   Review the objectives of his assignment with him. Let him know with *unconditional positive strokes* that he does a fine job and that you and his colleagues have a high regard for his capabilities. Using responsive listening, carefully lead him to discuss the present task in the light of past experiences. Try to enable him to see the possibility of long-term negative effects that might result from short-term efforts dedicated to pursuing a path that may not be adequately promising to the progress of the project and of his colleague's tasks.

Discussion. The last thing you want to do is demonstrate the annoyance and exasperation you must feel when you realize that Mind-set is beginning to repeat his habit-formed and less-than-rewarding methods. He really isn't a *child* any more than anyone else. We are all the products of our environments and teachings that began in our very early childhood. Blaming someone for a personality trait is nonconstructive, can be quite destructive. It certainly will not have the desired effect of causing a change or modification in behavior. If you keep cool this can be handled quite neatly with no losers.

Option a. Obviously, this is losing your "cool." You might even be accused of behaving like the *natural child* yourself, having been hooked by his *child*, as in transactional analysis. This could lead to an open conflict, with each of you saying things you might later regret. At the very best, if it does cause a change, it will be a forced and very temporary change, extremely short term.

Option b. There is some value in the incentive approach because it has inherent recognition and ego status factors. You might try it anyway. However, the strong probability is that Mind-set will just work harder and more diligently at his old method in an attempt to, at last, make it work! This option offers some benefits, but not directly related to the problem you face with Mind-set.

Option c. You neither have time to nor do you care to make "looking critically over someone's shoulder" part of your managerial duties. Very few, if any, professionals are able to perform effectively under this kind of supervision. It smacks of the Driver or even the Dictator style, neither of which seems to be appropriate to this situation.

Option d. It is almost obvious that this establishes an adult-adult relationship between you and Mind-set. Both of you are being logical, uncritical, examining facts, calling up data, looking at open options, and moving together toward optimization of the assignments you both have.

You recognize that habits formed over the years are not easily changed. Thus, you and he will periodically, as either of you sees fit, get together again for a look at progress and additional options that my be exercised. This looks very much like a no-lose option that is attractive to all parties.

Option d is preferred.

The Strangler

You wonder if your group leader, your subordinate manager, is too tough on his people. Is he instituting too many controls? Not that "controls" are bad. In fact, they are essential to the predictable management of any orginization. But one can go overboard and institute so many controls that creativity, ingenuity, initiative, and energy are diminished. Too many dos and don'ts, with regular reminders and disciplinary actions when one of the people does a "don't," can seriously impair morale and attitude, make it impossible for motivational influences to be perceived or received. One of the symptoms is a high rate of absenteeism (which you suspect is related to a high degree of moonlighting, or part-time consulting work being done outside the company by your professional staff). This might be evidence that they are not finding adequate satisfaction for their needs inside your department. It can't be the money. Your company is as generous as any in the industry and in the geographic area. You talk with your subordinate manager about his management style and the effects you perceive. "Is it possible," you explore with him, "that the series of rules are binding rather than guiding your group? Is a silent rebellion taking place? What are your experiences with adherence to your rules?"

He reports that despite his efforts to provide some controls, the rules are being broken quite often. He admits he is hard put to figure things out right now and what course to pursue.

"The Strangler" is asking for your help. There are, of course, several options. However, you must keep the objectives in mind: restore positive attitudes and constructive performance. Increase productivity of the group.

Rules, controls are necessary to the formation, development, and growth of any group of people. How can you and The Strangler keep them at a sensible level?

a Reverse all the rules and controls. Suspend them indefinitely.

Your staff are all grownups. Tell them what you expect from them and depend on them to do it.

b You should support your manager. After all, you appointed him to the position. Discipline those whom you can identify as the leaders of this "silent rebellion." You might go so far as to make an example of someone who has repeatedly broken the rules and elected to ignore the controls. The Strangler may not be right all the time but he is the *manager* all the time, not someone to be fooled with. He has the good of the company at heart. And your staff should be reminded they are part of the company. What's good for the company is good for them.

c Modify your tough stand in *option b*. Let your staff know you back The Strangler and those who ignore the controls will have their names posted on the bulletin board outside the lab. The threat to ego status and the negative recognition are certain to have a noticeable effect.

d Work with The Strangler to identify those controls and rules that are considered essential to the group's task fulfillment. If they are all "essential" (this is a possibility you have to recognize because The Strangler is an intelligent person), establish a set of priorities for implementation or elimination over a reasonably short time period. Decide which controls are truly essential to an effective operation. You might carry this an important step further. Involve the group members in identifying and setting priorities for controls and the procedures for implementing them.

Discussion. You must select an option that demonstrates continued support for your manager who, unfortunately, is referred to as "The Strangler." If you do not demonstrate this support, you must transfer, demote, or terminate him because he will have been rendered totally ineffective. You named him a "manager." Now you have to make a *manager* of him for everyone's benefit, including your own.

Option a. This means you have stepped in, taken over. Now The Strangler not only has lost the support of his subordinates, he has lost the support of his supervisor. If he stays with the company he will probably be quite bitter about the experience, learn nothing from it, and blame you for interfering with his job after you had given it to him.

Further, the *Laissez-Faire* style assumes that after you have told everyone what you expect of them, they will do it. In this case, it represents complete abdication of the manager's role; a complete reversal, when compared with The Strangler's style, that can leave most people bewildered, confused, and just as dissatisfied for a different set of reasons.

Option b.   Support your manager, of course. However, this "support" should not mean back him under any circumstances. He's been overdoing the controls. You know it. His subordinates know it. Probably others in the company, your peers, know it. "Make an example of someone who has repeatedly broken the rules" may work in a military organization (during wartime), but certainly will be disastrous in your environment. Do not do this.

Option c.   Like *b*, this can be disastrous. You may wind up having everybody's name posted on the bulletin board—all at the same time— as former employees now working at your competitors' labs! This option is the same as *b*, with a method of "making an example" spelled out.

Option d.   Very few people fail to recognize the need for rules, policies, procedures, and guidelines. The problem here has been overkill. It is sometimes surprising to a new manager to discover that his people do want such things as rules, controls, and guidelines. It is one form of stating expectations and the standards by which their performances will be measured, appraised, or even rewarded. Make use of the resource you have in human intelligence embodied in the members of your professional staff. Elicit their viewpoints with respect to the specific controls and standards. You might even try a brainstorming session, following the rules and controls for such problem-solving meetings.

Option d is preferred.

Granite Man

Planning a change and introducing it in a way that assures that your people will adjust, conform, modify their behavior accordingly, or respond without loss in time or productivity is one of the severest challenges of a manager's capabilities.

In this situation you have assured yourself that a change is necessary. The change is important. For purposes of our discussion, the nature of the change itself is not important. You've dedicated a considerable amount of your time and energy toward the conception of the change. You've planned well. You have the full approval of your supervisor to implement the change according to your plan and timetable. Documents and notices have been prepared and distributed. No physical detail that you can foresee has been overlooked. The entire process, you feel certain, has been well conceived, and announced. Many, in fact most of your people are accepting and going along with the change. However, one particular person, "Granite Man," is stubbornly resisting the change.

For reasons hard to understand, and certainly not predicted, Granite Man not only is resisting the change but he complains to anyone who will listen (and to some who don't want to listen but can't escape him). Granite Man is an outstanding engineer or scientist, distinctly an asset to the work group as a technologist. His work, you fear, is being affected adversely by his attitude. Worse, he is affecting some of his colleagues; some agree with him and some do not. However, you sincerely believe that if Granite Man would stop his resistance and the proselytizing, the change could be implemented with everyone's full cooperation and without adversely affecting work performance.

Unfortunately, by the time you realized Granite Man was the source of resistance, the project had slipped perceptibly and management was beginning to comment. You must take some action. But you don't want to take action that will just suppress the situation so that others do not notice the problem. You want long-term results. You also want to win Granite Man over to your side, make him your ally. In fact, you want all those who have been feeling some resistance, overt or convert, to agree with your approach, agree that the change was necessary, is necessary.

    a   You will talk to Granite Man to assure him there is nothing personal in the change, that he will benefit from it just as much as anyone else will. Maybe he is feeling some insecurity.

    b   Bring strong pressure down on Granite Man. No doubt you believe his behavior is childish. Advise him that if he persists in trying to oppose or undermine your authority, if it comes to a choice of him or you, you know exactly who will win! Remind him he has been well paid for his contributions to the company and you want him to stay but you alone are the *manager*. You cannot tolerate such behavior from one of your subordinates—

however vital his skills may be—and that's the way things are!

c   Make Granite Man face the fact that he is resisting change. You might even use such clichés as: "You can count on change"; "Change is the only thing that is constant"; "If you don't like the environment, wait a few minutes, it is sure to change." These attempts at semi-humor will make a strong point with him and make him see how unrealistic he is. He'll probably conform after this delivery. There are times, you think, when shock is the best way to problem-solving.

d   Create an opportunity for a staff meeting with Granite Man in attendance. Make it clear that the meeting is for information purposes. You intend to describe the condition that prevailed prior to the change, the need for the change, the nature of the options available to you and why you chose the one that seemed to meet the needs of the majority of the group, the time-table for its implementation, and the long-term benefits that will accrue to everyone involved. Perhaps this will make the change less objectionable, even more acceptable. Invite questions and discussion of all the options that had been considered and the process that led to the selection of the one now being put into practice. Take special care to respond to all the complaints that have filtered back to you, to Granite Man's gripes as you know them. It is possible that participation by the group will reduce Granite Man's objections, perhaps even win him over through your appeal to his intelligence.

Discussion.   Here we have the situation of the manager acting all alone in the planning process and expecting his subordinates to accept his plan and timetable without notice or comment on their part. The manager made a basic error at the onset. He would have been prudent to meet with his people, singly *and* in a group session, asking for inputs to solving the problem he perceives.

Perhaps his perception was wrong. Let's assume it was right. Change was truly needed. But since his subordinates are the ones who have to implement and live with the process of change, their assistance and cooperation should have been sought by the manager. His subordinates are the ones who have been living, so to speak, with the previous condition. Possibly they welcome a change. Very likely they would like to be consulted about the specific change and be given time to consider its impact on them. "Ownership" of the problem-condition should have been shared with the group. They should have been expected to "own" a share of the solution. This would insure implementation and a high degree of success for the planned change. The damage has been done, however. The manager realizes now how he should have dealt with this and he will probably do it more correctly next time. No more "Granite Man" for him! Is it too late? Not necessarily. Let's see how you can rescue the manager for short- and long-term benefits.

Option a. This will probably put Granite Man on the defensive. He might feel he is being attacked and may counterattack. If he is feeling insecure and this is the reason for his resistance to change, this direct approach to him as an individual might only heighten his feelings of insecurity. His reactions could be unpredictable, most likely unpleasant.

Option b. Spank! Spank! That's what you'd be doing with this option. You are accusing him of being a *child* and he will have "hooked" you as the *critical parent*. There is no move toward an *adult* relationship in this option. This is also the style of the *Dictator* manager; not appropriate.

Option c. The approach is oblique. The humor will probably fall flat and give Granite Man more to talk about—how bad your sense of humor is, for example. It is doubtful that he will get the true message because it is couched in language that is similar to (although not exactly the same as) the *Report-Command* theory, in which the weak humor takes on the nature of the *report* and the *command* is intended to mean "Accept this change because that's the way it is!" Very little benefit to be derived from this course of action.

Option d. Information meetings are extremely valuable devices for establishing communications among subordinates and their managers. (Doesn't every new manager begin his assignment by calling a meeting exactly for this purpose?) It is not too late to compensate for the fact that this manager overlooked the important value of the information meeting as a method for defining a problem and seeking solutions in which others are expected to take an active part. The manager should expect the participation of all members of the group because he has sincerely invited such participation. Although this meeting seems to be somewhat after the fact, it does bring conflict out into the open rather than allowing it to fester and contaminate the environment. In the open, conflict can be resolved, laid to rest, and the protagonists (Granite Man and any allies he may have won over to his invented cause) will have their "day in court" to express their defense of the way things were ("We've always done it this way"), and the prosecution of the change ("Who needs it?").

This is not to be a contest between you, the manager, and Granite Man and his unofficial aides-de-camp. If their reactions are born out of insecurity, they will be enabled to overcome their fears through the knowledge you willingly share with them at the information meeting. Many people view change as containing implicit threats. The fears that arise are often the result of incomplete knowledge. By sharing, quite openly and freely, all you know about the raison d'etre for the change you will help allay these fears and, quite likely, make a friend of your former covert foe. Granite Man will cease to demonstrate or feel resistance. You will have learned an important lesson in the management of change—participation in information collecting, option examination, planning, and implementing; truly the *Captain*.

Option d is preferred.

You have just practiced problem solving at the manager level

Each of these exercises in managing people has been drawn from actual case histories, real-world experiences. Recognize the element that was vital in value to you as you "tested" your skills on paper. This "vital" value is in the learning process of *how to solve people problems*. It is not at all in whether you agree with any of the options offered as "preferred." It is not at all in whether you chose a completely different option, one of your own invention. It isn't found in the possibility that you may have combined some of the "best" aspects of the proposed options to create an optimized response that might enhance the probabilities for long-term success.

Well, then, where is or what is the "vital value"? It is in the very simple fact that you have just learned valuable and very positive techniques in solving problems in interpersonal relationships.

Denied the use of drastic, final action such as *termination* or *transfer,* you were forced to develop solutions to problems from which there were no simplistic "escape routes." You had to exercise your knowledge-based authority and discard, temporarily, your power-based authority. You had to prove to your superior, your peers, your subordinates—and to yourself—that you could recognize the true nature of a management problem, define it, develop and evaluate alternative courses of positive and constructive action, present them to your superior for discussion and thereby prove your maturity and effectiveness as a manager, leader, supervisor of a professional staff.

The *vital value* is in your own growth, learning and doing in a nonthreatening way. A "paper exercise," perhaps—but as close to the "real world" as one can possibly get without placing one's self at risk. An "exercise," yes,—but designed to strengthen, vitalize, and hone your skills and your effectiveness.

There is little doubt that, if management is your career objective, you will have to deal with every one of the twelve examples of managing people that we have presented. And, quite probably, some we have not presented. However, the technique for solving the problems is not likely to change from those we described.

The theories are well founded, well developed. They provide a relatively scientific basis for practice that gives the maximum probability for effectiveness as a manager and for achieving the desired results.

12
Moving up

Look around you. Observe and describe to yourself the attributes of your superiors, colleagues, and subordinates, using these criteria:

1. Physical appearance.
2. Manner of speech.
3. Predictible performance.

Then, classify each of the individuals according to the following categories of opinion (your opinion):

1. Looks like a manager. (Yes) (No).
2. Sounds like a manager. (Yes) (No).
3. Will probably move upward in the hierarchy. (Yes) (No).

A simple exercise. What can one learn from it? One can learn that there are, without a doubt, certain superficial factors that appear to be common among those people whom you have identified as "Yes" people in the above process. It is improbable that you would rate an individual likely to move up in the hierarchy (No. 3) if he did not look (No. 1) and sound like (No. 2) a manager.

What are the "looks" and "sounds" that we tend to associate with managers? If we may consider that there is a definite relationship between upward movement in the hierarchy and "looks" and "sounds," and if we want to participate in this upward movement, it is worthwhile to investigate and, perhaps, emulate these factors regardless of their superficiality. It doesn't matter whether you are not yet graded by your company as a "manager," are in an entry position in management, or have been titled "manager" for some time. If you seek *upward movement* it is important to subjectively examine those who are effectively pursuing the career path you want to travel.

This is not purely attempting to succeed through imitation. Deliberate emulation of another's appearance and behavior is often impossible, unnatural, ineffectual, and self-revealing; it also contains high risk of embarrassment. We are searching for common denominators that characterize those who are succeeding (with "success" defined as *upward movement*) in the organizational hierarchy, gaining increased responsibility, authority, and whatever physical and psychological rewards may be made available to those who are operational in this mode.

The "look" of a manager

Is there such a thing as "looking like a manager?" We offer an opinion based on long and deliberate observation, first as a young engineer looking for identity, later as an operational manager, and then as a consultant to management at all levels of the organizational hierarchies, with companies ranging from one-man start-up sole-proprietorships to Fortune-500 corporations. Our answer is yes, managers do *look* and may even *sound* like *managers.*

Let's start with an imaginary situation. A stage play, a major motion picture, or a TV film is being cast. It concerns the human interplay among people within a business corporation. It dramatizes the expressions of the individual personalities (the "personalities" developed long before the individual characters in the drama joined the corporation), the problems in communication, the interpersonal conflicts, and the successful and not so successful efforts each of the leading characters (the "managers") makes to communicate effectively and to resolve conflicts. The person responsible for identifying the actors who fit these roles—in show business he is called a "casting director" while in the corporate world he is called a "personnel director"—searches his files, memory, resumes, photographs, and credits (credentials) from among those actors who might fit the parts to be cast. "Fit"? What are the very basic criteria that determine "fit" or "no-fit"?

We put them into question form:

1 Does the actor look the part?

2 Does the actor sound the part?

3 Does the actor have a parallel, successful trackrecord? (Possibly a typecast image?)

Ah! Is there a "sterotype image" for the "manager?" In plays and movies of the twenties and thirties the chairman of the board usually wore wing collars and striped pants; at the very least, an immaculately tailored suit, white shirt, and dark tie. In the forties and fifties, the "manager" had switched to a gray flannel suit. Charcoal gray took its place alongside the blue-serge suit as a symbol of authority. They implied knowledge that is associated with austerity, dignity, and maturity. Actors like Edward Arnold, for example, seemed continuously to play the role of the enormously successful business executive (always at the very top of a giant hierarchy; powerful and wealthy), giving commands to the subordinates who surrounded him wherever he went. They responded quickly, without challenge! One could never visualize or think of Edward Arnold, *chairman of the board*, in need of a shave or a haircut or without a jacket on, either at home or at the office. These superficial traits were automatically associated with the concept of "manager" . . . senior genre.

Then, too, I recall Gregory Peck, the man in the gray flannel suit. Sensitive, determined, when he spoke every one of his associates— superiors, peers, subordinates—listened closely to this well-groomed manager.

Can you imagine the casting director choosing a gum-chewing, tousle-haired, carelessly dressed actor for one of the "managerial" roles? No, you cannot, unless this particular "Manager" is intended to be a disrupting, challenge-to-authority character around whom much of the communications problems and conflicts are intended to revolve. Continuing the imaginary plot for the moment, this nonconformist "manager" is never proved wrong in his basic beliefs or in his behavior. However, here is the inevitable conclusion of the script: "Making a soft-spoken speech to his peers and superiors about rights of the individual, our rugged individualist, firmly upright but not racing away, announces his resignation and his intention of starting his own company in which individuality will be allowed to flourish because it will be nourished by him as the head of the operation! Nobody among his peers or superiors rises to join him. Some look at each other briefly and then out the window of their skyscraper board room, while others put their heads in their hands or stroke their chins as though in profound contemplation (trying to figure out what just happened, no doubt). Finis."

As the curtain rises on the sequel (a good story always leaves the reader, listener, or viewer with imagination-stimulating options for postludes), our rugged individualist is shown as general manager, president of his own relatively small company surrounded by managers who are physical reflections of himself. The ambience is that of a group of highly motivated individuals, engineers and scientists all, in shirt sleeves, bearded, long-haired. Not a white shirt or heaven forbid, a necktie among them. They might just make it to physical and emotional independence. This is the opening mood.

The sequel to the "sequel," which seems unavoidable, shows our rugged individualist talking to a consultant. Times have become difficult. Productivity is not where is has to be to satisfy the needs of the creditors. From the scenario, here is a conversation that we learn is far from an isolated one in this company:

> "Sure is a great place to work, isn't it?" (Note the statement and question all in one thought, as though the speaker is seeking assurance by converting a statement into a question.)
>
> "Sure is. But I don't feel any movement. Hard to get a decision. And even if the decision is made, it's hard to get action."
>
> "Can't figure out what's wrong. The boss used to be pretty carefree, but I hear we've got *mucho* problems with money."
>
> "Wonder how the market is for engineers and scientists out there? Maybe it's time to look around a bit."

The conversation provides a revelation that the "manager," this rugged individualist, nonconformist, maverick, didn't *look* like a *manager* because deep down he didn't *want* the responsibilities and accountabilities of a *manager*. He deliberately did not "look like a manager" because he did not want to identify with management. One of his favorite lines was: "The first myth of management is that it exists." His mode of appearance was an unconscious statement of his rebellion against the establishment. His experience as an entrepreneur is that management must exist. Even in a modest form it must exist. There must be those who can plan, organize, direct, and control (set standards

by which plans and people will be measured), and who will accept and
practice the dominant role in these processes. They happen to be called
"managers."

This manager's rejection of the role, his *Laissez-Faire* approach to
business matters, led to confusion, frustration, and brought productivity
to so low a level that creditors took note of the inherently high risks in
the enterprise. Thus with poor credit and no apparent easy solution, a
consultant was called in for an organizational diagnosis. Among the
processes that had to be implemented—after the cash situation was
ameliorated—was a more businesslike approach to the world inside the
enterprise and the relevant outside world. A manager was brought in to
run the business and to make or direct the making of decisions. As is not
unusual in such circumstances, the new manager may have been
installed by the sources of new cash, investors or capital-venturists who
recognized the true capabilities of the founder and gave him responsibility for technology and product development although he retained the
titles of president and general manager.

Of course, as you've already guessed, the new business manager
looked like and *sounded like* a "manager."

Like it or not, often you are assumed to be what you look like. What
you wear may be considered to be a visual expression of your acceptance
or rejection of your environment and its value system.

This doesn't necessarily mean everyone who is called or aspires to be
a manager must wear wing collars, white shirts, ties, striped pants, suits,
and jackets at all hours of the day and night until one reaches the total
privacy of one's own bedroom. There are exceptions to the need for
emphasis on "looking like a manager." One major exception is California industry, which has developed its own unwritten codes for dress. In
California, it is generally believed, long hair down to or even below the
shoulders may have originated. The informal, unstudied casual look, the
open neck, the open shirt front became acceptable business wear in
California almost before it was acceptable in comparable major metro-
politan areas that are not tropical.

Yet when a California manager does travel outside the state—or even
outside his own parts of the state—he usually wears a suit (even though
the jacket and trousers may not match) and usually has to go out and
buy (or borrow) a tie. He will resist buying a white shirt or even a
solid-color shirt unless it is a bright pastel. He will often appear at a
meeting "out of town" in a relatively bizarre outfit consisting of a

mismatched jacket and trousers, outlandish sport shirt and necktie that is obviously making him uncomfortable. Such is the nature of concessions made to the establishments that exist "back east" (Nevada and beyond). Thus we may exempt California from the need to *look like a manager* as we have defined the "look."

It is the conclusion of those who have made special studies of such matters that, in the manner of dress, there are implications of authority and dependability. From one extreme of the wing collar, striped trousers, and Prince Albert coat to the *macho* look of the open shirt front and totally mismatched color scheme, there ranges a very broad middle ground of acceptable practice. The dark blue suit, perhaps with a fine pin stripe, white shirt or subdued pastel shade, and a small-patterned tie present an image of a "solid person," dependable, responsible, and mature in thought and actions. A dark gray suit or a dark brown suit, with complementary-color shirts and ties present images of maturity and wisdom similar to, though not quite as strong as, a dark blue suit.

A green suit suits a carnival mood or scene better than it does an engineering manager's environment, with the possible exception of St. Patrick's Day humor. Leisure suits were once faddish, but were never quite accepted among senior managers. Translate "leisure" into "I don't really care." Bold stripes and "loud" checkered patterns have no place in the manager's wardrobe of suits or shirts. They imply that the wearer thinks like a subordinate, not a manager, at the bottom of the totem pole. Combinations of blazers and slacks may be acceptable, but never such combinations as red slacks and purple jacket, whether solid colors or patterns prevail. "Wild" combinations give the impression that the wearer is loud, boisterous, shallow in his thoughts and eager to be "heard." They convey the impression that the wearer may not have much to say, but he will be noticed!

Changing one's wardrobe, assuming one accepts the concept that the outer garments reveal the inner person, is purely a matter of emulation and money. Seek the guidance and suggestions of a good clothier, men's haberdasher, or tailor who displays "what the well-dressed executive wears." Pay careful attention to fit and appearance. This may cost a bit more than one has become accustomed to paying; after all, executive "looks" cannot be found in a bargain basement. However, judicious shopping, holiday sales, inventory clearances or closeouts often do provide opportunities for enhancement of the manager's wardrobe without requiring a disposable income equal to that of the chairman of the board.

The vital element is that if you would move upward in your company's hierarchy, it is important for you to look and sound the part of the participant at the level to which you aspire. Look closely at those at the level of management just above yours. Identify the surface common denominators. Adopt them. When you make the break and start your own enterprise, and are your own pacesetter, then and only then may you set the example for casual fashion and expression. Until then, to be in fact a *manager*, you must *look and sound like one.*

Personal comments and observations:

- I have not yet met a *senior manager* in a *successful big business* operation who wears open-front sport shirts at the office and sports a beard.

- I have met only one CEO (Chief Executive Officer) for a high-technology subsidiary of a major corporation who wears a Fu-Manchu mustache. It makes him look malevolent. He has great difficulty relating to his subordinate senior managers; has an unusually high turnover rate among his senior managers; and his P&L sheet reads like a disaster report.

- When I made the move from engineering-section leader to senior department manager, I was advised by an older, seasoned, and successful veteran, "You still look like an engineer." I was wearing a brown sport jacket, blue slacks, open-collar shirt and V-neck sweater (my usual dress at that time). His comment was the result of my asking him for help in developing a stronger "voice" during management meetings. I got the message and, as my budget allowed, asked him to help me select a new wardrobe—all suits.

- The founder (an engineer by training and inclination) of a small company that is now a world leader in its industry once told me, "I can't see any reason for spending more than $50 for a suit." His appearance always delivered that message without the need to say it. The company he founded became a "world leader" after he was neatly, inconspicuously shunted aside, removed from operational control, securely ensconced in a suite of offices and with his own laboratory, far from any of the locations of his company's executive offices and factories. He passed away, enormously wealthy, but with no voice of influence in operations of the giant corporation(s) that still bear his name. The succession of chief executive officers who have followed him always looked like, and still do *look like managers*.

- A doctor with a financially successful practice in a poverty-level district of an eastern city told me, "My patients gain special status from the fact that their doctor wears expensive suits and parks his Cadillac in front of his office."

- I have met many *senior managers* in *small struggling companies* who wear beards, long hair, sport shirts, and even dark glasses while indoors. Cause or effect?

- Make-up people in Hollywood have always been an elite group. A star will spend hours in the make-up man's hands before going before the cameras for a few minutes of shooting.

Yes, it's generally agreed that if you want to be a manager you must learn to *look like a manager*.

In his book *Dress for Success* (Wyden, 1975), John T. Molloy reports on responses to eleven written questions he submitted to 100 top executives of major corporations:

1 Does your company have a written or unwritten dress code? Ninety-seven said yes. Three said no. Only two had a written dress code.

2 Would a number of men at your firm have a much better chance of getting ahead if they knew how to dress? Ninety-six said yes. Four said no.

3 If there were a course in how to dress for business, would you send your son? All 100 said yes.

4 Do you think employee dress affects the general tone of the office? All 100 said yes.

5 Do you think employee dress affects efficiency? Fifty-two said yes. Forty-eight said no.

6 Would you hold up the promotion of a man who didn't dress properly? Seventy-two said yes. Twenty-eight said no.

7 Would you tell a young man if his manner of dress was holding him back? Eighty said no. Twenty said yes.

8   Does your company at present turn down people who show up
    at job interviews improperly dressed on that basis alone?
    Eighty-four said yes. Sixteen said no.

9   Would you take a young man who didn't know how to dress
    as your assistant? Ninety-two said no. Eight said yes.

10 Do you think there is a need for a book that would explain to
    a young man how to dress? Ninety-four said yes. Six said
    no.

11 Do you think there is a need for a book to tell people in
    business how to dress? All 100 said yes.

Mr. Molloy's book is one of several, recently published, that were
totally dedicated to the subject of how to dress to achieve specific
business objectives.

Like it or not, behind every management decision—possibly behind
every decision made by a human being—is a set of assumptions about
people. Like it or not, therefore, your future will most certainly be
affected by the assumptions your peers and your superiors make about
you, based on your appearance and mannerisms. These assumptions are
usually made at the very moment of initial encounter. You get only one
chance to make a first impression. You may have many opportunities to
alter the assumptions made as a result of the first impression, but it is
very difficult to achieve any significant alteration. The mind accepts the
first inputs it receives. The mind resists any inputs that represent
change. As previously mentioned, *change* represents *threat* because it is
intended to alter conditions or assumptions that have been accepted and
stored within the mind and with which we feel secure. Our retention
mechanism is strong with regard to impressions—if not with regard to
specific data, details, or specifications.

How shall I dress for the role of *manager*? The simplest, possibly the
most effective guidance comes from those who are successful within
your own company. Closely observe and evaluate your peers and superiors. Correlate appearance, manner, and probability of moving upward
in the hierarchy. The rest is up to you as a self-disciplinarian. It may
call for *change* in your own looks and manners.

The sound of a manager

The matter of *sounding like a manager* is more difficult to resolve; it
may cost less in dollars but certainly more in the development of

awareness and taking remedial action where it is indicated. No one is proposing that you must sound like Sir Lawrence Olivier or Sir John Gielgud reciting a soliloquy from Shakespeare. Even in England such superb elocutionary performance may be more distracting and more attention-getting than action-getting in a non-theatrical environment. The requirement for "sounding like a manager" has nothing to do with regional accent—no matter whether you speak with the famous Brooklyn or conspicuous Harvard accent. The content of your "sound" matters.

Note that the effective manager, the one who is worth emulating, is invariably a superior communicator of ideas, concepts, plans, and programs. He is direct and certainly makes his point. His sentences—whether or not grammatically correct—convey what he wants to say, without ambiguity, with exceptionally narrow margins for misinterpretation. His vocabulary may not be large, but his words and meanings are unmistakable and lucid. Given the floor for a ten-minute presentation, he makes his point in the first five minutes and then devotes the second five to straightforward, equally unambiguous answers to questions from the group to whom he has made the presentation. And primarily because his audience has little difficulty, if any, in understanding just what he means, the probability for acceptance of his plan, program, or project is significantly enhanced.

Listen closely. Analyze the technique. Learn to emulate this effective manager's "sound." Study and practice the communication of your ideas and concepts in nonthreatening environments. For example, take short courses in public speaking at local colleges and universities, or in other public school systems that offer adult courses in self-development. Volunteer to present a paper to your professional society's chapter. The question-and-answer period will reveal instantly to you whether or not you have been understood. Talk, then listen very closely to the types of questions that are asked of you. Analyze the questions. Do they indicate that your statements were not clearly understood? You covered the point raised by the question, but why then is it being queried? Were you unclear, transmitting a garbled message? Or was the receiver off your frequency, not listening "clearly" when you transmitted?

Take such incidents seriously (every speaker has them and they should not annoy or perturb him when they occur) as areas for self-improvement, signals that might mean the "transmission" needs to be improved. Volunteer as an "after-dinner speaker" at your social or hobby club meetings. You have much to talk about. Your "talk" doesn't have to be long. Half- or three-quarter-hour presentations are usually more than adequate. Join a toastmasters' club. Check out a Dale Carnegie or equivalent program that offers nonthreatening instruction and practice with people who seek the same self-development.

Attend a couple of how-to seminars. Read about the subject of effective speaking and presentations. Learn how to use graphics, slides, transparencies, charts, and chalkboards to enhance your communications skills. The successful communicator is not "born" as such. Although many may not have taken any courses in communicating ideas and concepts, they quite likely absorbed it from the fortunate circumstances of the environments in which they were nurtured or exposed. What may seem to be a "natural" speaker may actually be a person whose exposures during the personality development period were very different from yours and, only in this sense, can his development be considered superior to yours. It is never too late to learn how to communicate unambiguously. A large vocabulary and a superb knowledge of grammar may help but are not at all essential to effective communications. What is essential is a recognition of your need, if it exists, in this area and the will to do something constructive about it.

If you really do want to *move upward,* you may have to learn to manage your own change and overcome the resistance you may feel to implementing the changes. This may create an internal conflict among your Id, Ego, and Superego. Certainly you are adult enough to manage your own sense of insecurity that this change will cause. You may have to replace those assumptions you have made and stored within your own mind concerning "what it takes to be a manager." You can do it. If you want to.

Effective use of time

Pareto's Law—popularly known as the "*80:20 Rule*"—contends that 80 percent of our time is spent in accomplishing only 20 percent of the results. This might be loosely interpreted as "we spend most of our time wheel spinning!" Now this "wheel spinning" may not always feel like wasted time. But it would be more valuable time if we could improve the productivity of the energies we expend during 80 percent of our available time. People waste time everywhere—at the office, at home, at social activities, while traveling, or waiting for an event to start. Our theme is *effective management for engineers and scientists.* We would be remiss if we did not include the requirement for *management of time.* The objective, perhaps even one of the measurements of *effectiveness*, is *productivity.* If we can change the ratio of 80:20, say, to a ratio of 75:25, we will have made a significant advancement in our productive use of time and energy. Now 75 percent of our time produces 25 percent of the results.

As a side note, the 80:20 Rule often proves reasonably accurate with respect to the productivity of people engaged in parallel activities. For example, sales managers will report that "80 percent of their orders come from 20 percent of their salespeople." Putting this into another perspective, 80 percent of the salespeople generate only 20 percent of the orders. Test this rule within your own activity. You may be surprised to discover that 20 percent of your professionals are responsible for 80 percent of the positive results, the output of the group.

The same is often true of managers. While there may be complex reasons related to creativity (not a commonly available talent) of the individuals within the group, possibly only 20 percent of the group can be described as "creative" or "ingenious" professionals. However, the correct use of time must be examined. Time and productivity are inseparable in the sense that productivity is not instantaneous. Time cannot be frozen. The time base for the generation of units of product (concepts, ideas, hardware, software, goods, or services) moves inexorably. The closer the fulfillment of the task to the start of the time base-line, the more productive is the use of dedicated time.

It comes down to a matter of time management, or planning the way one's time is to be used. An effective manager deliberately allocates segments of time along the available time base-line to individually identified tasks. There is a simple methodology.

Start with a diary in which you record how your time is spent or utilized. On a lined page, dated at the top, establish quarter-hour time periods of your typical work day. For example, on the first line indicate 8 A.M.; second line, 8:15 A.M.; third line, 8:30 A.M—and on through to the end of the day. Then as each quarter-hour interval passes, make a brief entry of how you used the time interval. A review of each day's time usage may prove quite revealing. Do not, of course, draw conclusions on the basis of a single day's review. Consider a period of at least two weeks for review. You may discover some patterns of behavior on your part or on the part of your superior or subordinates who occupy much of your time, that indicate a need for improvements in self-discipline or self-control. You may find that you are going from one task to another without really completing any one task. You may discover that you procrastinate in taking definitive courses of action. Or that you spend too much time at lunch or on coffee breaks.

You may discover you have been tackling the easiest tasks first and putting off the tougher ones. This is human nature, the tendency to deal with those problems and people with which we are most familiar and with whom we have the friendliest relationships.

How do you discipline yourself?

Plan your time in advance!

Make the same sort of dated diary pages, one for each day, as you did in developing the self-diagnosis of how time was actually being utilized. This time divide the page in half, vertically. The heading for the left of the page is PLANNED TIME/USE. The heading for the other half of the page is ACTUAL TIME/USE. At the center of each horizontal line, list as before the quarter-hour time segments for your entire day. Now enter on the left half and in the appropriate time segments the individual tasks you plan to attend to or accomplish during the day. Be specific. State the *planned* intent and the objective for the use of the individual time periods. As the day progresses, enter information on what *actually* was done, attended to, or accomplished. If a planned task has been diverted or postponed, make an entry of these facts along with the reasons why. A review of your PLANNED vs. ACTUAL use of time may reveal you are being hampered by too many interruptions, people dropping into your office just to chat (the person who has time to kill usually kills yours) or you may be overly extending telephone contacts that could be shortened. Separate the essential from the nonessential. Finish things that you start. Don't be afraid to tell a drop-in visitor or telephone caller that you are quite busy at the moment or have a specific task to attend to at this time—that you will call back at the first opportunity, as soon as pressure is off.

We do not advocate a strait-jacket approach to your time. If your PLANNED TIME goes awry, don't let it throw you. How do you avoid being "thrown"? Immediately reschedule the task for another specific time slot, and record the reason for the postponement. Do not procrastinate. Identify and separate any of your procrastinations from those causes for delays that may appear to be entirely beyond your control. However, in either case, take control of your time. Within some period of time, not necessarily immediately, you will become the *manager* of your time as opposed to the reverse, in which time manages you. You are certain to notice a change in the *80:20 Rule*—for the better—as it applies to your own productivity.

The manager and red tape

When an organization is in its infancy, it is quite usual for an engineer or scientist to walk into the president's office with an idea roughly sketched on a sheet of paper and get a decision, reject or go ahead. When this organization is mature and more complex, the same engineer or scientist must complete project forms as requests for capital funding, present detailed budgetary forecasts, make written projections of total time and costs, and elaborately describe the benefits to the corporation to be derived from the successful completion of the project. The change in the approach is not caused by a disease or corporate illness that comes with age or maturity. The stakes have grown considerably. The corporate managers are responsible to investors, stockholders, and the law for the optimum use of available resources. Risks as well as the opportunities must be defined in full detail so that senior management can make manager-type decisions. As much as is forseeable, the "payoffs" must now be clearly expressed, whereas for the less mature company clarity and detail may be offset by massive uses of energy and enthusiasm. The need for documentation is often bitterly referred to as "corporate red tape."

It is generally in the organization's best interests to create sets of rules (policies and procedures) that regulate work flow and provide a discipline for those who must perform work as well as for those who are accountable for the performance of people. Rules are intended to relieve the manager of the burden of specifying repeatedly those things the corporation expects from its managers and employees. Rules facilitate communication and reduce the margins for error on the part of maverick managers and employees. Rules may also satisfy the need for an impersonal intervention between the manager and his subordinate. "These are the rules. Blame them, not the boss." It is probable that, in such instances of impersonal intervention, the relationships between managers and subordinates are strengthened. It is not the manager who "threatens," it is the rules.

Controls that appear to slow down the decision-making process may actually be preventing the making of hasty decisions on the basis of inadequate information or data, supported only by emotional rationalizations that could create significant risks for the company's resources.

Rules can go to an extreme. If overly prepared and enforced, they can paralyze an organization's people. The requirement for the completion of numerous "standard forms" each time an action is either proposed or implemented can become burdensome and severely discouraging to creative people. Complex red tape can drive such professionals to seek other places of employment less dedicated to the "paper mill."

It is possible, however, that those who protest most vehemently against red tape may reveal basic tensions and insecurities. They may have a limited view of the need for such "red tape" paperwork. Because of these highly personal perspectives, they may become careless about record-keeping and rebel quite openly, almost pathologically, about the organization's demands for conformity and what they interpret as "politics." They yearn for those good old days when informality, faith in a "man's word," and enthusiasm and confidence were all that were needed to get things done. An interpersonal "wedge" appears between the organization and the individual. If not handled properly, both may lose.

How does the manager enable his subordinates to cope with, to live with this red tape? The manager must learn for himself and believe in the reasons for the rules, policies and procedures, the red tape; why they were created. What are the benefits to be gained from following the rules? What are the losses that might be realized by ignoring the rules? It is then incumbent upon the manager to share this knowledge with his engineers and scientists who in turn must share it with their technicians, juniors, and aides.

Rules, policies, and procedures are prepared and published by senior management for implementation by their subordinate organizational managers, leaders, and staff members. Although reform must come from the top level of the organization, it is not likely that, as you advance from the lower levels to the senior levels of the organizational hierarchy, you will initiate the reform. You will learn more thoroughly that rules that are intelligently conceived and properly communicated have great validity. The difficulty usually lies in the chain of communicating the raison d'être from senior management downward through the organization to the lowest level on which the rules make an impact. Communication with your superiors and subordinates, up and down the channels, will do more than help you "learn to live with" the rules. It will make of you a staunch supporter of "red tape."

Moving out of management

As we have pointed out before, not everybody wants to be a manager. In fact, moving out of management and back into technical work may often renew the vitality and creativity of the individual. For example, at The Livermore Laboratory operated by the University of California under contract to the U.S. Department of Energy, there is a professional complement of 2,500 scientists and engineers out of a total work force of 7,000. Approximately 850 of the 2,500 professionals have doctoral degrees.

Livermore has no formal policy of moving managers back into technical positions. But in a relatively short span of time, approximately thirty of the professionals who had advanced to managerial positions in scientific divisions moved back into the technical ranks. Half the professionals who made the move *out* of management initiated the change voluntarily. The other half were required to move for reasons that generally can be described as "involuntary," though not necessarily for reasons related to competence in their managerial duties. In some instances the movement out of management revitalized a manager who had been coasting. In one unusual case, a successful director of the Laboratory took a year off for advanced study at a university. He returned as an effective associate director.

In some instances in which the managers returned to technical work after two or three years as managers, there were some difficulties in catching up to technology. Others also had difficulty in adjusting to reduced income and status. However, there was strong evidence that adjustments have been made successfully and that vitality and creativity were significantly renewed.

No doubt, you are truly a professional. Your roots are those of a competent, high-achieving engineer or scientist. You used to derive a special sense of excitement from direct participation in the technical work, problem-solving, searching for novelty, creativity, and ingenuity. However, you are now a *manager*. You may reminisce about the "good old days" when you were a designer, researcher, part of the technical-professional staff actively engaged in a new project, exploring new technologies, creating new processes, techniques, and products where they had not been before. The change in your career direction, the role of the *manager*, demands that you make vital adjustments in your perspectives and in your practices. Your relationships with those who were once your peers have changed. Now some are your subordinates in the hierarchy of the organization. Things will not again be the same for you.

For example, a super project, a dream of an R&D program has just been authorized. Especially exciting is the fact that you have been named *manager*. You know this particular science so well. You not only "cut your teeth on it," you made your reputation in it. You would very much like to keep a piece of the R&D action for yourself, "keep your hand in," so to speak. You even wonder about the possibility of having the company set up a small lab bench for you, just a corner of your office or an insignificant amount of floor space out in the "pen" for your use. You proved in the past you are productive as a scientist. You feel quite "turned on" by the unique challenges inherent in this new and important project. You are sure you could make valuable contributions.

Certainly, you could. But should you?

You could get so wrapped up in the task, your "piece of the action," that your relationships with your staff could skew in the wrong direction. Suppose the project were to fall behind schedule. Or suppose it were to go over budget at some finite point in time. Or some of the critical events in the multiple paths of your chart against a base of time were to go out of synchronism—some ahead of time, others behind time. In such a situation, although the aggregate or cumulative expenditures against total budget for the year to date might be right on the mark, a peer in the finance department who is equally professional in his own discipline might point out that the project is off-target with respect to the predetermined bench marks for the project. He's only doing his job in pointing this out. It can be devastating to have a financial manager (who reports to a superior who is peer to your direct superior) imply that the project is out of control from the financial viewpoint. He is saying that one manageable entity of the project, budget management in which he has expertise, *is not being properly managed!*

What do you say now?

This hypothetical situation is discussed at this time because of the many times it has been brought to me by participants in my seminars, "Effective Management for Engineers and Scientists," especially during coffee breaks or after hours when I have made myself available for individual and semiprivate discussions of specific situations in management.

No doubt, many of the managerial positions have been filled directly from the ranks of the technical-professional staff. The promotions have usually been the result of demonstrated competence in technical skills, communications, and interpersonal capabilities. The promotions have been happily, enthusiastically accepted as a welcome form of recognition and status. But the hands-on part of the former role as engineer or scientist is sorely missed after the "glow" of promotion has diminished.

It begins to become quite difficult to restrain one's strong, almost overpowering desire to join in the "fun."

The manager must accept the inherent isolation of his job. His subordinates are responsible for technical work. He is accountable for his subordinates' performances. If the desire to do technical work is irresistible, I suggest the manager set up a lab in his home, apartment, or garage. There he can do R&D, related to the job or not, to his heart's content. The manager must avoid the competition, the threat that would be inherent in his assumption of the role, however minimal, of the technical professional.

Is this role assumption the same as the *Driver* manager? Is this the Driver's behavior? Which leads to the important question, Is the Driver style appropriate to the situation? If the answer is yes, set up the mini-lab if you must. But if the answer is no, setting up your own lab is the same as delivering a message of "no confidence" to your subordinates; totally inappropriate, when the reason for the lab is egocentric. It represents an abdication, in part, of the managerial role in the project's "script."

The work of the manager is a full-time job. Who ever heard of a moonlighting manager?

There is occasionally a manager who also does hands-on work; he is often one of the owners of a business, perhaps the sole proprietor, the entrepreneur who can't let go, who says, "I don't want to become a big corporation. I don't want all those personnel headaches. I don't want others to make decisions for me, which is what will happen to me if I become 'big'." At some point in time, this entrepreneur-manager-engineer (who is also, incidentally, doing his own technician-level work) may discover that he is losing money faster than he can make it. His cash-flow problems are out of control. One reason for this may be found in the fact that when he is fulfilling the role of president, he is being properly compensated, paid an appropriate salary with respect to the company's capabilities to pay. But when he is doing the work of the technician, he is still being paid at the president's salary level, beyond the company's capabilities. A decision has to be made: "Am I to do technical work or managerial work?" Both are full-time activities. Attempting to fulfill both roles simultaneously may build a basis for conflict.

Are heavy readers high achievers?

Reading habits and achievement can be correlated, according to an RCA study of its engineering professional staff and supervisors. Approximately 3,000 professionals participated in the study, which attempted to correlate information-retrieval habits with achievement, and discovered some of the techniques used by professionals in keeping abreast of technological developments. The 3,000 respondents included researchers; development, systems, project, manufacturing, and service engineers; and organizational levels of engineer, leader, and engineering manager.

Being technically current is very important to engineers. But exactly what does "technically current" mean, not in the academic sense but in the real-life practical sense to the working professional? We might define the term "technically current" as being adequately informed so as to be able to apply a store of knowledge to the productive fulfillment of a task in an environment of rapidly changing technology. We live and work in an era that seems to be dedicated to the obsolescence of existing products and technologies. It is dangerous to one's career objectives as a scientist or engineer engaged in technical work to lose touch with discovery. According to a report attributed to the Harvard Business School, if we take the body of man's knowledge as it existed at the time of Christ as our point of reference, the rapidity with which things and knowledge are becoming obsolete is dramatically described in this way:

- By AD 1700, the "body" had doubled.
- By 1900, it doubled again.
- By 1950, it doubled again.
- By 1960, it doubled again.
- By 1968, it doubled again.
- By 1973, it doubled again.

The Harvard report did not go further. However, if this premise and geometric progression are accurate, the body of knowledge would have doubled again by 1976, and again by 1978, and yet again by 1979. From this point on the rate of change becomes quite overwhelming. One has only to read new product announcements and technical journals to recognize that this acceleration of the acquisition and practice of knowledge is creating an intensely dynamic situation, presenting the professional with special problems in keeping pace with changes and breakthroughs.

With express permission of RCA, here are some excerpts from the study presenting several of the relevant questions and answers contained in the survey. "Engineers" refers to all professional, technical, and nonsupervisory employees working in the physical sciences. It includes those working in research, design and development, and in manufacturing. "Leaders" refers to the first level of supervision. "Managers" refers to all the higher levels.

1 How important in your present job is keeping abreast of new technology in your field?

Importance	Engineers	Leaders	Managers
a Extremely	32%	39%	40%
b Quite	44	42	43
c Somewhat	18	15	15
d Slightly	5	3	2
e Not at all	1	1	0

More than three-fourths of each occupational group rated keeping up-to-date in the two highest degrees of importance. It is interesting to note that *leaders* and *managers* assign new technology a higher degree of importance for their jobs than do *engineers*.

2 How important to your future career goals is keeping abreast of new technology?

Importance	Engineers	Leaders	Managers
a Extremely	37%	38%	28%
b Quite	47	47	52
c Somewhat	14	12	18
d Slightly	2	3	2
e Not at all	1	1	0

Combining the two highest degrees of importance, *engineers* and *leaders* regard keeping up-to-date as more important to their futures than to their present jobs. *Managers* assign it only slightly less importance to their futures compared with their present jobs, but agree that it is quite important.

3 How much emphasis does your management put on the importance of staying abreast of new technology in your field?

Importance		Engineers	Leaders	Managers
a	Very strong	7%	7%	12%
b	Strong	21	27	28
c	Moderate	37	36	39
d	Minor	23	21	15
e	None	11	8	5

4 What percentage of your information is received through: Reading? Discussions with other engineers? Educational courses? Business meetings? Professional society activities?

(Note that in the following table, *job-related* information is that which is relevant to the specific task on which the person is working; *industry related* means concerned with the overall technology with which the respondent associates himself; *professional field* means that the information concerns the field of engineering, any aspect of the profession other than that which may be included as being *job* or *industry* related.)

Method		Job Related	Industry Related	Professional Field
a	Reading	40%	55%	51%
b	Discussions	34	23	19
c	Courses	8	1	19
d	Meetings	8	6	4
e	Societies	4	3	8

The columns do not total 100%, you will note. This is because respondents checked more than one method twice or did not respond completely. Conclusions were reached and may be considered valid because of the wide variances in percentages among the methods and the functions to which they are related.

Reading is clearly the primary source of information for all levels of work, with informal discussions second. Together they account for 70 to 78% of the information acquired. Reading is

most productive for acquiring information that is not directly
related to the job. Reading is also the most productive method
for acquiring information that is directly related to the immediate job.

5 On the average, how much time during and after working
hours in a typical week do you spend reading the various types
of material listed below? Also, approximately how much of this
total reading time is done during working hours?

		Engineers		Leaders		Managers	
		Total	Work	Total	Work	Total	Work
a	Job related	5.0	3.3	6.0	3.6	6.4	3.6
b	Industry related	1.1	0.3	1.6	0.6	1.9	1.0
c	Professional field	1.5	0.9	1.4	0.5	1.9	0.5
	Total	7.6	4.5	9.0	4.7	10.2	5.1
			59%		52%		50%

Numbers in the table are hours averaged across the responses.
Engineers average 7.6 hours per week in the three areas of
information related to their immediate jobs, their industries,
and their professional fields. *Leaders* spend somewhat more
time reading. *Managers* do the most reading among the three
levels of technical people. *Managers* also do the most reading
during work hours.

6 Which, if any, of the following are obstacles to you in keeping
abreast of new developments in technology by reading? Which
are the one or two you consider most important?

Obstacle		Importance
69%	I do not have sufficient time to read at work.	48%
47	I do not have sufficient time to read outside of work.	24
27	I keep abreast by ways other than reading.	9
21	Management does not condone reading at work.	11
13	I need a better grasp of mathematics.	6
9	I need a better grasp of science.	5
4	I lack interest in reading.	2
3	Reading wouldn't help in my job.	2

Time appears to be the major restraint or obstacle in reading, both at work and outside work. A surprising number report management as an obstacle to reading at work, which might also be related to the response, "I keep abreast by ways other than reading."

The study continued with the responses of *high* and *low achievers* and their views on (a) the importance of keeping up-to-date, (b) the influence on their career goals, and (c) the emphasis management puts on the importance of keeping up-to-date in technological knowledge. Achievement levels were related to such factors as:

- How do you rate yourself in terms of being up-to-date with the current state of the art in your technical field?
- How many awards or recognitions have you received of a technical-professional nature?
- How many patents (sole or with a colleague) do you have?
- How many papers have you as author or coauthor published in the past five years?
- How many formal paper presentations have you made to engineering or scientific groups in the past five years?
- How frequently do other engineers seek you out to discuss technical information?

1 How important in your present job is keeping abreast of new technology in your field?

Importance	High Achievers	Low Achievers
a Extremely	54%	15%
b Quite	38	43
c Somewhat	7	30
d Slightly	1	10
e Not at all	1	2

2 How important to your future career goals is keeping abreast
of new technology?

Importance	High Achievers	Low Achievers
a Extremely	51%	22%
b Quite	42	49
c Somewhat	6	25
d Slightly	1	4
e Not at all	1	1

3 How much emphasis does your management put on the importance of staying abreast of new technology in your field?

Emphasis	High Achievers	Low Achievers
a Very strong	16%	2%
b Strong	30	12
c Moderate	34	36
d Minor	15	32
e None	6	17

Three times more *high achievers* regard management's
emphasis as strong. Perhaps more significant, nearly half of
the *low achievers* believe that management's emphasis is either
minor or nonexistent. *Low achievers* did not find much encouragement from this level of management emphasis to keep
themselves up-to-date technically. Most people respond to or
try to respond to what they think is valued and expected of
them by their management. It is important, therefore, for the
manager to express his expectations, and for the *manager* to
understand how his people—*high* and *low achievers*—perceive
their *manager's* emphasis on being abreast with technology.

A call to action

There are several lessons to be learned from the opinions and data
expressed above. Here are some specific recommendations for the *engineer* who would become a *manager* through demonstration of his skills,
and for the *manager* who would grow in the hierarchy of the company.

- Accept the premise that keeping current in your field (not just your job) is important, now and in your future.
- Assess your information-gathering habits. Do something to improve them.
- Read more. Do not limit yourself to the "news" and easy things to read; read technical papers and reports outside your immediate area of expertise to broaden your horizons and perspectives.
- Learn how to use your library and librarian.
- Seek out knowledgeable colleagues and experts in other work groups at your own company and in other companies.
- Participate in technical committee work, technical symposiums, workshops, seminars, society meetings. Take an active part in your professional society.
- Don't be complacent. The technical world grows more complex and more competitive every day.
- Reexamine your actions in supporting effective information-gathering habits of your professional staff. Encourage reading and other constructive habits that might contribute to improved performance and personal advancement. You are accountable for their productivity.
- Develop interdepartmental plans for conducting joint information-sharing workshops and seminars for cross-fertilization and improved communications.
- Encourage your staff to participate in professional society activities.
- Keep yourself well-informed. Read. Write. Present papers. Go for technical-professional awards. Enhance your A_k. Become a manager who is sought out by his superiors, peers, and subordinates for his knowledge of all aspects of his work, industry, and profession.
- Be the role model for your subordinates.

Your superiors are certain to notice your efforts, effectiveness, and willingness to apply yourself to methods that enable you to grow. When opportunity for advancement appears within your company, you will be considered on the basis of your achievements and willingness to apply your time and your mind to growth in your chosen field. You are offered opportunity when your superiors believe the company will benefit by enabling you to move upward.

The *effective manager of engineers and scientists* is able to maintain a balance between the ever-changing, the dynamic loads and differentiated demands of *concern for people* and *concern for the task*. His ego derives satisfaction from the productivity that results from his skill at establishing and maintaining this balance. His own needs are his motivators. They will remain his motivational influences until he is able to satisfy them.

Are we capable of totally satisfying all our needs at the same time? Not likely. We are, as normal human beings, constantly pursuing satisfaction of one need or another: physiological, security, societal, ego, and self-actualization.

Back to your desk. Time to plan for your next upward movement in management.

Index